Pele's New World

PELE'S
NEW WORLD

by

Peter Bodo and *David Hirshey*

with

W · W · NORTON & COMPANY · INC ·
New York

First Edition

Library of Congress Cataloging in Publication Data

Bodo, Peter.
    Pelé's new world.

    1. Nascimento, Edson Arantes do, 1940–
2. Soccer players—Biography. I. Hirshey, Dave,
joint author. II. Nascimento, Edson Arantes do,
1940–   joint author. III. Title.
GV942.7.N3B6   1977   796.33′4′0924 [B]
ISBN 0-393-08758-1   76-46961

This book was designed by Jacques Chazaud.
Typefaces used are Perpetua and Electra.
Manufacturing was done by Vail-Ballou Press, Inc.

1 2 3 4 5 6 7 8 9 0

For the memory of my father, and my dear mother

PB

For my father, who taught me the game,
and for Gerri, who taught me the score.

DH

Acknowledgments

The authors would like to thank a number of people whose patience and unfailing support helped carry this project through.

Dave Hirshey would particularly like to thank his most demanding editor, wife, and best friend Gerri Hirshey.

Peter Bodo would particularly like to thank his family, Karol Kamin, Franz Schubert, Mrs. Paul, and Bill O'Mahoney.

The title of this book comes from a movie of the same name by Lawrence Solomon and Paul Gardner.

This book could not have been written without the constant help and encouragement of Clive Toye, who found the man we wanted to write about; Giora Breil, who delivered him; Ed Barber, who helped us fit him into these pages; and John Sterling, who guided us through the hard times.

Special thanks to Brian Glanville and Paul Gardner, two of the finest soccer writers in the world; Fred Schruers, Gordon Bradley, Professor Julio Mazzei, Jerry Lisker, Mike O'Neill, Dick Alford, Bill Brink, Sal Gerage, Paul Durkin, Greg Gallo, Mike Matthews, Jim Trecker, Pedro Garay, Aziz, Laila Magalhaes, Steve Marshall, Charlie Cuttone, Dick Schaap, Ted Howard, Lou Luca, Carol Harmon, Fred Klashman, Safi Newman, and John O'Reilly.

Also thanks to: Paul Thebaud, John Powers, Bob Savett, Alex Yannis, and all those others who have written about this beautiful game. *And this beautiful man, Pele.*

Contents

Photographs appear following pages 80 and 186

Pele's New World

Prologue

_____

*F*rom above, Ullevi Stadium in Gothenburg, Sweden, is a lovely and mysterious organism with an outer band of moving colors and a cool, green, empty heart. The still center is a flat logo of sod some 120 yards long and half as wide, dominated by a chalk circle of imperturbable correctness, softening the severe lines of the field.

It is different from ground level, where the pitch comes to life in inconsistencies. There is a slight, gradual rise here, a thin spot there, where dirt is visible. The mat of sparkling grass gleams with a thousand pin pricks of light from a recent hosing. There are patches of dark green and patches of light; resistant places and scar tissue, raw, self-renewing, breathing freshness into the the agitated air. There will be a soccer game here tonight.

Beneath the massive steel and concrete steps that form the levels of the stadium is a dark, mildewy tunnel, with a light at its far end, placed like a bright paneless window opening onto the field and its electric haze. The photographers are lined up peering into this tunnel, toward a door etched into the darkness by three fine lines of escaping light. Suddenly, sixteen men pour into the tunnel clad in short pants. Their spiked shoes clack on the cement, thighs gleam and smell faintly of wintergreen. Each man wears a perforated white jersey with a green and black logo, a stylized soccer ball in motion and the name, NEW YORK COSMOS.

Alliansen, the Swedish all-star team, has already been introduced and stands lined up at midfield, basking in the throaty roar of the spectators. One by one the Cosmos are called, each player sprinting into the harsh light. Finally, one player is left. He is why 35,000 people are in the stands. He is the greatest player the world's most popular sport has produced—Pele.

You still cannot see him clearly because the rest of the Cosmos' entourage dwarfs his five-foot-eight, bullet-shaped body. But you know he is trotting towards the mouth of the tunnel because flashbulbs are exploding everywhere, blinding him temporarily in a shifting curtain of green, blue, red, and yellow patterns thrust against his eyes. At the tunnel's end, with the tumult rising to a crescendo, he surprises the photographers by completing an abrupt about-face.

Turned around thus, he begins backing into the light and dim of the stadium, slow, crablike, one leg yielding to the other. His arms are raised, each hand locked into the "V" salute, as he backs implacably on, into the adulation of the fans. A sheen of sweat breaks over his forehead, above a deep, intoxicated smile. His forehead is narrow, gracefully meeting an even mat of short hair. The eyes are laid into high cheekbones, distinguished by a feline quality.

Framed and held out of context, the smile can be Delphic in its elegance and dignity. When the eyebrows are raised and knitted, the spirit of Cheshire Cat flickers over cheeks slightly pitted with acne scars. It is the smile and face of the Sphinx, asking you to choose between the innocent black boy descended from African slaves or the wealthy, enigmatic genius.

The body is a rugged driving wheel that begins with slumped shoulders and tapers out to massive thighs. It is the perfect body for a soccer player, minimizing the less important regions between neck and waist. This triangular power plant has a low center of gravity, enabling Pele to react to a ball rolling along the turf with maximum efficiency and minimum waste. It is as if the strength that is normally distributed throughout the body has been pushed down from above and pulled up from below.

By now, he has backed onto the field, turned around and run to its center and a circle of 100 children standing impatiently, each one with an orange soccer ball. As Pele arrives at the hub of this ring, the children suddenly kick their balls towards him. The first ball rolls in; he passes another off, flicks at another with the opposite foot, lightning-fast tries to fend off yet another and another and another . . . but it is too late, he is engulfed by balls rolling, spinning, bouncing crazily all around him like foam from a thunderous breaker.

The preliminaries are over; the referee places the plain white ball onto the lime spot at the precise center of the field. Pele casually draws his right foot back to kick off. All noise abates. Each player slams the mental door on everything which does not immediately affect the ball. The ball is here and now and always, a perfect sphere that will regulate the pith of life for the next ninety minutes.

Pele squibs the ball to teammate Mordechai Shpigler, who puts his foot on top of it and in an instant's time surveys the pattern forming in the Swedish end. Already, the defender is upon him; Shpigler sweeps the ball to the left, then to the right, a simple function, a small obedience imposed upon the least disciplined object in the world. Tak . . . he passes to Ramon Mifflin, twelve yards crossfield, ten yards into the Swedish zone. Heel and toe, the lash of a defender's leg and the ball runs off uncontrolled as the players downfield begin to draw back. Freedom! Here comes the ball, purring along the turf evenly, escaped from everyone and running headlong towards the refuge of the far side line and over the boundary. The Cosmos are awarded the throw-in; Tommy Rellis looks for his Brazilian striker.

Pele takes the ball confidently, bending back to trap it with his chest. It rolls gently down his torso and drops like a melted puddle at his feet. The defender chooses not to challenge and Pele begins his move. With a sudden burst, he makes as if to shove the ball to his right with the left foot but actually steps

3

over it. Then, carried forward by momentum, he efficiently taps it in the opposite direction with his right heel. Deceived, the defender lurches back towards the ball, arresting the very orders his body is just beginning to carry out.

Too late. The ball is running, sucking the eyes of the stadium along its trail. Mifflin has it as Pele races by, legs churning with a power that depresses the soil at every step, heading for a space that is not there yet but should be when he arrives, because he instinctively expects the Swedish center-back to pull slightly to his left, toward the ball that Shpigler is now about to receive.

Pele only half sees this and half hopes it; logically, the cumulative experience of every moment he has ever spent on a playing field dictates that a meeting between Shpigler and the ball will occur with favorable consequences for Pele. But it does not happen; the defender lunges with his left foot, pushing the ball wide of the onrushing Cosmo and right to the instep of a blue-shirted Alliansen defender.

For the next few minutes, the teams feel each other out, detecting certain patterns and tendencies. Each man has sized up the opposition and each squad is developing a feeling for the other's strengths and weaknesses. The Swedes know that they have in Pele a shrewd, tactical threat armed with a surgeon's surety, a creator and intimidator who must be counted as a factor anywhere on the field.

The Swedes move ahead with long, crisp passes while the Cosmos are inclined to stretch the midfield, creating and closing spaces, weaving baroque geometrics with the ball and imposing a hypnotic, skillful slowness on the play until the unexpected back pass or sudden chip reveals a fleeting miracle of free, dangerous space.

The ball favors the Cosmos through the first ten minutes. It somehow skirts the outstretched Swedish feet, runs cleverly through a forest of legs and only shows the impossible roundness of its surface to Alliansen. Tak . . . tak . . . tak. Metronomic passing. The ball is urged from foot to foot, the Cosmos build, create, encourage and force the ball along tricky paths that seem as preordained as they are spontaneous. Occasionally, the game collapses, as it always does, because the imagination is exhausted. Then the ball is afflicted by a puzzling lethargy, stagnation seizes the players and two men are left on the side line, bulling and gouging for an indifferent ball whose magic is momentarily spent.

In the fifteenth minute a chance materializes. Pele traps the ball with his abdomen in the Swedish end and shuffles it off to Mifflin as he surges through a small space cobwebbed by the arms and legs of two Swedes. In a split second he is free, open in a newly discovered space of twenty square feet; his mouth is already wide, but before the urgent word "Meee-flin" escapes, the ball is running back towards him. And here we are, at the top of the penalty area, with the Swedish goalkeeper frozen in a crouch at the prospect of a shot.

There is one defender to beat, but instead of challenging him Pele notices the keeper's commitment to a low, screaming cannonball and pulling up short, nudges the underside of the ball, floating it delicately over the surprised keeper. But it goes over the crossbar too, and flutters onto the top of the netting with a gentle swish. A miss.

In the twenty-eighth minute, Shpigler on the right side spots Pele running goalward, feeds him a beautiful ball and pulls up in the excitement as his teammate, off-balance and dueling shoulder to shoulder with a defender lashes out powerfully with his left foot and sends the ball by the diving goalkeeper; but it strikes the post and caroms out to a Swede. Pele clambers to his feet and dropping his head in a penitent gesture gives Shpigler a short, apologetic wave. The half ends without score.

Before a game, the locker room is the waiting room at the dentist's; faceless, drab, populated by a nervous company left to their individual fantasies. After a game, it is a laundry room, with wet clothing strewn everywhere, a solemn or chatty mirror of the events of the preceding ninety minutes. At half-time it is refuge and cage, a moment to catch the breath and scan the exhausted faces leaned against the wall between smashed insects, while the hands clutch a warm drum of steaming tea.

5

The Cosmos file in, clacking along the cement floor of the tunnel, passing into the puffs of tea steam and wintergreen waiting in the cold changing room, gradually warming it with body heat. The medicine chest with its cargo of amber bottles occupies a space worth two men. Coach Gordon Bradley speaks to the team, panning their deficiencies, encouraging them to shout more, to communicate and knit their individual perceptions into a fruitful attack.

"Okay, boys," he concludes, in a voice quiet and dignified, slapping the fingers of his upturned left hand into his right palm. "You have this team. You created many fine chances out there. You were one pass away from a goal a number of times and you controlled the tempo of the game. Now go out there and give it a good second half . . ." The voice rises. "Remember to shout. Make things happen. A win here is a good win and if we avoid costly, individual mistakes, we can win this by three goals. Believe me, we can win by three goals . . ." The voice has gone soft. Pele listens with his head slightly cocked as his friends, Cosmo trainer Julio Mazzei translates. Bradley is smiling now. It is time.

The tension in the stadium has evaporated as the second half begins; the yearning of the fans has mellowed into fragmented small talk. The beast does not come to life until the first goal of the game, by Alliansen, in the fifth minute of the second half. The score has a curious effect on the Cosmos; they come alive once again and seize control. They begin to take the game to the Swedes, to impose a complex architecture on the field. Tak . . . tak . . . tak, the passes are sure, the ball glides willingly from foot to foot, from instep to chest and back to foot again. It is beautiful soccer, the ball perpetually in motion, running in the controlled freedom afforded by a team which laboriously clears spaces for it in a hop-scotch pattern, moving ever downfield. It is bound to pay off.

Consecutive headers by Brian Rowan and Pele send the ball to Tommy Ord, who lunges around 180 degrees and catches it perfectly with his right foot, driving it past the goalkeeper from thirty yards out. Ord erupts, triumphantly flinging his arms into the air, staring at the back of the net to confirm what he already knows. He spits for verification and Pele and Shpigler are there, one hugging either side of Ord's body. It is 1–1.

The Cosmos continue to threaten as the game wears on despite the succession of small hurts, protesting muscles, futile creativity, and flickering rewards. They grow stronger as the game wanes; it is apparent that the Swedes will be lucky to escape with a tie. In the twenty-second minute, Shpigler is demonstrating his exaggerated, long stride down the right wing when his eye catches a white cloud floating in unoccupied green; the ball is passed left and Pele gathers it in with one man to beat to the goal.

He drifts left, stutter-steps to confuse the defender, and sets his right foot up with the left. He taps the ball to the right, catches the Swede going the other way and smashes a fifteen-yarder crossfield, into the lower right side of the goal. Two-one, but the best is still latent.

Only five more minutes have elapsed when Ord traps a high ball near midfield and passes to Pele, cutting a swath down the center of the field. It is a perfect pass which Pele collects without breaking stride, two vital steps ahead of a pair of blue shirts. He races downfield, slows, and decides against shooting just fifteen feet in front of the goal, with the surging defenders on his back. "Shoot," Shpigler is screaming from the wing, "shoot, shoot." But Pele decides to bring time and motion to a complete standstill.

A whole stadium is poised over the still ball as two defenders careen past Pele, reaching for the ball with four feet. But it is well protected and as he feints a pivot to his left, he uses the outside of his right foot to tickle the ball five feet to the right and forward. Both defenders have reacted left, effectively cleared. One more timeless moment as Pele makes the keeper commit himself to the far side of the goal and he effortlessly flicks the ball into the lower left corner.

It is a spectacular goal, a fitting game ender, both improbable and enigmatic. It has happened in movement that encompasses inertia, it is one act and a thousand acts, simple and impossible, past and present, perfection whose lesson is swallowed up and lost in the subsequent moment.

The name comes cascading down in a massive chant from either side of the stadium—"Pele, Pele, Pele"—lingering in the air like massive storm clouds. Pele's body is stretched high off the ground, his arm cocked in the famous goal salute, head bent back in jubilation, eyes wide against the hollow above the burning light stanchions.

It is the same stadium where in 1958 he made his World Cup debut as a seventeen-year-old who squirmed and cried in the arms of his teammates upon astounding the soccer world with two goals against the Swedish team in the finals. Now he is a thirty-four-year-old millionaire whose momentary joy has eradicated seventeen intervening years of fame and lifted him triumphantly one more time.

He is the poor man who has become the incarnation of soccer, a game which has personified the inarticulate passion of poor men like no other. He has just ended one of the shortest retirements in sports history to play for the New York Cosmos for three years at a price the press reported to be $4.75 million. It is the only major team Pele has ever played for besides Santos, his lifelong Brazilian club or his country's national team.

The decision to come to the United States—and back to soccer—gave him a new future, and offered Pele a final way to push his star higher in the firmament.

1

"I Only Wanted to Be My Father"

*M*any times, people ask me where I come from. This is very hard question, because the answer is nothing. I come from nothing, because where I grew up in Brazil was a very poor place in the middle of nowhere. Also my nickname means nothing. Pele. It is just a word. People always want to know how poor I was. But when you are poor, you do not know what it is to be rich. You do not know anything else, so you can be very, very poor and you are not aware of it. Only later, if you are fortunate, you can look back and see how things were. When I do that, there is always some nostalgia for me.

As young boy, I wanted to be my father. That is all. He was a player in Brazil, I would say a second division caliber player through most of his career. To me, he was a very nice player. He make a lot of goal. He still have one record in Brazil because in one game he make five goal by head. As a child, I remember everybody on the street saying, "Oh, Dondinho is a good player." I want much to be like him when I hear the people speak like this. I remember a picture of many people carrying my father off the field on their shoulders after he win once with goal late in the game. My mother Celeste is different. She was not happy, because my father was a football

9

player. *She was always afraid that my father would get an injury and the family would have many problem. My father make 90 cruzeiros [$4.90] for each game, and we must live mostly on this, but my mother not worry about the money so much; she worry about what happen if my father has an injury and then cannot work at anything.*

I never worry about this. I like my father just like he was. Always he was glad to see me going with the ball too and this was a problem for my mother, because he always encourage me to play. I don't have money for regular ball, so sometimes I play with a grapefruit, or other kind of round object. I do things which make my father mad; I take button off his raincoat when he is not looking to play button football, a little game with the hand. Also, I take my father's sock and put rags and strings into it to make a ball. But he have only three pair of socks, so when he see me he gets very, very mad. He shout, "I kill you, I kill you," so I have to run away. But he always forgive me fast.

The state of Minas Gerais is a sprawling province that nuzzles up against the rich coastal strip where Rio and São Paulo generate the images most of us associate with Brazil: Sugarloaf, exotic cariocas chattering away in sidewalk cafés, and the sparkling high-rise apartments and chalk white beaches of Ipanema, hugging the shore like a string of pearls. But to the north, Minas reaches into the hinterland and becomes one with a block of northeastern states—Bahia, Piauí, Gameleira—which yoked together constitute a million square miles of tropical and semiarid farmland. The thirty-two million inhabitants of this rugged, uncharitable geography represent the greatest concentration of poverty in Latin America, a vast mezzotint whose images of want are the dark side of Brazilian life.

The northeast is the great black father of Brazil. Most of its natives are descended from the black African slaves who hacked and bundled sugar cane for Portuguese landowners on the largest plantations in the colonial western hemisphere. Brazil gained its independence in 1822, but the vestiges of foreign economic control were still evident more than a century later. The nation began to stir in its sleep in the early 1960s, dreaming the "economic miracle" which blossomed in the following decade. Through a combination of state capitalism and local and foreign investment, Brazil catapulted swiftly and surely into the twentieth century, with the gross national product increasing by 10 percent annually since 1969. Although the miracle bypassed most of the northeast, Minas managed to seize its share by virtue of mineral nucleations below the dusted hills of its southern reaches.

As one travels north, however, the prosperity and activity gradually diminish. There is no exact demarcation line, but the town of Tres Coracoes sits precariously on the silver hem of the miracle. Today it has a population of 17,458 and counts as its most distinguished son Edson Arantes do Nascimento, known to the world as Pele, who was born there on October 23, 1940.

Celeste do Nascimento did not want another footballer in the family. That her husband played professionally was bad enough; her worries only doubled when her proud Dondinho peered over the edge of the cradle and beamed: "With those pretty little thighs, he can only become a football player." To Celeste, this was tantamount to saying that her first-born was doomed to a flattering but hazardous existence, a way of life that no respectable man would embark upon. Dondinho himself was a charming man, as well as a player of considerable gifts. Yet in 1940, the motivation of a professional soccer player in Brazil was grounded only in love of the game. Soccer, invented by the English in the eighteenth century, had been quickly embraced all over the world, but there was neither the demand nor the organization by which a man could turn his passion into an adequate career. Those who tried were looked upon as wastrels and vagabonds, suspect magicians whose skills smacked of charlatanism. Although the World Cup originated in 1930, it would take the communications revolution and the internationalism that followed World War II to ignite the game in the public imagination. Celeste's apprehensions about football were rooted in flawless logic.

But Dondinho would not desist. He looked on with pleasure whenever young Edson, affectionately called Dico, spotted a soccer ball and flung his body upon it with abandon. Edson was three years old when his father's career took an upward swing. Dondinho was offered a position on a team in Bauru, a railroad town in southern Minas. There was consolation in this for Celeste too. The team had also offered Dondinho a small job in the municipal service. It was with an air of optimism that the family packed and moved into a small one-story house with ocher-tinted tiles and a white-washed front on September 7 Street, in the workers' quarter of Bauru.

Edson would live in Bauru until he was fifteen years old. It was there that he developed and cultivated his "feel" for the ball, acquired his nickname, and wed himself incontrovertibly to soccer, causing his mother more than a little anguish. To make matters worse, Dondinho's career was shattered in 1950 by a knee injury which cast the family on hard times. This event and the subsequent hardships confirmed all of Celeste's misgivings. By the time Dico was nine years old, he showed little inclination towards school or a conventional career of any kind. She had lost the early battles, but the war was by no means over.

At the time, Bauru was just a railway station for the wilderness. You should see what the kids there used to do. Some would dribble with their heads all the time; the ground had no space because of all the children. This is how I grow up, playing in the street all day, juggling any object that was like the ball.

At this time, when I have maybe six years, I get my nickname Pele. Now I think it is lucky for me, because it is unusual. Nobody else has it, and it is so easy to say in all languages. But when I was a child, I don't like the name. At school I fight with anybody who call me Pele. And I used to fight all the time. Because of all this fighting, the teacher often make me stay longer for punishment. But it is the old story, the more you fight against the name, the more you have it. There was nothing I could do. I still don't know why I was called Pele in the first place.

There was an airport near my home in Bauru, and as a child I also wanted to become a pilot. It was the only thing besides football that I really ever want to do for a career. A child cannot go into the airplane to practice, but he can live in the street and play football, so I forgot about the airplanes.

For some years, my father look healthy and good, score many goals and the family have money coming in to feed me, my brother Zoca, and sister Maria Lucia. But then he have the knee problem, when I was ten years old, and I begin to work. This is when I begin to not like the school at all. First, I sell newspaper, and then work for a shoemaker as apprentice. But I don't like that. The job I like best was selling pastry and cold drinks by the train station. All day sometimes I stand and say, "Is very hot, very hot, you want to buy?" I also have the job of shoeshine boy. I still have at home the box I used. For me, it is a symbol of me as businessman.

In the street, we also make at this time many projects. For instance, we all go with bags to find the cigarette butts people throw away. Then, we collect them, take them apart and make from them new cigarettes, which we sell before the stadium during football match. One idea we also have is to steal peanuts from the railroad car and roast them for sale, so that we can buy a ball. But to do this we need a special place, because if our parents know they would be very, very mad. So we make from all kinds of junk a little house, like a cave, in the woods. We keep there the peanuts, roast them, put them in bags for the sale. One day, we are not far away when we hear a big noise, the little house is collapsing. We rush back, but it has fallen down and buried underneath is one of our pals. We try to dig to find him, but it was too late. He die of suffocation. When his mother find out, she is in kitchen making bread, her hands in a bowl of flour and I never forget the terrible picture of her black face, streaked with tears and flour as she cry for her son.

PELE'S NEW WORLD

The time of most difficulty for my family was when I am between eight and fourteen years. We were very poor, but I always have time for the game. All day Saturday and Sunday I play football and when I was in school, we have two hours for lunch so I stay in the street to play instead of eating. Then I rush home very fast to take off my dirty clothes and eat before I go to work. I remember many times I came home and there is nothing to eat because I am little bit late. Maybe I just have a banana with some sugar on it and bread.

A lot of times my mother and father didn't eat because there was not enough food for the children. Then we would look at each other, and say, "Oh, I'm not hungry." Also I remember coming home when it was dark after I play for many hours and I go next to a bar. I look in and see the people inside drinking beverages and see big glass cases full of pastry and cake. I go in and ask for a drink of water, hoping that maybe the man give me beverage. But it didn't happen that way very often.

The biggest problem was always for my mother, because my father still encourage me in football. He always teach me; I remember I was young, maybe eight or nine, when he was watching me in the street and he call me over and say, "Okay Dico, you better now, you must learn to kick with both foot, not just the right." This made many problem at home. I had a grandmother, and every time I go to practice or play with my father she stay home in the house and pray. Even later, during my last days with Santos, my grandmother never went to the stadium and watch games on television only one or two times. My mother was the same. In all her life, she come to see me play at the stadium maybe three times, once because she was guest of honor for a special ceremony for me. She always prefer to stay at home and pray.

You can imagine how hard it was for her when I was a child. I try all the time to make her feel better; I go to work, but I cannot stop playing. It is the only thing which I want. So we fight. I remember when I was twelve years old, my mother and father speaking about the family money problems. I go to her at this time and say, "Wait, mother, one day I buy for you a house." She smile and shake her head and I know she did not believe me. But I had a strong mind and even though I love my mother very much, I also love football and I kept on playing.

So while it was not a very easy life, it was a life which I loved and for which I have many fond memories. Some people say that because I was poor and then became famous when I was fifteen years old I had no childhood. This is wrong. It was a very worthwhile childhood and even after I became well known I was able to take pleasure in small things. There is a little Brazilian black bird called a Tiziu. They hop around in the streets when I grow up, not afraid of us. To this day, when I see such a bird I shiver because it brings back good memories of when I was a child, playing football in the street all day.

Edson dropped out of school in fourth grade because of poor grades, lack of interest and the family's financial straits. He played continually in street games organized by the children in the neighborhood. These games were called *peladas*, perhaps the most plausible clue to the origin of his nickname.

The conflict between Celeste and Dondinho over their son's future seemed only to strengthen Edson's character and sense of purpose. Despite the status of the game, every city and village in Brazil had a team at some level, even if the uniforms were faded scraps and the players had to provide their own shoes, or simply went barefoot. When Edson was eleven, a self-proclaimed "impresario" stopped by to watch a neighborhood *pelada* and was so impressed by Edson and his friends that he proposed to turn them into a professional team. That night Edson did not sleep, flip-flopping through imaginary uniforms, sparkling playing fields, and championship games.

But it did not go like that. The name of the club Ameriquinha (Little America), was impressive enough but the 4.50 cruzeiros per game each player received bought more pride than food. Still, it was a team, even if the promised soccer cleats were nothing more than the broken discards of the city's adult team, Bauru AC. Pele helped Ameriquinha to successive championships in the Infanto Juvenil league and received his first bonus—3 cruzeiros which he promptly gave to his father. His mother held two and gave Pele one for ice cream and candy.

Yet there was an advantage even in this primitive organization. Invariably, league games attracted all manner of spectators and idlers who turned out to watch the raucous, pell-mell games of Ameriquinha. They included former players like Valdemar De Brito, an acquaintance of Dondinho's and a former national team player for Brazil, who was now coaching in Bauru. He immediately noticed the rail-thin youth whose painful lankiness belied an extraordinary shot, a subtle, feline mastery of feints and moves and apparently inexhaustible stamina. De Brito stayed for the whole game and at the end is said to have turned to a companion and passed judgment: "I have found greatness."

De Brito signed Edson and gave him a place on Bauru's junior team, Baquinho. He coached, advised, and groomed Edson, and watched in astonishment as his protege helped Baquinho capture three regional championships. Edson had forty goals in fifteen games, and a future as big as all of Brazil.

Now we have big problem. I have fourteen and a half years, and Valdemar believe I should go to play for Santos. This is first time I realize that I am a player, because other teams want me. My father of course is very happy. But my mother, she say, "no, no, no" and mean it. What I do? Me, I am a little bit afraid, because they want to test me with the big team. Maybe I am only afraid to fail, about how I would feel if I go there and Santos say to go home. Because I was still boy, I dream of future, hope to become big player. Now the future is in front of me. Underneath, maybe I do not want to face it so soon. But my father and De Brito say all the time, "no problem." It is time for you to test with good players. Now, how do we make my mother change her mind? A director from Santos and De Brito come to my house for two weeks to fight with my mother. At first, she say, "No, he is too young, you cannot take him." But they listen, very polite, and then tell her how big a chance it is for me. She does not care for that. But they talk and talk and talk. Finally, she throws her hands up in the air and cry, "Okay, take my boy." My father is happy.

Santos is 300 miles from Bauru, so I must go by train. Now I have fourteen years, eight months. But I never go near São Paulo and I do not know what a big city is like. Valdemar go to Santos first, and tell me when to come and that he will meet me at the São Paulo train station. When the day came, I didn't eat, not because I was so happy but because I am afraid. I put on my good clothing, brown pants and a big shirt that hang on my shoulders like a tent. Also, the good shoes I have for church. I take with me little cardboard suitcase filled with personal things and some bread and bananas to eat on the way. When I see my father put my suitcase in its place on the train I cry a little bit. Then we go.

Across from me sits a drunk man. He look at me, point his finger and say, "I know you, you are Dondinho's boy. I read about you in the newspaper. So you are going to try your luck at Santos. Listen boy, one day I was also professional player and it was a good life until somebody break my leg. Then everybody abandon me, nobody care for me. Look out boy, the same thing maybe will happen to you, and you will turn out like me." Of course, this did not make me feel very good. All the trip I think about this and about things my mother and father fight about, the difficulties we have with the money because of football. When I get off the train at São Paulo station I look for Valdemar and say, "I don't want to go to Santos, I want to take the first train back to Bauru."

But it is better now, because Valdemar is there and he told me not to worry. We take the bus to Santos, and then we walk in the street. I see many people and I like it very much. I look at the big tall buildings and all the bicycles and cars and I feel a little bit better. Valdemar take me straight to Vila Bileiro Stadium so I can watch a Santos game. I see many, many good players. Again, I say to Valdemar, "Okay, I practice one time with team but then I return to Bauru." He laugh at this, but I do not think it is so funny.

The next day, I go to the stadium and into locker room. The players who I worship—Zito, Pepe, Vasconcellos—they look at me and speak to me, shake my hand and tell me not to worry. But I worry anyway. Then we have the practice. I have a little problem, because I am not used to playing on good grass field. It is wet, and I have experience only on dry, dirt field where ball run much more fast. To me, it was impossible. I did not know what to do, and I am very afraid to make the mistake. So I try to only take the ball and make good pass with it. One or two time I have a chance to dribble with it and shoot, but I try to make these things very fast. At this time, I weigh 103 pounds, and the Santos shirt is very big for my shoulders. It get all wet from sweat and feel like 50 more pounds on my back. After training, I am sure that the manager Lula will tell me, "Thank you, but you must return to Bauru now." He come over, look at me very straight and say, "Boy, you still have much to learn." My heart jump into my mouth. I nod my head. "Also, you must put on some more weight before you are ready to play in the first division. But if you want, we will make out a contract for you today."

This is very good, but I am not so happy. Some eight or nine days pass and I feel very much the saudade, a nostalgia for home. So one night I decide that I have enough of Santos and I will go back to Bauru, where they offer to my father to pay me the same money as best player on the Bauru adult team if I change my mind. For me, this would have been enough. I could have stayed with my family and friends.

So now it is very early one morning, maybe 6:00 A.M., and I pack my few things and sneak out of the player's dormitory. I begin to walk on the street towards the train station, when here comes the groundskeeper of the stadium. He was out to buy some bread, or coffee, something. He see me, and ask where I am going. I told him I have the permission to visit with my family, but he look at me very suspicious and ask where is my pass. I try to not be nervous, "Oh," I say, "it is right here in my pocket." He wants to see it, and I just try to lie some more but he knows now that I do not have permission. So he say,

"I Only Wanted to Be My Father"

"Sorry, Edson, you must go back." What can I do but listen? This was very lucky for me that he come along when I try to make my big escape, because if I go I think the Santos directors just say forget this boy, and maybe I spend all my life in Bauru. For a few more days I feel bad, but then things became better as I get to know the people on the team and I make some more games with the juvenile players. Soon I get my contract—5,000 cruzeiros for one month, which is about two hundred and seventy-five dollars American money at that time. But for me that was many money. Just two year before, when I work as apprentice to shoemaker, I get one fifth that much for four months of work. So I believe I am rich man, grow more happy and comfortable at Santos and pretty soon, no problems.

Edson's development as a player was paralleled by the accelerated growth of soccer. It was an era when sport provided order and peace to a world rocked by war and rapid social change. At one level, soccer was mere spectacle, a diversion for the working classes all over the world, save the United States. On another, it also helped reconstruct the illusion of international understanding and good will via the World Cup.

No matter that in the first World Cup, held in Uruguay in 1930, the entire Argentine team was searched for firearms before entering the stadium to play the final. Or that the world received a grim prognostication in 1938 when antifascist refugees showered the Italian side with boos and insults as the team gave the fascist salute before the game. Pozzo, the Italian coach, made his players hold the salute until the jeering stopped. Then he dropped his arm and a moment later barked, "Team, attention. Salute." The squad obeyed and again held their arms aloft until the din subsided. A year later the world was plunged into war and the World Cup was reduced to memory until 1950.

The convulsive years in between witnessed a revolution in communications, as radio and teletype chronicled the fragmentation of peace and the subsequent efforts to knit the world together again. This served to shrink the globe and turned its attention to international issues and concerns. The rebirth of the World Cup in 1950, in Brazil, was one of the first cautious indicators that nations could again meet on a pitch other than a battlefield. Certainly it was more of a bromide that a solution, but people looked forward to the tournament with optimism and passion. Brazil and Uruguay reached the final in Rio, with the hosts losing, 2–1. Back in Montevideo, three fans died of heart attacks during the broadcast, while another succumbed in the jubilation afterwards. In Bauru, ten-year-old Edson wept upon hearing that his heroes had been vanquished.

By this time, Brazilians were acknowledged masters of this game of foot and ball which had been introduced to their nation in the late 1800s by English sailors. Although Brazil had reached the final four of the '38 World Cup, it was not until the emergence of black players that the nation really became a superpower. Banned from the sports clubs in and around Rio early in the century, undeterred blacks took the game to the beaches and hard sand plateaus above the port city. There, they played all day and long into the tropical night.

Such dedication paid off. The blacks developed a stunning technical virtuosity, and played an abstract game of imagination and deception, a far cry from the straightforward, breakneck English game. While the dilettantes and tradition-bound players frolicked on the grassy fields of Brazil's commercial centers, blacks were quietly changing the face of soccer in the hinterland. By the late 1940s, they began to dominate Brazil's pro ranks. In the '50 World Cup, Italian newspapers headlining the play asked, "COME RESISTERE?" How to resist the brilliant Brazilian game?

Although the '50 final broke the heart of the host nation, it also intensified soccer mania as thousands of mostly black players erupted from the *favelas* sprinkled over the hills of Rio and the hundreds of villages like Tres Coracoes in the provinces. An unrecognized fever, fostered by poverty and energy, infected a generation, casting its symptoms across the breadth of this emerging nation. Before the decade was out, it would produce Pele.

The Santos Football Club was heavy with aging veterans in late 1955, and coach Lula was particularly interested in the young talent on his squad. The most promising one among them was Edson, a serious youth dubbed "Gasolina" for the enthusiastic way he carried out various errands for the team's veterans. Joyfully resigned to his fate and growing more comfortable with it daily, Edson lived in a boarding house with other *aspirantes,* junior hopefuls on the Santos reserve squad. When he was not in training or playing matches, Edson attended school. Each month, he sent his entire salary home to Bauru, covering his own meager expenses with the bonus money he received for his performances on the junior team. His most impressive qualities were enthusiasm and seriousness of purpose that seemed far beyond his years. Driven partly by doubt about his own abilities and partly by the apprehensions of his mother, he had resolved to seek security as totally as he sought football excellence.

Just about one year later—one September 7, 1956—Edson played in a regular first division game for the first time. The opposition was Santo André and Edson was called upon to substitute for Vasconcellos. The stadium announcer, puzzled by the appearance of this unknown youth told the crowd that the replacement was "Tele," a well-known Brazilian player who had never worn a Santos uniform. No matter. When Edson reported, the referee arched his eyebrows and smiled slightly at this wide-eyed fifteen-year-old hayseed. Just minutes later, fortune's child took a pass in the opposition's penalty area, shucked a defender with a head feint and drilled a booming shot into the net. Lula was both impressed and amused by the youth's auspicious debut, but the heavens did not part.

Lula knew that Edson was not ready for the rugged competition of the Paulista league, and used Edson only as a substitute when the team was safely ahead. In early 1957, Santos toured Rio Grande do Sul and Edson saw action at all of the forward positions. He had eight goals as a first division pro when Lula decided to give him his first official start, against São Paulo FC on April 26. Edson responded by scoring a marvelous goal in the 3–1 victory, and was promptly discovered by the Paulista press. Genius was now unleashed, and it burst with youthful fire all over the Paulista league. By the end of the year, he had sixty-five goals, thirty-six of them in rugged league matches. The brilliance of this feat is best understood in terms of American baseball; a soccer goal is roughly equivalent to a home run. It is as if a fifteen-year-old had broken Babe Ruth's record as a rookie. Now that he was a regular, Edson's teammates began calling him only Pele.

But ominous portents circulated in the rarefied air surrounding Pele. In a match against Flamengo, a frustrated fullback who had been unable to throttle Pele finally exploded in anger and tried to pummel the uncomprehending youth. Jair, Pele's paladin, was expelled for taking up his defense. In the locker room later, Jair draped his arm around Pele's shoulders and advised: "You must be prepared for unclean play, and for retaliation. It will be part of your life, no matter how unsavory. And you should never let it interfere with your ambitions. For this reason, you must meet violence and deal with it. You must show that you can defend yourself as ably as you can confuse their feet with your dribbling." Pele listened. As usual, he did not have to be told twice.

Intense interest in the upcoming World Cup spiraled at the end of the 1957 season. Silvio Pirilo, the national team selector for Brazil, had been duly impressed by the mercurial Pele, but the critics attacked when he picked the sixteen-year-old as a member of the Rocca Cup squad. This competition was a home and away series against Argentina, known for its uncompromisingly tenacious, brutal game. The critics blanched as Pele scored the only goal in the 2–1 loss in Buenos Aires as a second-half substitute, and added another score as a starter in Brazil's 2–0 victory at home. This established his reputation in the soccer centers of South America. The World Cup would be held in Sweden six months hence, and the countdown had already begun. In less than 200 days, Pele would become a startling new word in the vocabulary of worship. He was now sixteen years old.

I do not think I was prepared for what happened in 1958. I have no idea before of how my life would change in that year. It all happen very fast. It seemed like a dream. Really, I have no time to realize what is going on. In 1958, it was all a novelty for me. The first time that I go on an airplane in my life is the one which carry me to Sweden. But all this was good, because it meant that what happened to me was a growing together. My personality developed as my fame grew, otherwise, maybe all the attention would kill me. I go to Sweden as a simple youth, still learning, so it was not like I finally reach something for which I struggle for many, many years. All this make it easier for me to accept what followed.

When I think back now, I do not remember very much of what happened. I know that the goal against Wales was maybe the most important of my entire life. Also I am told that against France in the semifinal, when French score to make game 1–1, I run into net to get the ball, run up to the center circle and put it down, then make a hot speech to my teammates. What I said to team? I don't know. I recall only running into the net for the ball. They say that when we beat France, I suddenly become very famous all over the world. But I did not realize myself. I only stay with team, train for final, hope to win. The only sign I remember of the way I play in that final against Sweden is that after I make my number two goal, I hear in the stadium people chanting my name, "Pele, Pele," and staying on their feet.

After we win was a crucial time in my life for my personality. To come back home as a hero is not always easy. But I believe I was able to keep my simplicity and, how do you say?, sincerity, because of my family. The education my family gave me was very important to me always. When I became famous, they stay same. Normally, when something like this happen, family is the first to change. But when I return to Brazil, I find life just the same, and I am happy. My mother she still very worried and always behave like football is a big risk for me. But now she accept that I am a player and that my path in life is chosen. Nothing to do.

I think also our Brazilian attitude help me, both in the World Cup and after. Our team relax in Sweden, even though we work hard. Didi, Vava, Garrincha, all of them were like brothers to me and our training ground at Hindos in the forest far away from the city was quiet and peaceful. It put no pressure on us. We did not really know what is happening in outside world, because we Brazilians have our own approach to the concentration and preparation. We relax more than European team, maybe have more easy communication. Before our important game with Russia, the first one I play in, our fullback Nilton Santos look to Garrincha and say, "Okay, let's go, I know you will not let us down." But Garrincha look only at one official for the game. He say to Santos, "Hey, look this guy, he look like Charlie Chaplin." Me, I was more nervous and serious and I forget to laugh.

Brazil left for Sweden with a team of matchless talent, a potent mix of veterans and untried youngsters like Pele and Garrincha. In terms of sheer brilliance they were the odds-on favorites to finally break through and claim the World Cup. Yet few thoughtful observers of football would bet on them. In the course of its meteoric rise in the tournaments of the past, Brazil had proven two things: first, that they were consummate, unparalleled artists, and second, that they were vulnerable and prone to collapse, stumbling just as they approached fulfillment of their promise.

Brazil had reached the final eight in three successive tournaments, only to sputter and fail. In 1954, they had been eliminated by the Hungarians, 4–2. This was the Hungarian wonder team that lost the final to West Germany in what remains one of the most puzzling and cruel upsets in sports history. Not a knowledgeable expert in the world would deny that Hungary was a squad of destiny, an intense, explosive team which skipped cavalierly through the most formidable opponents. As a primer for the tournament of '54, Hungary had become the first team in history to defeat the English nationals on their home soil. In a return match, Hungary pulverized England 7–1 in Budapest. But in the final of '54, they lost 3–2 to the same West German team they had humiliated 8–3 in the opening rounds.

The word on Brazil was that they were charming wizards, but could be taken by decent talent mixed with fiery determination. Critics suggested that the blacks possessed marvelous skills, but lacked drive and discipline. To many in the English and European football establishment, the repeated failure of Brazil in the final rounds was a heartening vindication for their own grueling, often unimaginative game. In their thinking, hard work, effort, sheer will, and the forces of reaction would prevail over creativity and free-floating talent. To a large extent, it took Pele and Garrincha, two personifications of all that seemed suspect in Brazilian football, to destroy that myth.

Brazil came to the World Cup with its most organized, balanced team ever. The only roil surfaced when Didi, the inspired father of the *foglia secca* (falling-leaf) kick was nearly left off the team. He was criticized for being too old at thirty, for marrying a white woman, and for alleged lack of effort. "It would be funny if they left me out," said the heart of the Brazil attack, "after I paid for their ticket." As for Pele, he arrived in Stockholm nursing a knee injury sustained just days earlier. It did not matter much, because he did not figure highly in Coach Feola's plans. Brazil wanted to play it safe with a veteran lineup, and Pele was untested in the crucible of the world's most illustrious tournament. Because his reputation had not passed Brazilian frontiers, the foreign press considered Pele dunnage.

The determination of Brazil to make a concentrated, well-planned run at the trophy was evident when they arrived in Sweden with a team psychologist and the kindly, even-tempered Dr. Hilton Gosling. The latter had scouted the Swedish countryside months in advance before settling on Hindos as the ideal headquarters.

As for the psychologist, he was a likable iconoclast who wandered about Hindos unshaven, clad in a bulky gray sweater. He neither believed in lecturing or criticizing the players as a group, nor in taking them to task individually, because this only made things worse. He did believe in making players draw pictures. Everybody in the Santos team had to draw a likeness of a man for analysis. The psychologist felt that the best wing partners would be a cerebral player, who drew sophisticated pictures, and an instinctive one, whose renditions were mostly matchstick men. By this standard, Pele and Garrincha, who thought this artistic exercise very amusing, were two of the more instinctive players on the team and Feola well knew that spontaneous talents were often inconsistent ones as well.

Brazil got off to a good start, steamrolling Austria 3–0. But England subsequently held them to a tie, and Feola felt the earth trembling beneath his feet. Forwards Joel and Mazzola had been unable to crack the British goalkeeping, and Feola decided that he might experiment with a more creative lineup for the game against Russia. This was also encouraged by the team. When Nilton Santos led a delegation of players to request that Garrincha be given a chance on the wing, Feola decided to give Pele a start as well. From the opening minutes, it seemed a stroke of genius. Pele and Garrincha romped through the Russian defense, hammering at the goal. At one point, Garrincha, the "little bird" who had been partly crippled since childhood, held five Russians at bay, controlling the ball as they braced in bemused embarrassment. Pele assisted on the second goal in Brazil's handy 2–0 victory.

When the preliminaries were over, Brazil found itself in the quarter-finals, against Wales. It took sixty-six minutes for Brazil to wear down the rugged Welsh defense, and it was Pele who snapped the deadlock. The goal came during a flurry of hectic activity in front of the goal, and if it was by his own estimation Pele's most important goal, it was also one of his luckiest. The goalkeeper had the angle safely covered, only to see the ball deflect into the goal off the foot of one of his own defenders.

The major obstacle had been surmounted, and the next two games hurtled by in double time, with Pele caught up in a mad whirlwind that would deposit him on top of the soccer world. Against France his three goals carried the day for Brazil. On the wet and gloomy finals day, Sweden coach George Raynor cheerfully predicted that if Brazil went down a goal early, "they would panic all over the show." Brazil did go down a goal early, as a result of a glaring defensive error. But instead of folding, the Brazilians arched their backs and attacked the game with pantherine extravagance.

Vava equalized in the tenth minute, following a fine run by Garrincha. Brazil stepped up the tempo and the game burst from the cocoon of cautious, defensive play. In the thirty-second minute, Garrincha again threaded the Swedish defense and placed the ball at Vava's feet for the lead goal.

Ten minutes later, Pele gave the '58 tournament its most memorable goal. Trapping the ball with his thigh in the Swedish penalty area, he let it fall to the crook of his ankle and in the same motion looped over his own head and that of a stunned defender, cracking a volley into the net. The ball had not touched the ground. The rest of the game was an afterthought.

Pele still believes that he played that whole game in a kind of trance, as if the future was unfolding before his own disinterested eyes. His feeling is confirmed by newsreel footage of the Brazilian squad moments after the final whistle. As he twists and turns in his teammates arms, Pele's youthful face is gripped by an almost pained wonder. He looks like a child, caught in the tortuous grip of some unnamed, private ecstasy. Each time he looks at the camera, he turns away quickly.

Brazil's victory stayed the critics. Yes, it had been the product of creative genius, but it had also been tempered by a controlling measure of organization. This final wedding of disparate elements was symbolized by Pele. While he possessed a staggering imagination and consummate skills, he also showed him-

self, at seventeen, to be a rugged player with a fund of detached, clinical knowledge. He was neither a scatter-shot
offensive threat, nor a peak-and-valley prodigy. His approach to
football was total and if his game was Brazilian, it was also informed by intelligence, stamina, and determination. The gravity
with which this child had approached life translated into his
athletic systems. His was not a crippled genius, like that of Garrincha, and his individual excellence and exploits were all the
more remarkable for his complete understanding of all aspects
of the game.

Pele returned to Brazil a hero, and promptly renegotiated his
contract with Santos, receiving $22,000 for signing, a $40,000
home, and a Volkswagen. The club was happy to do this, because they now literally held the keys to a gold mine. At his
age they could avail themselves of Pele's talents for as long as
two decades. Foreseeing packed stadiums at every Santos game,
they began laying the groundwork for what would be a year
round, global touring schedule. Eventually, their dream materialized as Santos became a traveling definition of soccer brilliance, playing some 200 games a year under all conceivable
conditions before all conceivable kinds of people.

Yet there were still skeptics in those early days following
Brazil's World Cup triumph, including those who felt blacks
were incapable of playing on an equal footing with whites.
Many of those who had only listened over the radio during the
World Cup would wait for their own eyes to finally convince
them. Pele rendered the evidence, often by the most dramatic
means. In August of 1959, Santos played a game against
Juventus, another top rank Brazilian club. At the opening
whistle it was clear that the host club's supporters had selected
Pele as their target. His first shot on goal hit the outside of
the net, triggering a shower of laughter and boorish remarks.

"Hey Negrinho, get off the field, you're only an apprentice,"
screamed one leather-lung. Unfortunately, Pele was having a
bad afternoon. His passes were imprecise or a split second late,
his rhythm floundering. "Palhaco [clown], go back to Bauru,
your place is in the forest." Pele missed a header. "Macaeo, forget soccer, it isn't a black man's game." It continued like that

until Pele took a chest-high pass at midfield and eliminated one defender by backing off and chipping the ball over his head. He was now under the ball in full stride, and each time a defender challenged, he flipped the ball over or around him, advancing it fifty yards unmolested, without letting the ball touch the ground. Finally, only one opponent was left, the goalkeeper. As he came out to challenge, Pele feinted right, juggled the ball left and contemptuously headed it into the net. Immediately, he dashed to his adversaries in the grandstand, held up both hands in triumph and screamed, "That's how a monkey scores goals." In the estimation of many, it remains his supreme performance.

By late 1960, a whole nation was convinced. The gifted Coutinho, who Pele would later call his greatest teammate, arrived and Santos became the most celebrated club in Brazil. By now, the rest of the world had taken great notice and prepared to move in. Wealthy Italian clubs had a habit of skimming the talent off the top of the South American leagues. Economically, Brazilian clubs could not match bankrolls with Europe and it often took only the wave of a few thousand dollars under a director's nose to purchase a developing talent. The players, uneducated and grafted to their clubs by what amounted to slave-labor laws, had very little say in the matter of transfer and only marginal compensation. So in 1960, it was not surprising that Santos received an offer from three Italian clubs who had pooled resources to seek the services of Pele. The only surprise was the size of the offer—the equivalent of one million American dollars. Santos never even had a chance to think about it, because the Brazilian government promptly declared Pele a nonexportable national treasure.

By now, every club in the world knew that a game against Santos and Pele insured a sellout, and they lined the mailboxes at Santos's headquarters with lucrative offers, all of them contingent on Pele's presence. As a result, Pele and Santos worked out a joint profit-sharing scheme which boosted him into an income bracket comparable to that of any athlete in the world. By necessity, he also developed a secretive life-style, frequenting back-stairs and service elevators, slipping into theaters after the curtain and leaving before the lights were turned up. But it was only a practical device; whenever Pele was caught in public, he graciously and patiently signed autographs and chatted for hours on end.

The new Brazilian team manager Aymore Moreira had a prediction for the upcoming 1962 World Cup. "The World Cup could be terribly rough and violent," he said, "and I don't think we will see very many goals." This was a reference to the increasing negativism in football, the growing impulse to play a physical, defensive game. Still, Brazil left for the games in Chile in fine form. Pele was now an idol, the acknowledged focal point of this marvelous team. Most of the '58 veterans were back, including Garrincha, who had by now fathered eight daughters, and detonated the love of popular singer Elsa Soares, who pursued him as doggedly as any defender and finally marked him for marriage.

Brazil began its cup defense with a 2–0 win over Mexico with the twenty-one-year-old Pele fulfilling the sternest expectations. Italy and Chile confirmed Moreira's forecast in another early match featuring players who spit in each other's faces, a broken nose from a left hook, two expulsions, and ugly outbursts of hooliganism on the field. It seemed that the relatively docile Brazilians might have a rugged time dealing with this style of play. The fears escalated into paranoia when Pele, shooting a powerful twenty-five-yarder on the post against Czechoslovakia, severely tore a thigh muscle and limped off the field and out of the tournament. But despite the foreboding Brazil would not be denied and again it was primarily a Negrinho who carried them. Garrincha played magnificently, right through to the final, as did his wing counterpart Zagalo. The latter also sprang from the destitution of the northeast where, according to Dr. Gosling, he developed his phenomenal lung capacity by swimming in the murderous coastal breakers. Pele's substitute, Amarildo, was brilliant and when Brazil desperately needed a digger, a reliable, intelligent and precise player who could shoulder the responsibility left by Pele, they found him in Zito, Pele's Santos teammate.

"I Only Wanted to Be My Father"

I have my first girl friend when I have twelve or thirteen years, in Bauru. She was fifteen, a Japanese girl whose father owned a grocery store near my house. We have a very nice time together, but then I go to Santos and we must forget each other. When I arrive at Santos, I don't think of girls too much, I worry about how I play and my chances to make the team. Then, after the World Cup of 1958, I met Rosemeri Cholby. I was nineteen and she was fourteen and from the beginning I like her very much.

I met Rose for the first time at a basketball game. The Santos team sleep then in a dormitory where she is a player on the basketball team in the same gymnasium. Many Santos players see Rose, and they all like her. Rose sat on the bench, she did not play much the first time I saw her. This was good by me, because I get a chance to look at her very close, while all my teammates shout, "put her in game, put her in game." I found out that she work in a record store so I begin to go over there and I am embarrassed. I want to talk with her, but I think I should also buy the records. So I make a good record collection and get to know Rose very well.

We like each other, and I would like to go with her to dinner, or the theater. But this made a problem, because now I am famous and if the journalists see me with a girl I know it will be in every newspaper the next day. Also, I did not realize it at the time but I think maybe I wanted to be sure that Rose like Edson, not only Pele. So if we go together quietly, with no big circus, I find out for sure how she feel and how I feel.

So I go after the training sessions to see Rose play basketball. Later when we start to go out more serious, Rose would go with her aunt to a movie theater. They go in, and keep one place open for me. After the lights go out, I sneak into movie and then near the end of film I sneak out. It was little bit strange, and it was very old-fashioned. I come to know Rose's family, and I go there for lunch sometimes. We build a relationship.

I have some things in common with her father, Señor Guilhern, who work for the harbor authority in Santos. Both of us like to hunt and fish, so many times we go fishing together, in a little rowboat. Maybe that is where I got my best physical training, because I row and row all day, and think I am rowing closer to Rose. One day, sometime after the 1962 Mundial I decide to arrange a little fishing expedition so I can speak to him of my courtship of Rose. At this time we like each other enough so I feel I must get his permission because we cannot hide our feelings anymore. Perhaps I also want somebody besides Rosie and myself in this confidence, because we must do so much in secret that we are like the ghosts. I want to explain to her father that I don't like or intend to court Rose in secret. So we go fishing one day and I say over and over to myself, "Today I sink or swim."

When I tell him, Señor Guilhern say that Rose is very young and he would have to speak with his wife about this. At the time also the footballers are not so well-respected as today, even though the situation was getting always better. It is same story; they like me, but most worry about what happen if I get serious injury or my career is suddenly destroyed. Rose is at this time only about eighteen years old, so for her it is the biggest step in life. We wait a little bit, her father told me. So it is a good beginning, and some time after that we decide to marry in 1966, during the Carnaval when everybody is busy, and before the World Cup.

My wedding is a problem because in Brazil it is in all the newspapers and we want to have nice, quiet ceremony. So we make some stories to create confusion and decide to make the event at my house on the morning after the biggest day of the Carnaval, when everybody is tired and have hangover.

Still, it is big problem. Every newspaper put one man to watch my house and one man to watch Rose's house. My manager then, a man called Pepe Gordo, also tell some people. When Rose arrive, there are photographers everywhere, on the balconies nearby. One Turkish guy even fall off a balcony in all the pushing. Then there is the wedding, with many TV camera and crew. In the middle of the ceremony one cameraman tries to get behind altar to make picture of Rose and me, but his cable go over the altar and he knock off a big statue of a saint—crash—it break right in middle of ceremony. But by now I am used to this kind of thing, so I don't worry and my marriage was just the old and beautiful story which happen to millions of people all the time but for everyone it still has some special meaning. After the ceremony we go straight to airport to a plane to Munich, where we begin our honeymoon.

I believe my marriage was most important to bring maturity into my life. When you begin to live with another person, that is a radical change. Before, I was a happy kid, with no responsibility. But then I must become more mature because I have a daughter, Kelly Christina in 1967 and son Edinho in 1970. I have new responsibility and I must think more seriously about the business and security of the future. This Rose help me very much in, because she is quiet woman who prefer to stay in the background. Because I travel so much, she help to look after the business. But most important, she is very good mother for the children. I like very much to fool around and roll on the floor with the kids, but I was always afraid that if they get hurt a little, they feel it is hostility from me because I am home so little. So Rose and I make decision that when the kids need a little guidance, she is the one who speak and I support her. She knows the psychology very well.

Pele entered the 1966 World Cup as a man of twenty-five totally in concert with himself. Able to demand anything of his body, he was also armed with a new tranquility stemming from his marriage. The cup was held in England and Brazil loomed as the pretournament favorite, although astute witnesses questioned the side's apparent reverence for the aging standouts who engineered the '58 and '62 victories. The increasing trend towards conservatism in football had even infected Brazil. Although their game was still based on imagination and skill, they added to this slow-paced, artful style a yeomanly defensive line. And still there were skeptics. "Sooner or later," the 1962 Czech team manager Rudolf Vytacil predicted, "Brazil's nerves would crack."

What did finally crack was not Brazil's nerves, but Pele's

knees. Brazil faced Bulgaria in the first round of the tournament and won 2–0 on a pair of perfectly executed falling-leaf free kicks by Pele and Garrincha. Bulgaria had assigned the pugnacious fullback Zachev to Pele, and he dealt hurt on the Brazilian at every opportunity without so much as a word of caution from the referee.

A French journalist watching in the press box foresaw the problems Pele would encounter. "Pele won't finish this World Cup," he remarked, "it is amazing that he hasn't gone mad already." The physical punishment he faced was so severe that he had to sit out Brazil's next match against a Hungarian side whose brilliance was on the wane. The result was Brazil's first loss in a World Cup match since 1954, in a 3–1 match that succeeding generations would remember as one of the finest to ever grace the games. It was daring, attacking football from start to finish by both sides, moving one journalist to write, "Football that day found an expression of its truth which touched on absolute art."

But Brazil's invincibility had been shaken, and the team now faced Portugal and Eusebio, who was touted throughout Europe as the successor to Pele. Although Pele started, he was only half-fit and Portugal controlled from the outset. Drained from its match against Hungary and plagued by inadequate goalkeeping, Brazil fell behind 2–0 with twenty-five minutes to go. This rendered the ensuing destructiveness of the Portuguese totally odious. The player assigned to Pele was under orders to neutralize him at any cost. He fouled repeatedly and flagrantly, and his efforts came to fruition twenty-five minutes into the match. He and another defender sandwiched Pele viciously as the three of them fought for an air ball and crashed to the turf in a tangle of churning arms and legs. Pele did not get up. He lay there, clutching his right knee, a victim of plain brutality. The hush that fell over the stadium at Wembley, lasted long after Pele was carried off the field.

Later, watching the incident on film, Pele would reconfirm what he had said just hours after he was carried off the Wembley pitch. "For me, there will be no more World Cups. Soccer has been distorted by violence and destructive tactics. I do not want to finish my life as an invalid."

Pele's attitude was all the more poignant given his durability as a player. This was the same man who had once played a series of games in Paraguay with his arm in a sling. Ever since Jair had warned Pele of what lay in store, he had taken an eye for an eye approach to unsportsmanlike conduct. He retaliated when an opponent fouled intentionally, once angrily seizing the offender and butting heads with him. Yet he never fouled intentionally himself and he finally discovered that there was no practical reply to a perfectly executed "cheap shot."

Pele and Brazil were now out of the tournament, as host England went on to win, beating Portugal in the semis and West Germany in the finals. The winners were the first to admit that they could not match the technique or artistry of the Latin Americans. They had kicked and scratched their way all the way to the semifinals only by virtue of hard work and determination. Yet in all fairness, the team had brilliant moments and in the final two games became worthy champions.

Despite the neutralization of Pele in two successive World Cups, his legend grew steadily and irrepressibly. Between 1962 and 1969, Pele led Santos to a number of World Cup championships, South American titles, and right along the yellow brick road to financial success as a touring club. He had become a uniquely global celebrity, one whose influence extended far beyond the touchlines.

In 1960, the duke of Edinburgh paid an official visit to Brazil, wanting to watch Pele play and perhaps exchange a few words with him. This put the Brazilian Foreign Office in a quandary. Should the visitor go down the field to greet Pele, or should the twenty-six-year-old footballer step up to the dais to meet the duke? The prince himself solved the problem, deciding to kneel to royalty on its home turf. He walked down to the field.

Zaire declared a national holiday when Pele came to play and the city of Belgrade also took the day off. On a trip to Brazil, Senator Robert Kennedy visited the Santos locker room after one game and embraced Pele just as he stepped out of the shower, lathering the front of Kennedy's suit with soap suds. The prime minister of Gabon refused to pay Santos its guarantee money until he could have a private meeting and conversation with Pele in his office.

Everywhere it was the same. The Nigerian chief of state received Pele and upon the entrance of the footballer, this stately, conservative patriarch could only gaze at him, muttering, "So you are Pele . . . you are Pele." King Faisal of Ryad, a more practical man, simply offered to hire Pele for one year, ostensibly to give soccer demonstrations to the local street urchins. He offered Pele $3,000 monthly, a bonus of $400,000 at the time of signing, a palatial home, and chauffeured limousine.

When Pele met the pope in private audience, the pontiff reportedly said, "Don't be nervous, I am more nervous than you because I have been waiting to meet Pele personally for a very long time." France gave Pele a ticker-tape parade and appointed him chevalier of the Order of Merit. Later, local hostilities in Biafra were suspended for three days while Pele played two exhibitions. First there was a game on the Nigerian side. Afterwards, he was put into a boat in the river that separated the warring nations and escorted halfway across by a Nigerian officer. Waiting for Pele was a Biafran launch, and the rival officers saluted each other crisply as Pele changed craft. Pele then played a game on the Biafran side. That the war resumed after he left was not his fault.

After his bitter experience in the '66 World Cup, Pele began to pay more attention to his business interests. He played in Paulista league matches and toured, but close observers felt that he was holding back, still living beneath the clouds at Wembley. Occasionally, Pele would reveal his genius to demonstrate that it was still very much intact. But he seemed not to offer his talents as completely and selflessly as before.

Meanwhile, incentive clauses and tour bonuses had turned Pele into a millionaire. He also signed endorsement contracts with various companies, including Puma shoes, the TV Colorado, and Athleta, a manufacturer of sporting clothes. Eventually, he would own some fifty apartment houses. Often, he allowed poor families to live in them rent-free. He also purchased a large farm a hundred miles from Santos as a retreat, and custom-designed a modest ranch-style house in Santos.

It immediately became a regular stop for tourist buses and had a twenty-four–hour police guard posted at the front door. One radio station became a Pele property, and among the songs it played were several Brazilian top-ten tunes written and recorded by Pele. In 1966, his mother received the house her young son had promised her so long ago, together with a monthly check for $1500 and an apartment house.

It is mildly astonishing that this uneducated child of the impoverished Brazilian heartland was nicked in the commercial marketplace only twice. The first time, it was by a generally inept business manager who succeeded in bankrupting a buildings material business Pele had invested in. This was in the mid-sixties, and it marked the last time Pele would give any business associate carte blanche.

The other fiasco stemmed from mutual ownership of a rubber company, Fiolux. Pele had unfortunately signed a universal liability clause, assuming personal responsibility for any debts the company incurred. He lost well over a million dollars in that venture in the late 1960s, but extracted himself and turned his attentions to a successful export-import business.

As the decade came to a close, Pele was acknowledged as "the goose that laid the golden egg for Santos" by the Paulista press. But the incubation was never easy. On one typical tour-week Santos spent 120 hours in the air and played in temperatures ranging from 103 degrees to 13 degrees in less than twenty-four hours. There were stops in New York, Los Angeles, Honolulu, the Fiji Islands, Sydney, Ryad, Qatar, Bahrain, Khartoum, Dubai, Nuremberg, Liege, Coventry, London, Rio, and São Paulo. Of the fourteen games Santos played usually in forty-eight–hour intervals at places thousands of miles apart, the team lost one.

But there was another dimension to Pele's productivity. He was now approaching the 1,000th goal plateau, a mark that had never before seemed possible, even for the finest players in the world. When the Paulista press took count and realized that the landmark score would surely come before the end of 1969, the eyes of the football world became riveted on the countdown. On October 22, Pele scored his 995th and the hunt for goal number 1,000 began in earnest. Hundreds of journalists trailed Santos to every stadium, as the total climbed to 999 on the eve of a game against Bahia, where the natives hoped that their celebration along All Saints Bay would put Rio's Carioca Carnaval to shame. Among the planned festivities would be a Thanksgiving mass. But the score did not materialize, and Santos returned to Maracana for a meeting with Vasco da Gama on November 19 with Pele still one goal from immortality.

Despite torrential rains, 80,000 Cariocas jammed the ground. The stands bristled with the nation's television cameras. Pele took twenty minutes to overcome a case of nerves and then settled into his usual, incomparable game. A superb lob was turned over the bar in the last agonizing second. Minutes later, Pele banged the crossbar with a furious shot. But time ticked by and Pele was shut out until the closing minutes of the game, when he split the defense and ran onto a perfect ball from Clodoaldo. Only a desperation tackle, a foul in the penalty area, saved a sure goal. Now the world could watch with complete attention. Pele placed the ball on the penalty spot and took a few extra moments of concentration to plan the shot. The goal was anticlimactic, a simple banana kick that curved gracefully into the lower left corner. After a frozen moment, Pele sprinted into the net for the ball and hundreds of newsmen poured onto the field, clustering around him. For a few moments, Pele was speechless. Finally, he opened his mouth, speaking in a strange, almost hysterical voice. "Remember the children, remember the poor children."

The next morning, the Brazilian press divided its front pages between Pele's feat and the landing on the moon by astronauts Conrad and Bean. Forming on the horizon was the 1970 World Cup, which would test Pele with one of the most unsavory experiences in his life before providing the perfect donouement to his career as an international.

After the experiences of '66, it take me maybe two year to change my mind about the World Cup. I do not want to play in '70, but I realize that there is not much choice. I am footballer, this is my life, I must accept. I was ready to wear national colors again when the problems begin.

The team manager, Joao Saldanha, was very temperamental man. He feel, I think, that many of our veteran players too old but he also believe they are greedy, something I do not agree with. First, he drop from team four tested defender in November 1969, even though Brazil had not played international match for past four months. Then, he also come after me. At first, he want me to play a different position and change the kind of game Brazil play. This was very unnatural for me and not so easy to learn, therefore Saldanha think I am just not trying, and that I am over satisfied with past achievements. He say Pele is not good, is greedy, he is not going to play for national team. This okay by me, because I think is just a personal problem. But then come only one or two people to defend me. This make me very disappointed. For twelve years, they ask me to play for Brazil, and I am player that make many goals, try to do everything best and now everybody turn against me. You know, I say to myself, what am I doing here. When I play good, everybody come to me and say, "Yes, Pele, you are wonderful, yes, we love you." But if they have idea that there is problem, or that you cannot make for them glory, they drop you.

So Saldanha want to make purge, but it make so many problem that he must go out as manager and Zagalo come in. By this time, there are many problem. One trainer from Flamengo club criticize Saldanha and so Saldanha go after him with a gun, try to shoot him. This is big scandal, and also help turn the mind of people to Zagalo. This finish problem, but I never forget, and I keep it in my mind when it comes to '74 World

Cup. I decide to play in '70, try very hard to help Brazil to third World Cup and then to stop playing while nobody can say, "Forget Pele, he has nothing more to give."

We win the cup in '70, is very satisfying for me, because for me it is personal victory, but also a thing which help Brazil very much. In '64, we have the revolution and Medici eventually become our president. At this time, Brazil struggle to develop itself further, and to show progress to the world. One way to unite country, make the pride and enthusiasm to begin a program is to win World Cup because it gives international prestige and helps to bring all the people of Brazil together. When we win, people in streets everywhere have Brazilian flag. Not so long after this begins the big advance of Brazilian economy. I like to think the '70 World Cup have some responsibility for this.

The high, hot climate favored the South American entries, because their slow, chimerical game was developed under like conditions and could be more easily sustained at the elevation of Mexico City. But the internal power struggle in the Brazilian federation had resulted in a puzzling club. People wondered if Brazil might not be a team whose best games were behind it. England looked as if they might repeat. But there were two factors working against the defenders; the climate, and an unseemly feud with racial overtones between the Mexicans and English organizers. Another question was whether Pele would survive the violence of the game or be driven to the side lines for the third successive time.

In the opening round, Brazil trounced Czechoslovakia, 4–1, displaying what the contemptuous Czechs later called "basketball defense," because Brazil simply drifted back as a unit at every advance of the Czechs and clogged up the backfield. Pele exposed the faulty logic which had argued for dropping him off the team. One aspect of his all-around brilliance, were his frequent retreats from his forward position to help direct the most creative midfield any World Cup has seen.

The luck of the draw found England matched against Brazil

in an early game which many retrospectively called the real final. The game began with the experts choice as the greatest save ever turned in by a mortal goalkeeper. Jairzinho, a worthy successor to Garrincha, broke free and darted down the wing to the end line, whirling and centering perfectly to Pele, who rose high and headed the ball down, on the bounce towards the left-hand post. He was already shouting "goal" when Gordon Banks launched himself across the length of the goal and tipped the ball over the bar with one outstretched hand.

"He leap like a salmon," Pele said later, "it is best save I ever see, it is a pity it came to nothing in the end." And so it was. With temperatures reaching ninety degrees, the two heavy-weights of the tournament played a spectacular game. Brazil's goal in the fourteenth minute of the second half proved decisive. Tostao dribbled past three defenders on the left wing and shot the ball over to Pele near the goal mouth. Pele passed up the shot with a deceptive fake and pushed it over to onrushing Jairzinho for the easy score. After the game, England reported that not one player had sweated off less than ten pounds that afternoon.

Brazil advanced to the final against Italy, and since both sides had won the World Cup twice the victor would become the first team in history to retire the Jules Rimet trophy. The game also had the overtones of a morality play. Italy, with its *catenaccio* defense was the embodiment of conservative football. *Catenaccio* was predicated upon scoring early and then lying back, turning the game off. It was negativism of the worst kind, in which the team banked heavily on the hopes of the opposition making a mistake instead of taking the initiative with aggressive play. Brazil, with its suspect defense and traditionally unexceptional goalkeeping was the ideal mark for this philosophy. If Italy could score early, the World Cup final could become a dreary exercise in keep-away.

But it would not be; Brazil's creative genius rose to the occasion, and Pele orchestrated a dazzling exhibition of daring, joyful soccer. He scored one magnificent goal, created two more and at twenty-nine played the most incandescent football of his career. Back at home, President Medici listened to the game on earphones during Sunday mass. Brazil went ahead after eighteen minutes, as Pele climbed an invisible ladder against the taller Italian defenders to head home a cross from Rivelino. But one of the lapses Italy had hoped for occurred seven minutes from the half, as Clodoaldo carelessly back-passed—right to an Italian forward who scored easily on the breakaway.

The teams played to a stand-off until the sixty-sixth minute, when Gerson hit a tremendous drive to put Brazil up, 2–1. This ended Italy's hopes, because now they would have to come out of their conservative formation and play Brazil's game. Pele and company leaped upon the opportunity, exploiting the new breathing room and scored again in the seventy-first minute. Pele slipped Gerson's free kick to Jairzinho. The final goal of the '70 World Cup came from Carlos Alberto, who ran onto a sublime pass from Pele. It was all over, and more than one journalist found the result gratifying. Wrote Brian Glanville, correspondent for London's *Sunday Times*:

The Brazilian jubilation afterwards was as spectacular and memorable as anything one had seen on the field: a joyful, dancing invasion of fans milling around their victorious players, pulling off their bright yellow shirts and hoisting them, bare to the waist, on to their shoulders. In this exuberance, this unconfirmed delight one seemed to see a reflection of the way Brazil had played; and played was, indeed, the word. For all their dedication, all their passion, they and their country had somehow managed to remain aware that football was, after all, a game; something to be enjoyed.

So the Jules Rimet Trophy, won by them for the third time, went permanently to Brazil, who had shown that enterprise, fantasy, attacking play were still compatible with success; provided you had the talent. . . .

Overall, despite the abominable [heat] conditions, the 1970 World Cup had been a marvelous triumph of the positive over the negative, the creative over the destructive. The final itself took on the dimensions almost of an allegory.

At the apex of Brazil's accomplishment stood Pele, whose contribution to the life of the game is best summed up by a moment from the early play-off game against Czechoslovakia. The game was tied at 1–1 and the Czechs were threatening. Pele, taking a ball near midfield, dribbled towards the center circle. Suddenly, he stopped a full fifty yards from the opponent's goal and chipped a high lob downfield.

Both teams and 80,000 spectators stood aghast as the ball floated serenely through the humid air. The Czech goalkeeper whirled and rushed desperately back towards his own net, and at that moment Pele's genius descended on the stadium with the impact of a bludgeon. From fifty yards away, Pele had detected that the Czech keeper had ventured just a few steps too far out onto the field. Missing by inches, the ball drifted over the crossbar, carried by the crowd's spontaneous roar of amazement.

Now there could be no encore. With the feud of '69 in the back of his mind, Pele retired from the national team on July 18, 1971. He last wore the national colors against Yugoslavia, playing the first half of a match at Maracana. The chant, "fica, fica" (stay, stay), reached a deafening crescendo of 180,000 voices as Pele lapped the field, waving his No. 10 jersey in triumph, tears streaming down his face. But it was to no avail. Neither was the petition he received signed by 100,000 school children, nor the fervent arguments of his friend Zagalo as the '74 cup approached.

Pele would continue to play with Santos, but he already saw an end to that too. This time, he wanted a simple parting. "One day, soon, during a game, I will decide that this will be the last one I will play until the final whistle. In the dressing room, after the shower, I will shake hands with my pals as usual and I'll say to them: "Meet Edson Arantes do Nascimento." That is how he imagined it.

My retirement from Santos was perhaps the most difficult decision of my life, because I know how emotional a time it would be. I decided to myself one month before that I stop on October 4, in our last home game. I did not want it to be a big circus in Maracana. I speak with my friends and family about the decision, but I don't tell them when. Physically, I feel I can play more, many more games. But there were other things involved in my decision.

I play for eighteen years in Santos and I see many change. More and more, as players make a lot of money and become heroes fast it is less like family and close friends and more like business. Everybody want to be a big star. The team, I know it is not so big and good as before, but the players think it is. But by this time, I do not want to fight with anybody and I have my own peace. As I become older, I become more expert in seeing the problems. When you are young, you only want to play. Later you see yourself in the young players. You go to give them advice, but the players no want to pay attention. Maybe this is because they are too proud in their new status.

When I start to play, players were bad people in the eyes of almost everybody, like drunken bad men. If you have a girl friend and her father find out you are football player, he tell her, "Sorry, you cannot go out anymore, you must find a good man." Players then were like the singer stars today. After I start, I have many chance to do things for soccer. For instance, before the '58 Mundial, all the children want to stay with me and speak with me because I am child too, only sixteen years old. This change the mind of fathers also. After we win in Sweden I make new contract for what is very good money in Brazil at that time people think maybe is a good idea for son to be a footballer. My big fame help also, and the honors from kings and politicians, all kinds of people. Little by little, football player became respectable man.

But then in the early seventies things change much, new generation of footballers are different and I feel not in place I never say, "It is me or this guy;" I believe all players on all teams are my friends. But I also feel last great Santos team is past and that I am only trying to stay where I do not belong, in an era that is the past. So I make the decision.

"I Only Wanted to Be My Father"

For me, it is like discovering Edson again, and I have seen Edson very little in my life. Even at home, I was not Edson but Dico. Edson is just the boy who arrive at Santos wearing short pants and very soon become Pele. People come to kiss Pele, to stroke his head for good luck. I have always asked why that happen to me, and I do not know. It is strange feeling, to think that so many people believe I can do no wrong. But I have my own fear, and always it was that I would try to do something beyond my capacity. For so long I have been lucky man. My father have no luck, his knee injury kill his career. But I never even have operation. So more and more I think it is maybe smart to stop.

In days before I retire, I feel sad confusion and great tension. People come to me and say, "Not to worry, I will still be your friend." I wonder then, is this farewell a rupture, a barrier that will divide me from the way of life that I am used to? The real tension begin in game on twenty-second of September, because I know then I do not turn back. After that game, I cry some tears. Later, before a game against the Corinthians club, I was in concentration, in a room shared with Marinho and Bianchi. I feel the urge to cry and cannot stop it. I am not sure if my friends see this. I think yes, but they were sensitive and not say anything.

Finally come October 4 and I live the strangest moments of my life. It is difficult to say what I felt, because it was pure emotion, not something I think. I look at public and players and say to myself, "No more," and it sound like the voice of other man.

Julio Mazzei met Pele in 1962, when he arrived in Santos to work as a trainer. He became a close friend and advisor to him as Pele's career progressed, and spent the most time with Pele through those last few days. Mazzei remembers:

> There is a lot of speculation about whether this will be Pele's last game, because he managed not to tell anyone, including Rose, until very close to October 4. A month earlier,

he told me he did not want to finish in a big stadium but at Santos's home facility, which hold thirty thousand. All that week of his retirement the newspapers and TV speculate on how much Pele would play and what he would do. People in streets, in bars everywhere said, "Well, this is the last chance to see Pele," as the game come close and the news leak out.

All that week, Pele was very tense; I know because he play the guitar a lot when he is tense. Also, he was not completely fit because of a muscle pull in his leg and he was afraid he would play badly. We talk a lot that week, about what Pele would do to tell the people he was leaving. I suggested that if he score a goal, he take the ball and run around the field. But he answered, "No, professor. My feelings will tell me what to do and I want it to be spontaneous."

Finally came the night before the game. Normally, Santos goes to a clubhouse in the mountains, where it is very peaceful, with a lake on both sides. The players relax, play cards, chess, billiards, watch the TV. Pele went only for dinner and asked if he could spend the night at home. This is when everybody found out that something is up.

The next morning, he is so nervous, that he send the whole family out to the farm. He wanted to be alone. He did not go to his business office, as was his habit. Only his home was comfortable for him, and the police give him two guards to stand by the house.

Inside, he watched television and played the guitar. I went to visit him in the afternoon, and I tried to make the mood more humorous and happy. But I see that it cannot be, so I left him with his thoughts and just sat with him. At 4:00 P.M. we went back to the clubhouse in the mountains for the pregame meal. Edu asked Pele how long he would play that night and Pele answered, "I don't know." Clodoaldo asked him how he will signal his final play and Pele said the same thing. Then Carlos Alberto tried to make a joke, saying, "Pele, don't stop yet. Without you we lose all our opportunity to make the money. Nobody will want us for a foreign tour anymore." Pele smile at this.

When we arrived at the stadium, the vendors outside were shouting, "Hurry, people, last chance to buy Pele button,

Pele flag." All over were hand-painted bed sheets, saying, "Pele, thank you." The scalpers sold tickets for thirty dollars and all over the field were journalists and cameramen. They pushed the microphones in his face, but he said nothing.

All the people brought fireworks, and when I looked up the skies were exploding. The game was against Ponte Preta. Of course, everybody expected Pele to make a goal despite his injury. The game began and by the twenty-fifth minute, Pele had only touched the ball twelve times. Then, near midfield, somebody gave him a high pass. Pele caught the ball in his hands, ran to the midfield circle and knelt down. He put the ball between his knees and made the cross with his arms, slowly turning to face every side of the stadium as a thank you.

Now everybody is standing up, and they began to shout, "Pele, Pele, Pele." Pele shook hands with the referee, the opposing players, and his teammates and started to run around the field. When he ran about fifty yards, he stopped and took off his Santos shirt. He waved it and the people and the crowd roared. All the newspapermen run around the field with him. But he didn't say anything.

Then everybody in the stadium begin to wave white handkerchiefs, a Brazilian symbol of farewell. Pele ran into the tunnel to the locker room and went into it alone. The door had been guarded, but one photographer managed to hide in the bathroom. Pele came into the room and put his head inside his locker, crying for five minutes. Then, dressed in his game shorts, with no shirt, socks, or shoes, he walked out to the car waiting for him and went to join his family on the farm.

So it was over. An era that soccer fans will remember as the equivalent of the Romantic period in music or the Renaissance in art had come to an end. One enthusiast ventured that "the generation of the sixties had been the luckiest to walk the face of the earth because it had seen Pele play."

After I retire, it was hard time even though I still train all the time with Santos and make the Pepsi clinics. Just the travel, concentration and game change. Still, everybody make the invitation for me to come and play in exhibition game and all-star game, so this make it little easier for me.

To see me at home was big adjustment for the family. When I play with Santos, I am always with the team on weekends, and now those days were free. After eighteen years, I have a Sunday with my family. I think, how you say, family deserves this? It was a little strange, because on weekend I do not know what to do. It is like this [Pele pressed his hands together and withdrew his body to indicate tension]. All the time, I find myself tight, and then I say, "What are you doing, you don't have game, why do you feel like this?"

My son Edinho did not want to go to games, but want to stay with me all the day. So we make a family program for every weekend because Edinho want to go by the beach and my daughter Kelly Christina want to go to restaurant to eat on Saturday night. I begin to know my children much better. I notice that Edinho all the time want to stay with ball, like I was as a child. But I see also that he has a different personality. When I was a child, I joke much more. He is serious. He has more concentration and is more quiet—maybe because he is son of Pele and all the people want to know him. In my time, I go to street and play all the time and have many friend that come to my house. Edinho don't have too many friend, even home in Brazil. He never bring friend home to play.

I believe I have lived a decent life. It did not take me long to learn when people try to take advantage of me, so I never become bitter about my fame. I started to watch this situation when I was very young and saw that it might make problem. Now I hope it doesn't make problem for my children. But I also decide that I would not put anybody in a bad spot in front of other people. I know I am not perfect man, so I believe I should judge others that way too. For me, the great satisfaction is that through my career I have many friends, and if I lost everything tomorrow I know I can get a job and support my family. For a boy born poor, this is very important thing. In my retirement, I decide to continue business interests because my father tell me, "When you are making money, do not stop to count it." But I also never did anything just for the money. I never really had the ambition to be a rich man. NUNCA.

One more thing I realize was that I never felt the solitude of an idol. I always liked my situation, even though sometimes it make having a personal life very difficult. I have good reason to be proud of my career, because I sometimes had an immediate effect on lives of people. Like when they stop the war for soccer game. This is good thing, and maybe it help a little bit.

I hope I served the children, because for me youth is something sacred. This is why even in recent years I have faith in young people. When they revolt, it is only because they want to build, but not along the same road, the safe road. Because my desire to be a soccer player was also a gamble, I feel for this. Life did not permit me to be like these young people today because since age fourteen, I have been occupied with training, travel, concentration, games. I did not have the time to reflect as much as others during that very important period in life. And I became a footballer, no more, no less.

When we are young, we are always rushed, in a hurry, running all the time. We, I, you ought to do something to change the world and we can only do this in small ways that are part of our real self. I don't believe any honest man ever believed he did enough to help others. Probably those who feel they did very little actually did the most. Technology, science, everything evolves except the mind of the man who is late. I think this is why young people did so many protests. They did not want to be late.

When I retire, I have a chance to think of all these things. I realize that a man cannot stop either, no matter how far he goes or how much he accomplishes. All the time I felt like other people, like my talent was a gift of God and my luck unusual. But for me, fame became a way of life and it was a fate which I tried to accept as the best fate. After I retire, I see that for me, what people call the normal life would be abnormal. It is already too late for me, I am far along my path.

For me, football was life for more than twenty years, and even though I am very active and involved in business, the game stay in my blood and I never really leave it. I love the game; my father and brother are both players and I have never been tired of the sport. Only this—the challenge went out for me, because so much had been accomplished. Playing more years with Santos would have become maybe a little bit boring. I also have the merchandising and business, but this is different, have a different feel. When I retire, I am in unique position. I have thirty-two years and already I am finished with one life. What is next? It must be something, because if I do not play, if I do not do something, I die.

2

"Clive, You Are Crazy, My Friend"

*I*n February 12, 1971, the mercury in Kingston, Jamaica is a pulsing ninety-two degrees; the humidity is 88 percent. This is not a climate that Clive Toye is used to; yet, as he steps squinting into the heat, the general manager of the New York Cosmos is smiling, as if he is enjoying a private joke with the lizards on the veranda of the Sheraton Hotel. If so, he has little else in common with the colorful Jamaican environment. His chubby English face, now pink from the sun, his well-tailored English suit, and his Charles Laughton portliness seemed better suited to a paneled library. There is, however, no time for a library in Clive Toye's near future.

In fact, Toye is about to become a gray-flanneled astronaut who will fly the equivalent of seventeen times around the earth in the next three years. He will become soccer's Great White Hunter, wired into international flight schedules, and a maze of Western Union and Watts lines that pipe the world into his office. He will swing between three-star restaurants and musty locker rooms beneath stadiums in strange lands. His telephone bills will rise to $800 a day. His great chase will cost more than all of Queen Isabella's expeditions and make him a man of intrigue in the midst of many whispers.

But today the most startling sound is that of tow-headed youngsters splashing about in the pool, as their mothers tan nearby. Otherwise, the area is deserted. Several feet from the veranda is a green almond tree, tall and festive, with glossy clumps of fruit hanging from its branches. Five wicker-backed chairs and a table have been arranged beneath it; three of the chairs are empty.

Kurt Lamm, secretary of the United States Soccer Federation, sits in one chair while Phil Woosnam occupies the other. Woosnam, a slender, intense man drums his fingers on a smooth bamboo armrest. He is the commissioner of the North American Soccer League, having emigrated to the United States from the farm country of central Wales, well endowed with traits his job demands—relentless optimism and mulelike tenacity.

Commissioner Woosnam, Lamm, and Cosmos General Manager Toye have come to Jamaica ostensibly to arrange a United States tour for the celebrated Brazilian soccer team Santos, in Jamaica for an exhibition game. By signing Santos, they hope to pump a little adrenalin and a lot of cash into the NASL. On an earlier tour in 1968, Santos and Pele had proven a fine draw, attracting 109,882 spectators for six games; their record that year against teams from all over the world was 58–5. Amazingly, two of those losses came against American teams, the New York Generals and the Cleveland Stokers. Everybody—Brazilians, Americans, the spectators, and NASL officials—looked back in wonderment on those events.

So did Pele. He would remember his first brush with American soccer in black-and-blue technicolor. After Santos lost to the Generals 5–3, he was moved to say, "I am surprised at how far American standards have come up." It had been an unexpectedly frustrating afternoon for Pele, who was shut out by the Generals' Gordon Bradley. A robust, aggressive defender, who sometimes seemed almost as interested in kicking the man as the ball, Bradley wrapped himself around Pele like an overcoat, shadowing his every move. Five times during the game, Pele was sent sprawling from a robust sliding tackle, and each

"Clive, You Are Crazy, My Friend"

time he brushed it off with the annoyance of a man flicking dandruff from the lapel of his sportcoat. Asked what separated Pele from the world's other great players, Bradley never hesitated, "He can take a kick better than anyone I've seen." Seven years later, that same truculent Bradley would coach Pele on the New York Cosmos.

Persuading Pele and Santos to trade a few more kicks with American teams might not, then, be such a difficult task. But there was another reason for this visit to Kingston, a granule of cockeyed hope lying beneath all the smooth sunny talk. American soccer urgently needed a superstar to carry the sport, to pack the stadiums, to plug into Mainstream, U.S.A. Only one man could do that: Pele.

So, they would meet on this lush neutral ground and quietly sound out each other's desires. The meeting had been suggested by Julio Mazzei and Pele had readily agreed. Mazzei is Pele's personal guru, a curious hybrid of fan, business manager, and protective *duenna*. For one of Pele's stature and public acclaim, a Mazzei is totally necessary. Pele needs someone to shield him from his own munificence, to draw him back into the cocoon of the famous when he tends to oblige every fan, quick-buck artist, or political hack that comes his way in the celebrity freak show.

Almost anyone can see Pele publicly. But to see him privately is as difficult to arrange as a papal visit. You must go through Mazzei.

Known as "Professor," Mazzei attended Michigan State and earned a degree in physical education, but he distinctly gravitates toward the spiritual, investing his friend Pele's actions with metaphysical significance. His favorite topic is Pele as "a phenomenon," and he is fond of saying that Pele "would be a genius, whether as a sportsman, a poet, or a scientist." He truly believes it. Thus, it is not surprising that Mazzei will frequently embellish a quote in translation, filtering it through his own perspective. Yet he remains one of the very few men whom Pele trusts completely.

His everyday duties are decidedly practical. Mazzei is the

53

man who translates the jabberwocky of a thirty-page endorsement contract into simple daily obligations. As an unofficial bodyguard, he disperses autograph seekers, scouts backstreets, arranges travel and appointments, and devises elaborate security systems. Mazzei is perceptive, protective, devoted, mysterious, shrewd—and always on stage.

For him, Pele has not changed since the day they met. He is still the same simple boy who came to play for Santos in 1958. As Santos's trainer, Mazzei felt paternal tenderness for this genius from a dusty Brazilian shantytown. Nineteen years later, he feels the same way.

The Professor approaches the almond tree in long, measured steps, a model of nonchalance behind his turquoise-tinted sunglasses. There are murmured greetings, followed by Mazzei's assurance that Pele "is just now on his way here." Nobody yet knows that in the months to follow, Toye will spend countless hours waiting for the man who is always just now on his way, noting as he paces hotel rooms and playing fields that Brazilian time and North American time are at war. Relax, do not worry, my friend. Listen to the sounds of the soft Brazilian night, Pele will say. My friend, you run along so, always run. The Brazilian approach always won the time war. Mazzei, Toye, and Woosnam sit in the wicker chairs, waiting.

Mazzei fills the time, asking a few neutral questions about the NASL and American players, offering a few asides on the finest moments of Brazil's third World Cup win. He had been surprised when Toye called to say he was leaving his post as a sportswriter for the London *Daily Express* to come to the United States chasing rainbows, because Toye was not just another huckster. He was a respected journalist whose tough, witty pieces on English football had received wide acclaim. Why should a man like that emigrate to the vast wasteland of soccer known as America? Surely, the impeccably tailored Englishman knew how to avoid the messy results of failure. It was worth a couple of hours of Mazzei's time to find out.

Mazzei straightens in his chair as Pele is just now on his

way across the wide veranda, swinging his legs in a slow, economic gait. The crease in the trousers of his crisp white linen suit is scarcely disturbed as he strolls toward yet another contingent of the vast world that wants so much to meet him. He has learned that they are always waiting for him somewhere. At last, he arrives under the almond tree.

"Hello, Clive, how are you my friend?" "Hello, Phil, Kurt, how are you?" Pele says, embracing each of them. Toye's eyebrows arch in surprise. They had not seen Pele in two years, and then only for an ephemeral handshake, yet he remembered their faces, their names. Or the Professor had, anyway. The subsequent conversation lasts for three hours as the tree's soft shadow moves steadily across the veranda tiles. It is amiable, but somewhat fragmented, drifting into nostalgic glimpses of World Cups past, turning toward discreet inquiries about Pele's long-range plans, veering erratically into the murky future of American soccer. Toye and Woosnam are cautious and courteous, two new but ardent suitors trying to woo subtly beneath the watchful eye of a knowing chaperon. As always, Pele is gentle yet his mood is aloof, detached. For a moment, he is vaguely stirred by Pepsi's plans for youth soccer, saying that he derives great pleasure teaching the game to children.

But the almond-eyed smile subsides as Woosnam mentions Pele's retirement from soccer, now only months away. He seems prey to that inevitable fear of tiring, quitting, and being forgotten that haunts every great athlete. "I know I must retire one day," Pele says in a voice as low as the dragonflies. "But it is the one day you do not wish to think about ever until it is here." Noticing the change in the unlined calm of Pele's face, Woosnam shifts his line of conversation to a lighter topic. "Pele, I just want you to know that we have a lot of ideas for soccer in the United States and that you're a part of those ideas." There is a weighty pause as Toye searches Pele's face for a hint, but it reveals nothing. Rising, Pele says, "Thank you, thank you, my good friends," very softly, and turns to leave.

Under the circumstances, it is the most enthusiastic response

Toye might expect. Pele's career had recently built up its fullest head of steam, barreling worldwide through stadiums that echoed "PelePelePele" in hoarse hysteria. He was in the flower of fame and reverence, leading Brazil to immortality by way of a third World Cup championship just months ago. To envision him in a uniform other than that of Santos was at best quixotic —at worst, lunatic.

"What do you think?" Woosnam asks Toye as Pele and Mazzei disappear into the hotel. His question holds the wistful resignation of a nine-to-five grease monkey who has just been allowed to drive a Maserati.

"I don't know, Phil, I just don't know," answers Toye. But it's not entirely true. Deep down he knows—it's just a hunch but he can sense it. The die's been cast. He keeps the thought to himself, wishing to avoid being cast as a madman in the high Jamaican sun. In any case, the exhibition game has been set.

One month later, the principals met again, when Santos played the exhibition at Yankee Stadium. It was to be a great occasion and a watershed event of sorts. On June 6, 1971, 25,000 people showed up at the stadium to watch a double-header between the Cosmos and Rochester, and Santos and Deportivo Cali of Columbia. When Toye arrived with his teams, they found the gates to Yankee Stadium locked. Frantically, Toye called Yankee President Mike Burke, plea-bargaining for his games. It had been raining the night before, and Burke exercising his legal lease options, had ordered the gates locked in fear for his turf. Toye tried to explain that there were 25,000 excitable soccer fans waiting to get in, and besides, it had *stopped* raining. Burke acceded, but warned that if just one more drop fell . . . Just as they opened the gates, a few drops trickled down, and the throngs were told to go home, on the verge of riot. The games were rescheduled for the following night. Under clear skies, only 7,000 showed up to see Pele. It was the smallest crowd on the tour. Toye's enthusiasm had become mortification. Even so, before the Santos game, Toye held a small ceremony at midfield, presenting Pele with a

No. 10 Cosmos jersey. The Cosmos had carefully chosen their team colors—green, yellow, and blue—the same as Brazil's. Just as Pele turned to go back into the dugout with his gift shirt, Toye stopped him. "Maybe someday you'll wear that shirt here," he said. A wide smile materialized on Pele's face. "Clive, you are crazy, my friend."

Perhaps he was. The thought had certainly occurred to Toye as he looked back on his long, complicated odyssey in colonial soccer. It began in 1961 when the London *Daily Express*, dispatched him to cover a number of sporting events in the United States, among them the opening of the International Soccer League, a summer tournament consisting of six relatively anonymous foreign teams. Researching his story, Toye met with the league's erstwhile impresario, Bill Cox, who informed him someday there would be high caliber, widely popular professional soccer in these United States. Toye returned to England thinking Cox an incorrigible dreamer, but harmless to small children.

Five years later, in 1966, Toye saw Cox again. By then, Cox was gathering a swarm of detergent and ball-bearings moguls in whose heads danced visions of trophies, television contracts, and champagne with movie stars in the owner's box. They thought they might like to start a professional soccer league in the United States. Could Toye help them find players, coaches, and general managers in Europe? Nothing flashy or high-priced, just road-worthy and solid. The first person Toye put Cox in touch with was Woosnam, who was then still a player with Aston Villa in the English Football League's First Division.

Over the next few months, Woosnam and Toye, plying their respective English trades, would repeatedly pick up a ringing phone and hear an American voice say, "Hey, Bill Cox told me to get a hold of you. We're in the market for an inside right." But Toye could devote only cursory attention to these matters since he was fully occupied with writing about the upcoming 1966 World Cup in England. The prospect of an English win in the Cup represented not only a binge of chauvinistic satisfaction, but the zenith of his career in sports

57

journalism. Each day he wrote the paper's lead story, every word pored over by a nation of soccer loyalists. He often ad-libbed 2,000 words to meet severe deadlines. It was a heady, rewarding but enervating period, culminating in England's overtime victory over Germany, and the riotous celebrations afterwards.

Two months later, when the English season started once again, Toye felt like a man who had scaled Mount Everest and had then been pushed back down. "After the drama and excitement of the Cup, I was finding it extremely difficult to write with any enthusiasm about meaningless opening league matches. I felt I had done all I could do in England with soccer. I was looking for new challenges."

The challenge appeared like a fractious child, daring him to step over a line toed in the vast Atlantic. Jerry Hoffberger called and asked him to run the Baltimore franchise in the fledgling National Professional Soccer League. Soccer in Baltimore, home of Lord Baseball's Orioles? Here was a challenge indeed, though few people on *either* side of the Atlantic took it seriously. When Toye walked into his editor's office at the *Express* and announced that he'd taken a job in the colonies selling soccer to the heathen, he got no reaction. Knowing Toye as a sharp-witted man with an appreciation for the sardonic, his editor never looked up from his desk. "I've been meaning to tell you, Toye, your final wrap-up on the World Cup was a bloody good job."

"I'm leaving at the end of October," Toye persisted. "I'm going to be general manager of a new franchise in Baltimore. Baltimore, Maryland. Maryland, U.——S.——A."

"I heard," his editor snapped back, "and Joe DiMaggio is coming here to be the new center-back at Arsenal."

No one took Toye seriously until he piled the contents of his desk into a large leather bag. His colleagues organized a farewell party on Fleet Street and assured each other they'd see him in two years—at best. The reasoning behind the smug assumption was indeed sound. What did America want with an international sport like soccer? Americans dreamed up baseball, basketball, and football, and quickly consecrated them as national institutions. They would only be shared with the world at large as a take-it-or-leave-it version of Manifest Destiny. By making up our own games, and working out our own rules, America had neatly become isolationist in its sporting interests. Thus, the "World Championship" of baseball in 1975 was decided between Boston and Cincinnati, two American cities 849 miles apart.

It did seem odd, that a nation able to infect the islands of Puerto Rico and Japan with baseball madness, and incite nations like Russia and Sweden to greater effort in hockey and basketball, never seized upon soccer. Ever isolated, ever practical, Americans were preoccupied with inventing their own culture. They could ill afford being cast into world-wide competition with countries that had passed the game to their progeny with the reverence of Moses handing down the tablets. The nation seemed singularly unmoved upon learning that in 1930 a United States team reached the semifinals of the World Cup. They don't remember that in 1950 a band of free-spirited Yanks partied into the wee hours and the next day recorded one of the most stunning upsets in Cup history by defeating England 1–0. "This is what we need to make the game go in the United States," decided U.S. Coach Bill Jeffrey after that game. He was naive. Soccer needed a good deal more than one memorable triumph to hook into a mass audience.

One such need was an antidote to the American love of clutching things and its subsequent emphasis on hand-eye coordination. Soccer had action and speed, skill and violence—virtues Americans found appealing in baseball, basketball, and football. But it offered nothing one could do with one's hands. And idle hands, Benjamin Franklin told us . . . Soccer asked Americans to think with their feet, something they could not do. When they tried, as in their own brand of football, they succeeded in inventing the ineffective kick with the toe, which has since become passé.

The game was thus doomed to languish, played in St. Louis and in places like Astoria, Queens, and Harrison, New Jersey, where neighborhood social clubs needed a topic of debate for

Sunday beer and bratwurst fests. Those who played and argued, argued and played, were the hyphenated Americans: the Greek-Americans, the Philadelphia-Ukranians, the Los Angeles-Maccabees. For them, soccer was a recognizable link to the old country, a fleshy, careening bit of flotsam to cling to in an alien world.

Many clung to it too desperately. The Sunday game became a catharsis for immigrant rage—a megaphone for orphaned nationalism. Frustrated pride ran amok in ugly battles whose motives went beyond a missed penalty kick; the wars of fifty years in Balkan history were refought on the soccer fields of Chicago. And in New York, a bunch of Haitian exiles sat down on the field at Downing Stadium on Randall's Island for four hours, until the red and black Haitian flag, a symbol of Duvalier's dictatorial reign, was removed. Newspapers refused to cover these local games, but devoted entire back-page photo displays to the riots that frequently accompanied them.

Unfortunately, the ruling body of the United States Soccer Football Association (USSFA), the only world-recognized American soccer organization, could do little to squelch these nationalist brushfires. Baseball Commissioner Bowie Kuhn had gone so far as to bar the owner of a major league team from his own clubhouse because he had been convicted of a felony. In American football, delay of game, and intent to decapitate are both punishable crimes. But USSFA itself was largely made up of hyphenated Americans who had a deep understanding of the passions involved. In the face of hot political issues, rules could easily melt away. And until the spectators became totally Americanized, the game would remain an ethnic maelstrom.

Saddled with the task of educating America to the game they loved, USSFA officials were forced to bring in a well-known Italian, Greek, or German team for a series of exhibition matches to assure a reasonably high standard of play. There simply weren't enough good American players to create a market. That only Italians, Greeks, and Germans would attend those games was a foregone conclusion, but there seemed to be a great many of them for the right game. In 1966, 41,598 people paid an average of six dollars a ticket to watch Pele and Santos play powerful Inter-Milan of Italy. But 41,598 is 41,598, and since no one went around checking birth certificates, here was proof that soccer had potential as a major spectator sport in America.

In fact, when Toye arrived in January 1967, the soccer fraternity was awash in reckless optimism. The World Cup championship game, televised live via satellite drew ten million U.S. television sets. The investors were panting. Armed with saddlebags full of industrial and private cash, no less than three separate groups of moneymen ran over each other in a scramble to stake their claims. Not once did they doubt the solvency of their mission. In this gold-rush mentality, three separate groups hoping to become America's first recognized pro league battled to win sanction. It was the crudest kind of problem, a symbol of the helter-skelter structure of the American game. But only one group could be recognized. USSFA, operating on a yearly budget that never exceeded $50,000, decided to go with the highest bidder. It proposed a franchise assessment fee of $25,000 plus 4 percent of the live gate and 10 percent of the television revenue. Only one league, the United Soccer Association (USA) was willing to meet USSFA's terms.

The United Soccer Association was led by people like Judge Roy Hofheinz, owner of the Houston Astrodome and oil baron Lamar Hunt, owner of other parts of Texas. USSFA reasoned that Hunt was a sound investor. Should things somehow go awry and the teams lose, say, a million a year, Hunt might file for bankruptcy in 150 years. Hunt himself was firmly convinced that given enough time and petrodollars, soccer would produce a gusher of cash-paying customers. "I really like the game," he explained, "but that's not the reason I'm in it. I see no reason why it shouldn't be as big as American football." Yet, subconsciously, he might have realized the possibility of failure. Why else would he name his franchise after a natural disaster—the Dallas Tornado?

Hunt was not the only sports mogul to hear the music of distant cash registers. There was John Allyn of the Chicago White Sox, the Madison Square Garden Corporation, Jack Kent Cooke of the Los Angeles Lakers, and Gabe Paul of the Cleveland Indians (now of the New York Yankees). These men had two traits in common; all were embarrassingly wealthy and none knew anything about soccer. But at least they had USSFA's blessing, one clear advantage over the closest competitor, the National Professional Soccer League. Rejected by USSFA, the NPSL had two choices; fold quietly or continue without sanction as outlaws. They opted for the latter, but not before engineering a major coup—a television contract with CBS.

Suddenly, USA owners had official sanction, but the NPSL had the clout to reach the American public in a much more meaningful way. The rebel league taunted from behind its TV coverage. Just as NBC and Joe Namath made the American Football League, CBS and its vagabonds would do it all for the NPSL. Additionally, the NPSL decided to get the jump on the USA by beginning its season in late April 1967, some six weeks before the USA opener. To do this, they needed players quickly. This problem was solved by importing a roiling bouillabaisse of overage mercenaries and underage recruits who were willing to risk suspension from their national federations by playing off-season soccer for a few Yankee dollars and a chance to see Philadelphia in the spring.

The 179 players in the league represented some thirty-eight countries. There were six Americans. The Chicago Spurs led the league in cacophony with eleven nations represented, followed closely by the New York Generals with eight. Given this ethnic mix, communication on the field often resembled a UN debate without interpreters. "It took me six games to figure out why I wasn't getting any passes from the Argentinians on my team," said Mickey Ash, an English forward with the Generals. "I was calling 'Mas' 'Plas' and 'Plas' 'Mas.' I had the two blokes mixed up." Soccer philosophies, as well as languages clashed on the field in a crazy quilt of defensive and offensive patterns. For instance, the English players favored a long-passing defensive game, the South Americans a more flamboyant, attacking style.

Despite these exotic adversities, the caliber of soccer was simply ordinary. Danny Blanchflower, a former Irish international player brought over by CBS to assist Jack Whitaker with the television commentary for NPSL games, compared it to Third Division English football. But Blanchflower found out quickly that the only commentary CBS wanted from him was fulsome praise of the product. Three weeks into the season, he was called into the office of CBS Vice-President Bill McPhail.

"We didn't like your commentary Saturday," said one of McPhail's aides.

"What was that?" asked Blanchflower.

"You criticized the St. Louis goalkeeper. Couldn't you be more positive?"

"No. The goalie made a mistake."

"That's not what we mean. You could have said it was a good shot on the part of the attacker."

"*That* would not be the truth."

"We don't want you to tell lies. We think there are two truths: a positive truth and a negative truth. We want you to be positive—to say it was good rather than bad." Since this was before the days when telling-it-like-it-is became de rigeur for incisive sportscasters, Blanchflower's contract was not renewed.

Still, CBS had a much more pressing problem beyond choosing the right announcer. Since they were paying the NPSL $500,000 for the right to televise games, CBS planned to recoup their investment through commercials. Soccer matches consist of two forty-five–minute periods of continuous play with a ten-minute break at half-time. This format failed to provide any natural intervals for commercials the way time-outs in football and basketball did. CBS officials decided to use goal kicks and delays for injury as starting points for commercials, running the risk of missing an exciting sequence or the game's only goal. Unfortunately, the players didn't always remember that they were expected to stay on the ground long enough for the commercial to finish.

This lack of rehearsal became obvious during a telecast from Toronto when a left-winger on the Toronto team tripped and fell. Referee Peter Rhodes, equipped with an electric device that beeped when a commercial break was about to begin, whistled a foul and waved his arms at the CBS producer, signaling all was go for the commercial. But the Toronto player wasn't really hurt, and got to his feet while Rhodes was motioning to the producer. Panicking, Rhodes pushed him back to the ground. The crowd sensed that this was not in the rule book and jeered the referee off the field.

Rhodes later admitted to "coaching" the players on the art of feigning injury. The Toronto player had just not been listening. "The cat was not only out of the bag," wrote Paul Gardner, "it was among the pigeons. NPSL Commissioner Ken Macker jumped in immediately to absolve CBS from any blame." The Federal Communications Commission investigated the incident later and found CBS innocent of any illegal manipulation. Despite the advertising difficulties, however, CBS was able to console itself. Its ratings were surprisingly strong, with an audience of almost five million for every game. At the gates of the two leagues, statistics were less encouraging. People were complaining about the level of play again.

Meanwhile, the USA, sanction and all, felt itself falling behind in the race for ownership of the game, lacking the time or resources to comb the world for good players; they decided instead to import eight supposedly top European and South American teams. Naturally, top teams often were unavailable, and thus the USA sometimes brought over eight bottom teams, hyping them as powerhouses. New York was represented by Cerro of Uruguay, the third best team in a country where only the first two matter. Cagliari of Italy fought fiercely for dear old Chicago and with almost anyone. Lamar Hunt got himself Dundee United of Scotland, while Judge Hofheinz had the opportunity to applaud his team, Bangu of Brazil, in the near solitary splendor of the Astrodome. The Shamrock Rovers of Dublin went to Boston and Glentoran, the champions of Ulster, were dispatched to Detroit. The USA was not merely importing soccer, it was relocating a civil war.

Still, the USA strategy worked after a fashion, attracting an average of almost 8,000 a game, about twice as many as turned out for NPSL games. In fact, the NPSL couldn't even give tickets away. On nights before a New York Generals game, the sports editor of the *New York Daily News* took a thick stack of tickets from his drawer and offered them around in the office. When no one came forward, he took them downstairs to the composing room and pressed them upon the Spanish printers at work there.

When the accountants got around to adding up the revenues and subtracting league expenses by the end of the first season, all NPSL teams reportedly lost money, up to $600,000. They had gone on wild spending sprees to sign players, and woke up three months later with fiscal hangovers and no fan support. When the aptly named Pittsburgh Phantoms vanished for good, the most common answer to man-on-the-street interviews, concerning their death was, "Who were the Phantoms?"

Clearly, something had to be done. A merger seemed to be the only answer and in December 1967, the two leagues agreed to share their lack of wealth. The new league would be called the North American Soccer League and would consist of seventeen teams. CBS extended its contract for the 1968 season and owners began talking once again about crowds of 15–20,000. These predictions proved extravagant when 336 fans trickled in for a 1968 game in Chicago. In New York, where the Generals played in cavernous Yankee Stadium, the few spectators who did turn out were strung like sentries among the empty seats. "I had the feeling," said Bradley, then of the Generals, "that most of our crowds arrived in the same cab."

As ticket buyers waned, so did the owners' enthusiasm. By the '68 season's end, only five clubs remained intact. Dallas, Atlanta, Kansas City, St. Louis, and Baltimore still hoped to cash in on the soccer "boom." The league still had a negotiable asset in Lamar Hunt. First, he convinced his fellow survivors to install the experienced, sober Phil Woosnam as the league's commissioner. Woosnam promptly spirited Clive Toye away from his job as general manager of the Baltimore Bays, to be his assistant. The two of them set up the league's headquarters in a locker room at Atlanta Stadium.

Strewn about the dank subterranean office that still reeked of liniment were long walnut conference tables, plump leather chairs in mint condition, and two sixty-watt overhead light bulbs. The entire place had the look of a bargain basement, crammed with the remains of a bankruptcy sale. "We were ashamed to bring anyone there," said Toye, wincing at the memory. But that was no problem, since the only people visiting NASL offices were close friends and next of kin. Almost all the millionaires who rang the doorbell three years before had scrambled for the back door when the overnight profit did not materialize. Unlike football, whose early pioneers invested their hearts as well as their wallets, most of the soccer owners loved only the bottom line on a ledger sheet. Now drastic measures were needed to salvage what remained. As a start, Woosnam asked all owners to pare their operating budgets to a realistic $200,000. "I could tell things had changed," said Ken Bracewell of the Atlanta Chiefs, "when we started to get food stamps on the road instead of team meals."

Sitting on their couches in Atlanta, Toye and Woosnam talked endlessly about things that had to be done, both short- and long-term to make American soccer go. They were a couple of dreamers, sculpting success in stale air.

"How about announcing our application to hold the World Cup in the United States in 1982," Toye said.

"How about expanding to thirty-two teams?" Woosnam countered.

"How about getting Pele to play here?" Toye said, and they both laughed like hell. Then they went back to the office and worried about where they were going to get the money to pay their telephone bill.

In their sane hours, the two men carried out an intense campaign to recruit new franchises, talking, pitching, cajoling, for up to sixteen hours a day. The one they desperately needed was in New York since a longstanding axiom of American sports in that no new sports league makes it without a strong Media City franchise. And the NASL didn't even have a weak one.

Casting about, Woosnam and Toye got in touch with David Frost, the English talk-show host and soccer fan whom Toye knew from his days at the *Express*, hoping to scare up the money for a New York club. Frost said the man they wanted was Nesuhi Ertegun, an Atlantic Records executive who was also a life-long soccer fanatic. When Woosnam was introduced to Ertegun at a cocktail party following the 1970 World Cup final in Mexico City, the men talked soccer, drank, talked some more soccer, and one week later Ertegun infected his fellow executives at Warner Communications with the curious international affliction known as soccer madness. The enthusiastic executives, most of whom had never seen a soccer ball, plunked down $25,000, and Clive Toye became the New York general manager. On January 5, 1971, the words "Gotham Soccer Club, Inc." were painted on a door at the Roosevelt Hotel and the new team was in business. Of course, they had no name, no players, no staff, no schedule, no home field, and no coach. The first of the list was most easily obtained. The name "New York Cosmos" came from a contest which included, among 3,000 entries, names like the Empires, the Diplomats, the Kickers, and the Peles. Cosmos did not mean cosmopolitan—nobody had ever accused the NASL of possessing that quality. Rather, it stood for the universality and inevitability of the game. Bradley of the late, great New York Generals and the athletic director of St. Bernard School signed on as coach. As for the staff—she was on loan from Office Temporaries. The home park they chose was Yankee Stadium, which then seated a modest 65,000, and is controlled by the baseball Yankee Organization.

Toye should have known better. As general manager in Baltimore and assistant commissioner in Atlanta, he had worked closely with the Baltimore Orioles and the Atlanta Braves and had seen their shallow commitment. Since the soccer season ran from May to August, it was in direct competition for the entertainment dollar with baseball. If soccer was to make it big, it would be at baseball's expense. In Baltimore and Atlanta, Toye often felt that the baseball people were bent on keeping soccer small-time even though it meant a loss of potential stadium rental revenue. "Baseball was the only sport I felt any real animosity from," said Toye. "They were definitely looking down their noses at us. I'll tell you, I could have punched some of the Braves' people right in the bloody snoot." Which was nothing compared to what he would have liked to do to the Yankees. This club was beneficent enough to rent the Stadium to the Cosmos at $40,000 per game. In return, the Yankees postponed five of the fourteen Cosmos games due to wet grounds.

Professional soccer in America was still out in the rain.

3

Preludes

*T*he Year of Enlightenment, 1972, was a watershed season for American soccer. After fifty years of immigrant status, the sport decided to shed its ethnic image and step into the American mainstream. The first step was to pass a league rule requiring each NASL team to have two American or Canadian citizens on its eighteen-man roster with an increase of one each successive year. But the greatest step toward Americanization was the institution of a college draft, a viable marketplace where franchises might shop for top-grade talent to buttress their teams—and meet the American quota.

"We realized we had been trying to build an inverted pyramid," said Toye. "We were working from the top down instead of creating a base of fan support on the youth and college levels." Toye was not the first to recognize the potential of the colleges. Thirty-two years earlier, Branch Rickey, ranking Lord of Baseball had made a curious prophecy. Addressing the coaches convention of the Nebraska Teachers' Association, Rickey proclaimed, "In fifty years, soccer will supplant football as it is now played in college." The audience shuddered, as if Rickey had announced that crab grass would replace grain as Nebraska's number one resource. When the stir subsided, a deep voice tolled from the back, "Which college?" and an explosion of laughter rattled the hall. But Rickey retained his pinstriped composure. "You will see, gentlemen," he intoned, "you will see."

What Rickey had seen was the growth of youth soccer in St. Louis where the Catholic Youth Organization had been running its parish leagues as far back as 1902. Once a solid groundwork had been laid, he believed, it was only a matter of time before the remaining layers would be built up. A strong youth level would give rise to a strong amateur level, which in turn would foster a strong college movement. The inevitable product of this pyramiding had to be a good pro league. This had proven to be the American Way in sports. Professional football and basketball were whelped by the elaborate farm systems of the colleges which gave instant prestige and a storehouse of talent to the nascent leagues. Theoretically, this all should have worked with soccer.

But something happened. Or didn't. High school, amateur, and college soccer did not boom. The roots, which were supposed to nourish a healthy pro league did not take in American soil. The three legs of the tripod which were supposed to support pro soccer were shaky to begin with. Youth soccer at the most basic level could provide a budding athlete with fundamental techniques and an introduction to the game. But the system dried up at the next level. There simply were no qualified people at the middle region of the game—coaches, trainers, and league organizers—to further the growth. The lack of organizational talent was especially acute in the great American heartland that cradled baseball, basketball, and football. The case of St. Louis was isolated and uncharacteristic. Soccer just happened to fit into the social machinery of that city.

None of this dissuaded Toye from spending every free hour scouting, panning the country in hopes of finding just one gleaming nugget of pure American talent. His search wasn't made any easier by the fact that there was no phone in the Cosmos' new offices for the first six weeks. The Cosmos had moved from their one-room suite at the Roosevelt Hotel to two cramped rooms on Park Avenue. Not exactly on the Park Avenue of Lever Brothers and the Waldorf, but Park Avenue nonetheless. To make a telephone call, Toye routinely culled a stack of dimes from the office kitty and walked two flights to the lobby, waiting his turn at the pay phone.

Finally, after a country-wide search lasting nearly three months, the Cosmos found a Golden Boy, right in their own back yard. As their number one draft pick, they chose Stan Startzell, a three-time all-American from the University of Pennsylvania. Clever, wily, and insouciant, with long straw-colored hair, wide-open blue eyes, and a bright smile, Startzell became the Cosmos' image maker. He posed for publicity stills and uniformed action shots, then announced he wanted action as well, a chance to prove that Americans do belong in professional soccer as something more than PR men. "I'm not here to tie anybody's shoes," he said upon arrival. "I want to play. It'll be good for me, good for the team, and good for the game. Kids have to identify with players before they can really get into any sport. Whoever heard of a mother telling her son to eat his Wheaties so he can grow up to be like Abaddia El Mostofa?"

As it turned out, Abaddia El Mostofa (a reserve forward for Montreal) was paid more for his services than Stan Startzell. The Cosmos signed Startzell to a contract for seventeen games at $1700 plus added $3,000 for publicity work. Startzell economized by doing without electricity for a month. In hindsight, he realized the die was cast as soon as the ink dried on his contract. The Cosmos were paying him more for his charisma than for his soccer skills. And well they might.

Startzell was terrific on talk shows, where English always came in handy and he was more resplendent than the foreign players, most of whom were likely to show up for an interview in bush jackets, sweat pants, and screaming ties. Startzell gave clinics, speeches, autographs, handshakes, soulshakes, kisses, busses, and Dutch rubs to thousands of boys and girls in the New York area. He smiled at everybody and although he appeared in only two of the Cosmos' first ten games, he appeared at all their press conferences. "I was incredibly naive," he would say three years and three clubs later. "They kept talking about my potential. I thought they meant on the field, not on billboards. I'm not saying I should have been starting. I know I wasn't in a class with some of the foreign players. But I think I deserved more than posing with Harold."

Harold, who came to most of the Cosmos' home games at Hofstra Stadium on Long Island, was easy to spot, although he was only three feet tall and weighed forty-five pounds. He was usually found eating bananas and climbing over seats. Off the field, Harold lived in the Monkey House of Jungle Habitat, a wild-life park in West Milford, New Jersey. Harold was someone's idea of a publicity stunt. Startzell remembers posing with Harold at a press luncheon once and feeling a warm pool around his shoes. But Harold was only five years old. That was excusable. The monkey business in another five-year-old, pro-fessional soccer, was not.

After all the promises of Americanization, it still helped to have a visa in the NASL in 1972. Eighty-five percent of the players were foreigners. There were eight native-born Americans in the league, and of these, maybe three played regularly. For an American player to make it, he had to be very lucky or better than he had any reason to be, like Kyle Rote, Jr. "You've heard of token blacks," Startzell says bitterly. "Well, we were token Americans. The league said you had to have a minimum number of Americans on the roster but it should be the other way around. Why not put a restriction on the number from overseas?"

If there had been a limit on foreign players, the Cosmos, rather than vying for the championship, would have gone quickly into the tank. At the soul of the team was Bermudian striker Randy Horton, Scottish midfielder John Kerr, and English goalkeeper Richie Blackmore: an incongruous mix whose only bond was a love of the game and its camaraderie. Horton, a towering black man whose gentle amiability belied the threat of his massive body and fierce eyes, once summed it up as he peered through a purple haze of smoke at a team party. "We're just a bunch of crazy dudes who love to play soccer and have a good time. That's all, man."

On August 26, 1972, these crazy dudes from Bermuda, Scotland, England, Germany, Czechoslovakia, Brazil, and Ghana played the St. Louis Stars for the title. "The only thing that worries me is that we might be overconfident," said one player before the game. "After all, we're playing a bunch of bloody Americans." The game was played in rain which sluiced across the field, making the Astroturf at Hofstra Stadium slick and treacherous. Players skidded across the surface, sending spumes of water to their teammates along with the ball. Three minutes from the game's end with the score tied 1–1, Horton was chopped down in front of the St. Louis goal. The Cosmos were awarded a penalty kick, and Josef Jelinek calmly converted the winner. Jelinek was a Czech who played in Mexico before the Cosmos purchased him midway through the season. He was known as much for his artistry off the field as on it. Always in the company of exotic women, his social life was a source of voluble speculation for his teammates. "Josef knows three expressions," said Horton. "Hello, I love you, and goodbye."

But for all their color, the Cosmos were unable to carve out a niche on sports-crazy Long Island. They averaged a modest 4,880 spectators during the season, and while the weather was certainly an intimidating factor, drew only 6,102 to the championship game. By moving their home field from Yankee Stadium to Hofstra University in Hempstead, they had severed the umbilical cord tying them to the ethnic fans in New York City. They were orphans once again, but orphans on their way to finding a family. Scarcely a foreign accent was heard in those Hofstra crowds, which consisted mostly of young boys who played little-league soccer and their parents. It was an American crowd watching Czechs and Germans play a foreign game. This told the Cosmos that they could use an American drawing card.

Enter Joey Fink. What name could be easier to pronounce than Joey Fink? It sounded even more American than Stan Startzell, who had been traded. Fink came to America with his Austrian parents at an early age and settled in a pre-

dominantly German neighborhood in Queens, New York. He
began playing soccer at age nine and enjoyed it enough to stick
with it despite the allure of America's traditional sports. He
was drafted number one by the Cosmos out of NYU and had
paid his dues playing on the pitted fields of the German-
American League in his spare time.

"I chose soccer just because I loved the game," Fink said. It
doesn't bother me that we aren't famous or make a hundred
thousand dollars per year. Sure, I'd like to have a three-year, no-
cut, two-million-dollar deal like a basketball player, but really,
I'm just playing for the love of the game, kicks, cheap thrills,
whatever. The money is pretty bad, around $3,000 or $4,000 for
the season for guys like me, so we try to work second jobs.
There isn't much security and the injury risk is high. But last
year kids who had been watching soccer and knew me from my
rookie year would come up to me and ask for an autograph. It's
the first time in my life that something like that happened. The
feeling falls behind pretty fast, but you know, it's a pretty good
feeling while it lasts."

Fink had just the kind of fresh-faced, short-haired choirboy
looks that would appeal to the solid citizens of Long Island. He
was a safe role model. What's more, in his first start for the
Cosmos, Fink scored three goals and later fraternized with his
teammates at Joe's Meadowbrook, the Cosmos' after-game bar.
High on the game, full of pride and self-esteem, Fink lifted his
stein and turned to Horton. "This beer is gonna taste better
than any beer has ever tasted." Horton smiled. Fink kept right
on guzzling. After several more, he turned again to Horton
and said confidingly, "You know when I scored that third
goal and looked up and saw all the people cheering, it felt so
good, I thought I was Pele."

"No shit," drawled Horton, nodding abstractly.

Three days later, Joe Fink went back to being Joe Fink:
quick, aggressive, erratic. He scored a goal early and then all but
disappeared from the game. Next game, he did not play at all.
By then, Clive Toye had realized that the colleges were not

going to furnish an American Pele. If he wanted one, he would have to go after the genuine article.

It seemed the hallucination of a lunatic. But Toye knew that it was often just the momentary tremors of timing that etched a hairline division between success and failure in the affairs of men. Columbus was a beautiful dreamer—just another jester until a restive Queen Isabella felt the need for mercantile expansion. A man had to dream or sleep the dull slumber of the dead. The time had come to galvanize a becalmed, drifting league.

The time was ripe for Pele as well. He was under enormous pressure at home. It had been almost three years since the meeting with Toye in Jamaica, three tumultuous years for Pele as he grappled with his decision to retire and with trying to explain to an adoring public that it had to end some time. Toye knew that Pele was too encumbered with such matters at home to consider any offer to play in America. Toye just had to be patient, a white-linen El Exigente, content to sit in the shade and sip a drink while the soft fingers of one more Brazilian night worked their magic on the slowly ripening coffee beans. Rip them from the branch prematurely and the taste would be bitter.

By May 1974, Pele had retired from the national team and had announced this would be his last year with Santos. He had signed a reported million dollar contract with Pepsi-Cola, Inc. to head up their International Youth Soccer Program, but he was otherwise a free man. In New York, the moment seemed right. After seven years of gasping for survival, the NASL seemed to be holding, though shaky. The league was making plans to expand to eighteen teams. It was winding up a marketing campaign that would win lucrative promotional tie-ins with hitherto coy Madison Avenue image-makers.

Philadelphia, with an American coach and partly American team, had become the first expansion team to win a championship in its first year in any major sport by beating Dallas 2–0 before a crowd of 18,824 in Texas Stadium. They made the cover of *Sports Illustrated*. And if Dallas lost the title, they came up with something far more valuable: a genuine, homegrown superstar; William Kyle Rote, Jr., son of the former all-pro flankerback with the New York Giants. It seemed that America was starting to develop an appetite for soccer, and Toye wanted to serve up the pièce de résistance: Pele in a New York Cosmos uniform. For Toye, the distinction between dream and reality had all but dissolved. Working for Warner Communications, Inc. allows you to think like that.

In less than ten years, Warners had completed one of the most remarkable metamorphoses in Corporate America. It was a Cinderella stock, waltzing upward through the Dow Jones average with a clutch of blue chip acquisitions and glamorous properties. Warners had gone from coffins and car rentals to rock-and-roll and cable TV, from window washing and real estate to publishing and show biz, from embalming to *The Exorcist*, the Rolling Stones, and Bob Dylan. Warner Communications had its fingers in a dozen or so diverse corporate pies—but its real business is making money. In 1975, Warners placed 279th on the Fortune 500 list.

At the center of Warner Communications is Steven J. Ross, chairman and chief executive officer. Ross is forty-eight. His thick silver hair is well groomed, without the studied funky effect so common to seventies executives. He is a tall, well-muscled man, whose body had once been laced, strapped, and taped into a Cleveland Browns football uniform. Ross still has a broken nose and a metal plate in his arm to remind him of those years. His forays on the fiscal field have not been without risk or injury either. He readily confessed a tendency to go for the game-breaker rather than try to establish a steady, careful ground game. Yet his failures have always been overshadowed by a string of successes.

Ross, who had been selling children's clothes, married Carol Rosenthal in 1955, and went to work shortly after for Carol's father, owner of Manhattan's Riverside Chapel. As an executive trainee his range extended from the funeral parlor to the garage, where the nightly sight of idle limousines made him uncomfortable. Why not rent them out? Soon Abbey Rent-A-Car was added to the corporate holdings and Ross then negotiated a deal with Kinney Rental Systems, enabling him to offer free parking with his rentals, a boon in crowded New York City. He went on from that to gain controlling interest in Kinney in what had proved to be a geometric progression in the finest capitalistic tradition. It was not long thereafter that he pulled off his biggest coup, purchasing Warner Brothers–Seven Arts Limited for 400 million dollars in the spring of 1969. This was a considerable gamble because it consisted of two properties, one of them a floundering movie company, Warner Brothers, and the other, a pair of lucrative record companies, Warner Reprise and Atlantic Recording. These were the twin pillars of Warner Communications and the kinds of businesses that Ross has found continually rewarding. He had found his niche.

Thus, when Bob Dylan first warned that the times were a changin', Ross commissioned a long-range planning committee to study some of the newer "growth industries," such as air travel, entertainment, and communications. On studying the results, Ross's skull began to click with ideas like a geiger counter over uranium. He finally sold the Riverside funeral chapel and severed his ties to the past, and the new conglomerate began in earnest with the concerns of the living: movies, records, television, cable TV, and publishing.

Ross soon gained a reputation as a dreamer with a good grip on the realities of cash-flow profits. Warners had made its mark with a string of low-investment, high-return successes. On a hunch, Warners bought the movie rights to a musical gathering of young people up in the New York woods and ended up with Woodstock. When women's lib was young, Warners invested in Gloria Steinem and *Ms.* magazine. In 1974, carefully planned promotional movie investment turned the 1971 low-budget *Billy Jack* into a multi-million-dollar payoff.

You must, of course, have a good team to win, and Warners boasts a roster of entertainment all-stars. The glamour that gets Warners into syndicated columns these days is a happy residual of its living, breathing holdings, like Aretha Franklin, Frank

Sinatra, Bob Dylan, the Rolling Stones, and now, Pele. All one-of-a-kind personalities.

Ross prefers to describe this artistic collective as a loose, unstructured company that's more a family than a conglomerate. His policy in handling the stars is one of "love with understanding," making the artist comfortable, attending to his or her best interests with a minimum of pressure and a maximum of breathing space. It seems to work. How else could one company hold on to Sinatra, when all of Australia once expressed its desire to pitch him into the Pacific?

Ross once thought he might also like to own a football team. Then he heard about the $18,000,000 market price. But also this: as an NFL owner, Ross would be just one of a gaggle of sportsminded businessmen. As far as the impact went, he would finish in a dead heat with a dozen or so other owners. But soccer, like cable TV, Warners' other hot-house growth market, was virgin territory in America. After all, a NASL franchise cost $17,975,000 less than one in the National Football League. If anyone could unlock the secret of soccer's success in this country, it was Steve Ross and his salesmen. "This was the first time just one particular artist was needed to make a project go," Ross felt. "One person in the whole world, and that's Pele. For a movie, if you can't get Jack Nicholson, maybe you can sign Al Pacino or Dustin Hoffman. But we had to go for the top."

Ross saw his first professional soccer game in 1971, when his Cosmos played St. Louis. A gate of 3,000 was announced but the true attendance was perhaps half that number. Ross, Executive Vice-President Jay Emmett and Nesuhi Ertegun, Warners' record chief and resident soccer pundit, cheered their team as the only spectators in a section of seats equal to one third of the stadium. On the other side of the field the stands were empty. By traditional standards, Ross should have been despondent. He wasn't. "It was a wide-open market," he figured, well aware of the irony in his comment. "The growth potential from ground zero was tremendous. When the risk is small on the down side you're crazy not to take it."

And if you lose?

"So you're down a couple of bucks. But it was a hell of a fight."

On May 14, 1974, Toye taxied to the Warner Communications building at 75 Rockefeller Plaza and took a high speed elevator to the twenty-ninth floor, the executive suite. As the doors closed behind him he was met by the first of three security guards, and continued down the corridor between walls of brushed steel, retracing steps taken before by Robert Redford, Mick Jagger, Frank Sinatra, Dustin Hoffman, and a healthy assortment of the famous and powerful in a dozen walks of life.

"Mr. Ross is expecting you," smiled Carmen Farragano, the chief of three secretaries sitting behind paneled desks in the reception area. She led him to a pair of brown doors to the right of her desk and gracefully ushered him into the throne room.

At the far end of the room is a kidney-shaped leather desk, barren except for three or four thick portfolios and a sterling silver elephant—the homiest object in the room. There is no art on the walls; it is, after all, an office. Behind Ross's desk is a Bunker Ramo Market Decision System, an electronic video ticker on which Ross can summon up current Wall Street quotations at the touch of a button. There are other buttons within reach of the desk. Press one, the doors slide smoothly closed or open. Another opens the panels on the far wall to reveal a television set. Still another unlocks a closet outfitted with a complete quadraphonic sound system, a playback tape deck, and a set of video tapes. Adjoining this office is a private conference room, appointed in utilitarian elegance, with a marble table and four contemporary chairs in bold upholstery. Fastened to each corner of the table is a beige phone for conference calls. In the corner presides a silver statue of *The Exorcist*.

Ross and Emmett are seated in one of two matched pigskin sofas in the center of the office; as Toye walks in Ross puts aside a leather-bound portfolio and rises to greet him. Toye settles into a facing couch; between them is a leather table with four more phones suspended under the protruding edge. The only other items on the table are a striking piece of sculpture, some fifteen identical S-shapes which swing in endless, nonrepetitive patterns when one of them is spun, and a large crystal bowl filled with chilled carrot and celery sticks.

Ross walked over and opened a bar lined with decanters of brandy and Scotch. Few of the liquors have seen less than twelve years on earth. This is standard hospitality, less striking than two big glass jars in one corner of the bar, one filled with Baby Ruths and the other with Milky Ways. Toye declined a drink.

"Steve, I want to go to Munich next month," he said.

"For the World Cup?"

"For Pele," said Toye. Funny how the two syllables required so much wind.

"Pele?" asked Emmett. "I thought he retired."

"He did," answered Toye, "but he'll be there for Pepsi-Cola."

"Let me get you straight," questioned Ross. "You're going to Munich to speak to Pele?"

"About what?" asked Emmett.

"About playing for us," said Toye, chomping on his cigar.

"How much is he going to cost?"

"A lot," admitted Toye. "Three, four million."

"Is he worth it?" Emmett asked.

"He can take us and the league to the top."

"In one year?" says Ross.

"No, I want to sign him for three years. That way LCA can do a lot with his name."

The air in the room seems to lighten, as if a zephyr had passed through. LCA is Licensing Corporation of America, a division of Warners that deals in licensing.

"Would we own his name?" probed Ross, more animated.

"That would be part of the contract," said Toye.

"Then we could market a whole line of Pele endorsements, soccer shoes, sneakers, games, clothes."

"He could also help generate TV income."

Pele scores in one of his first games as a New York Cosmo, leaping into the waiting arms of teammates Americo Paredes (No. 9) and Mordechai Shpigler. PHOTO BY TIM CONSIDINE

Action during the 1970 World Cup: Pele crashes to the turf in front of the Czechoslovakian goal. PHOTO BY DOMICIO PINHEIRO

Jubilant fans hoist Pele after Brazil's 4–1 victory over Italy in the '70 final. It was Pele's last World Cup game. PHOTO BY DOMICIO PINHEIRO

Pele scores his 1,000th goal, on a penalty kick against Vasco da Gama before 80,000 fans in Rio de Janeiro's Maracana Stadium. PHOTO BY DOMICIO PINHEIRO

After the historic 1,000th goal, a weeping Pele, embraced by his brother Zoca, could only mutter, "Remember the children, remember the poor children." PHOTO BY DOMICIO PINHEIRO

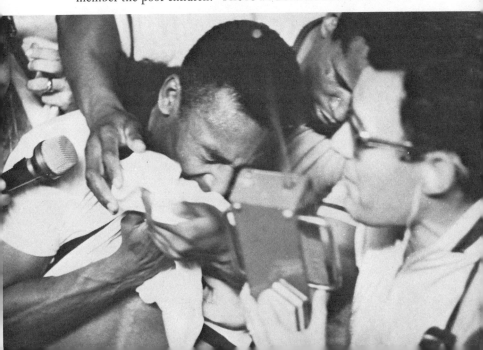

"The goose that laid the golden egg for Santos" acknowledges his fans before one of his final games for his lifelong club. PHOTO BY DOMICIO PINHEIRO

A statement to the press following all-night negotiations. *Seated around the table*: Zoca, Clive Toye, Julio Mazzei, Warner Communications Vice-President Rafael de la Sierra and international tax expert Jim Caradine. *Standing, from the left*: Xisto and Aziz, along with journalists and photographers. PHOTO COURTESY OF NEW YORK COSMOS

Warner President Steve Ross signs his name for the last time, as Emmett gives Pele a bear hug at the conclusion of the official contract signing ceremony in Bermuda. PHOTO BY WIDE WORLD

The official press conference at the "21" Club in New York almost triggered a riot, but the principals remained cool. *Standing, from left to right:* New York Commissioner of Civic Affairs Neil Walsh, Emmett, Cosmos Coach Gordon Bradley, Pele, Cosmos Public Relations Director John O'Reilly, Mazzei, Toye, Ross, de la Sierra. PHOTO BY WIDE WORLD

The Cosmos Pele joined for his first game against Dallas. By the end of the year, only five remained to play with the Cosmos in '76. *Standing, from left to right:* Tony Donlic, Barry Mahy, David Primo, Jorge Siega, Kurt Kuykendall, Sam Nusum, Werner Roth, Mark Liveric. *Front row, left to right:* Julio Correa, Johnny Kerr, Mané, Americo Paredes, Pele, Tony Picciano, Joey Fink, Mordechai Shpigler, Luis de la Fuente. Missing: Juan Masnick, Alfredo Lamas. PHOTO BY TIM CONSIDINE

Pele's first game with the Cosmos. He scored to tie the game 2–2 on a header. PHOTO BY ANTHONY CASALE, NEW YORK NEWS

Pele enjoys a rare, quiet moment
with his wife Rose and son Edinho.
PHOTO BY TIM CONSIDINE

"And help us in cable TV," Emmett added, suddenly sounding very much like Toye.

A smile began to crease Steve Ross's tanned face, the same kind of smile that he yielded ten years ago when he bought Warner Brothers Motion Pictures.

"Well, if he's that good," said Ross, "what the hell are you doing here?"

4

The Big Crocodile

*I*t was June 1974, well into shirtsleeve weather, and the New York Cosmos had been drilling unnoticed for two tepid months on the Astroturf at Hofstra University on Long Island. Instead of the swarm of sportswriters and television crews that usually haunt professional athletics, there were only a few neighborhood kids who hung around the practice field, peering through the chain-link fence.

Clive Toye took a final glance at his team as they jogged laps around the track, then slid into the back seat of a waiting car. He was on his way to Frankfurt, where the weather was cooler, and the soccer climate boiling. All Europe was mad with World Cup fever; West Germany had become a raucous, multilingual convention of soccer aficionados, and every hotel within miles of the four competition sites was crammed to capacity. The Brazilian team was there to compete. Pele had come to watch, and to make appearances for Pepsi's Youth Soccer Program. Henry Kissinger and Willy Brandt were there to see a match or two and smile for photographers. On June 30, ten days into the three-week-long competition, Clive Toye appeared, to seriously begin the chase.

Toye checked into the Frankfurterhof, wondering if his

smoke-screen would provide enough cover. He had told reporters that he would be going to the World Cup to scout players, especially a Yugoslavian winger named Dragan Djasic. Only a small knot of Warners and Pepsi executives knew his real mission. Toye phoned Pepsi liaison Giora Breil from the frenzied lobby and asked him to arrange a meeting with Mazzei. Breil had been expecting the call. Certainly, something could be arranged.

The next day, they met in a corner booth at the coffee shop of the Frankfurt Intercontinental, lingering over breakfast well into the lunch hour. Toye planned a low-key approach; he could sense that Pele is not a man to be pushed. All he really wanted was for Pele to come to the States and have a look around. To this end, he offered the services of the Warners jet for Pele and his family, but Mazzei was not impressed. A 6,000 mile flight to attend a couple of mediocre soccer games in New York? It hardly seemed worthwhile. Toye dangled a trip to Disneyland, and Mazzei brightened at the joke. Next to Pele, Mazzei said with a twinkle, Mickey Mouse is very big in Brazil. The two men laughed, and parting, Mazzei promised he would speak to Pele that evening.

The following day, Pele was to hold his customary nonstop interviews with a phalanx of journalists and soccer high rollers from around the world. Toye, still on New York time, was the first appointment scheduled, summoned to appear at the incredible hour of 9 A.M. in the Pepsi hospitality suite. When Toye entered, Pele came over to embrace him. "Clive, my friend, how are you? Of course, I remember. Jamaica. Three years ago."

Toye, who was serious then, was even more serious now. Both of them were, despite the fencing. Drawing Pele aside, Toye launched into a solid and well-rehearsed litany of reasons why Pele should come to America. It would be good for soccer, of course, to have the best player in the world teach Americans the game. It would be good for Pele, because America is a challenge worthy of his talents. He has done all he can for soccer in Brazil. Besides, the children would go to fine American schools, and all the family's needs would be well attended to. Finally, Toye played his trump card: Warners would like to buy the rights to his name. As puzzlement clouded Pele's face, Toye tried to define the marketing machine that is Warner Communications, rhapsodizing about Frank Sinatra, Superman, the Rolling Stones, Cher, and what Warners had done with *their* names.

Through it all, Pele remained inscrutable. Toye couldn't be sure he had even heard of the Rolling Stones and Cher. What is all this talk about a man's name? And how can another man buy it? Toye fleshed out the idea with examples of endorsements, personal appearances, and sporting goods chains. However, Pele remained coy. After listening to Toye's pitch, he nodded graciously and said, "I do not think so, Clive, my friend. Is not for me, but thank you."

"Thank you," Toye replied. "And please remember—the invitation to America is always open. Don't forget. Disneyland, too!" Pele smiled and walked Toye to the door, greeting the next contingent. It was headed by Genadi Radchuk, a Russian journalist and interpreter. "Even the bloody Russians," Toye muttered to himself as he walked down the hall. On the plane back to New York, Toye prepared his report to Warners. He recalled his first real opening on Pele, a brainstorming session held one month prior to his trip to Frankfurt.

It was May 24, 1972 and the executive dining room on the thirty-second floor of the Warner Communications building had been oddly stark and silent. Normally, it hosted a genteel clatter, but that day it was empty, except for a long, bare table and eight carefully placed chairs. To the initiated, this meant business. To Toye, it meant a brief discussion that could make or break his soccer team. After seven years at the grindstone, trying every promotional stunt from Harold the Chimp to free records, Toye felt he had finally set the stage for a major breakthrough. This one man could do what he and an army of soccer promoters could not. It was that simple, and it had all come down to this—a tense, forty-minute meeting to assure his final go-ahead.

Warner Vice-President Emmett wanted to know more, lots more, about Pele before making any commitment, particularly of the whopping size Toye was bandying about. Since Pepsi-Cola International had been the only American company to have dealings with Pele, a meeting was arranged with Pepsi executives familiar with the subtleties of the account. Emmett also wanted to know more about the extent of Pepsi's involvement. The market value of Pele's name could drop to zero if the two giant conglomerates were to lock horns over a conflict of interests and endorsements. Emmett knew he would have to touch on the subject casually, and listen hard.

The meeting was arranged by Cartha (Deke) de Loach, formerly number three in the FBI under Hoover, and now a Pepsi vice-president. De Loach and his employer, Pepsi Chairman Donald M. Kendall, had been instrumental in Pepsi's negotiations to sign Pele. Kendall was also a member of Washington inner circles, close personal friend to Bebe Rebozo, Robert Abplanalp, and their mutual friend, Richard Nixon.

It had been Kendall's mission to prove how much Pele could do for Pepsi, world-wide. Kendall quickly got Pele on the Johnny Carson show, and soon after, on the Richard Nixon show. On May 9, 1973, just two days after Watergate had spilled on an unsuspecting public, Nixon returned from his Bimini refuge to greet Pele, who had been whisked to Washington on the Pepsi jet. Pele's chaperons were Kendall and de Loach. His meeting with the president lasted ten minutes, and Kendall stayed on to chat for about twenty. On May 10, the *New York Daily News* ran a front-page photo of Richard Nixon, with Pele. Soon after, Pepsi signed its contract.

Toye recalled the incident vividly, and knew the power he was to deal with at the Pepsi/Warner summit. He had been most comfortable keeping silent, listening while Emmett assayed the Pepsi connection in a series of polite, yet pointed questions. In less than an hour Emmett had ferreted the essential facts: Pepsi would be glad to work with Warners, "for the good of soccer," and mutual profit; Pele himself is a pleasure to work with, sincere, obliging, accessible, and never temperamental—just occasionally tardy. His game is still in top form. The meeting was deemed a great success.

The Frankfurt meeting had been a direct result of that earlier conference and after these first surges of optimism, Pele's cool reception sent Toye's spirits plummeting. As soon as he reached Kennedy Airport, he phoned Warners to arrange still another meeting. There was a lot of work to be done.

In Frankfurt, the festivities accompanying the Cup semifinals had moved into high, high gear. Each day promised a series of tense, electric matches, followed by rounds of celebrations at night as world-class players met and reminisced, and beer-swollen fans toasted the afternoon's heroes. Amid the merrymaking, Pele seemed uncharacteristically glum, foundering in the grips of decisions that would govern his future.

Almost a year before the Cup games, Pele had announced his decision not to play for Brazil in the World Cup due to his retirement, and remained steadfast, despite public outrage and a plea from Brazil's president to reconsider. All of Brazil was in mourning for the fortunes of the national team which had recently lost a spate of pre-Cup exhibition matches. The coaching staff had fallen prey to political infighting, and the players were in a state of paralyzing hypertension. For Brazil to lose a World Cup after its three earlier victories would be a fate more ignominious than a thousand Watergates. Cardiac patients were advised not to listen to the games. All eyes were on Pele, hungering for a reason, any reason, to thwart his retirement. And he was silent.

In fact, Pele was in torment. Each day the frenzied tabloids picked at him with a new accusation. Por que, Pele, por que? Edson Arantes do Nascimento of Tres Coracoes had all of Brazil furious with him, and he knew it would only get worse. The Santos team was scheduled for a world tour in June of 1974 before the Cup, probably their last chance to showcase Pele before his October retirement. But Pele had made other plans. The Brazilian television station, TVTUPI, hoping to scoop the larger TV Globo network, offered him $400,000 to serve as their color commentator during the matches. Pele accepted. When news of this leaked, all of Brazil gasped. He was theirs; they had loved him. Money was never a factor. If Pele loved Brazil, how could he sit coolly in a booth high above the game and describe his team's defeat—a loss he himself had invited by his absence. Shame, que lastima. Betrayal.

Acting on this inflamed logic, Brazilian authorities responded swiftly to Pele's decision. The Brazilian Journalists Syndicate refused to allow him to appear on TV, reasoning that he was not a registered journalist and was therefore robbing another of a job. The papers were ablaze with stories branding Pele as a greedy ingrate, a son who turned his back in his country's darkest hour of need.

Ultimately, the TVTUPI project dissolved, but Pele's political discomfort was far from ended. Pepsico, holders of his lucrative promotional contract, stated that they wanted, very much, for Pele to participate in the opening ceremonies at Munich. It would be a classic opportunity to give the Pepsi logo (and, of course, the Youth Soccer Program) world-wide exposure. But this was a delicate matter. Pepsi did not wish to be blamed for Pele's absence from the World Cup. It would be best to negotiate the matter quietly. Breil assigned Pele a code name for telex messages from Pepsico headquarters in Purchase, New York, to the Santos office. The code name— "Big Crocodile"—pleased Breil. A crocodile is safe in the Amazon swamps. When the leathery reptile spots a piranha, it swims upside down to protect its vulnerable belly. A piranha can't get through the crocodile's tough upper shell. And neither can a journalist.

Pele and Pepsi were learning fast and the low-profile strategy worked well until newsmen learned that Pele planned to wear a Pepsi blazer to the opening ceremonies. German television does not allow any such commercialization on its broadcasts. Thus, another scandal was brewing across the Atlantic. German headlines screamed, "REISEN KRACH UBER WELTMEISLERSCHAF EROEFFUNG ZEREMONIE" ("Giant Trouble Over World Cup Opening Ceremony"). Back home, Brazilians had never stopped screaming. On June 13, when the games opened, the brouhaha was resolved in a split second. Just as Pele stepped to the center of the field, the cameras switched to an overhead zeppelin shot. Pele became a tiny dot on the swirling field; the blazer was invisible.

Now, as the ceremony was behind him, and the Cup proceeded, Pele could still see no end to his dilemmas. Toye had gone back to America with his confusing offer, but he was only the first of a swarm of international bidders, each of who came waving salaries and fringe benefits that most men only dream of.

Into the middle of this heavy bidding, and knowing nothing of Toye's pursuit, lumbered American millionaire Lamar Hunt, along with Bill McNutt, co-owner of the Dallas Tornado. Hunt met with Pele and Mazzei in Frankfurt and outlined a pitch for American soccer he knew was a strong one. First, there was the money, an endless stream of Yankee dollars that would surpass anything bankrupt Italy or peanut-sized Portugal could come up with. Second, America was virtually the last place on earth where soccer was a novelty. What's more, that place was already a sport fanatic's paradise. Americans spent more time and money on sporting pursuits than any other people in the world. All the elements were there—Pele had only to say the right word. The right word for Pele's state of mind was puzzlement. "But Lamar, my friend, why you no speak with Clive Toye? He makes offers for me to come to play *futebol* in America. Talk to Clive." These Americans, with all their money, don't they speak with one another? Even if he were to consider playing in America, he couldn't do it in Dallas and New York. Hunt, not a man accustomed to disappointment, nevertheless pledged his complete support to Toye. No matter what team Pele might end up on, his presence would benefit everybody in the league.

Back in his New York office after host West Germany won the '74 World Cup, Toye blocked out the next move. He believed he had laid the groundwork and approached Pele on the broad terms his quarry would find most congenial. But he also wanted to demonstrate that he meant business. So the next strategem had to be strong, decisive. Pele was scheduled to return to Santos for a rest before heading to Toronto and a Pepsi youth clinic at the end of August. Toye, knowing he would be passing through Kennedy Airport to change flights, placed a call to Mazzei's secretary regarding the Big Crocodile. The two men arranged a meeting in the Air Canada terminal.

After a tense, anticipatory two weeks, Toye arrived at Kennedy Airport at the appointed time, and found Mazzei and Pele in the executive lounge. The encounter lasted a mere fifteen minutes, in which time Toye informed Pele that Warners was still ready to talk seriously about a contract. He felt that Pele had surely given the matter a lot of thought: he must have made some tangible progress toward arriving at a decision. He was wrong. Pele listened, attentive but cool. He could not think in such terms as Clive described, he replied. "I grow up in Brazil, and play football only in Brazil. You ask me to leave my country. Is very big decision, too big. I have no interest in so big a step. I'm sorry, Clive."

Toye left in a dark mood. But as the tenacious man drove back on the Long Island Expressway, he reappraised the situation, turning it over, examining every facet. The largest problem would be in breaking through that shell of national-hero status in Brazil that protected Pele and kept other possibilities locked out. By now Toye had realized that he might be Pele's friend Clive, but he wasn't exactly his buddy. Despite what he wanted to think, an offer from Warners obviously failed to captivate Pele.

Two weeks later, in early September, Toye decided he would have to swallow his pride and go courting again. He phoned Mazzei, asking if he could come to Santos. Sighing, Mazzei said yes. "But Clive," he added, "I must warn you that you are wasting your time, and your company's money. Pele will not change his decision to stay in Brazil."

Dauntless, Toye flew to Santos on September 9, and was met at the steaming airport by Pele's driver Aziz who drove him to São Paulo. When they arrived, Mazzei was effusive in his greeting, but sorry to report that Pele had had to leave for another appointment. "We will go in one hour to Pele's office," he explained. "It is only an hour back down the mountain. Meanwhile, tell me what is new in New York."

After an hour's small talk in which Toye waxed enthusiastic about the NASL, they got into a red Fiat and left for Santos. Half a mile into the drive, a grey Mercedes hissed by going the other way. Toye did a double-take. The man is the passenger seat looked astonishingly like Pele. In fact, it was. Toye was starting to worry.

"I see you are a little bit worried, Clive," Mazzei said. "There is no need to worry, no need to rush. Pele will arrive in time for lunch." Seven hours later, Pele arrived in time for dinner. He apologized to Toye for being a little late. "Ah, Clive, my friend from America. So sorry. We talk now, yes?" Toye was nothing if not ready to talk after a ten-hour flight and another ten hours of alternating chase and wait sequences. He came directly to the point: When is Pele coming to America?

Pele started to laugh and Toye went for the soft spot. "Pele, I know you love children. Why not come and teach soccer to American boys? You'll make a lot of kids very, very happy."

Pele said yes, this would be very, very nice to help the young boys. But . . .

"Oh, come on now, Pele. Teaching and playing are as different as *talking* about making love and *making* love." They laughed again, but Pele seemed unshakable. "I like very much to make love, Clive. But no. Please, no thank you." Pele was still laughing when Toye left for the airport, and Toye was already mapping his next move.

On December 9, Toye telexed Mazzei with a message for the Big Crocodile. The Cosmos wanted Pele for three years, and asked when they might make an offer. Pele would not even look at the telex, and Mazzei telephoned Toye with another, final "no." He is sorry, my friend, so sorry, but you will understand. Still, by the end of 1974 Toye understood only that he would not give up.

During the time Toye had been so handsomely supporting

the international airlines and firing off Cosmos offers, the rest of the world had not been idle either. Pele had a score of suitors. Every day, Mazzei received a different bid for his friend's talents. In one month alone, Pele had been courted by Real Madrid of Spain, Bayern Munich of West Germany, Marseilles of France, and a Mexican club. Mazzei, slipping into his role as duenna, screened the callers and their credentials. Most were shown the door immediately, firmly, and politely. Real Madrid, a traditional European power, strutted in with an offer of a million dollars for one year. Bayern Munich topped that by $500,000 and Marseilles simply sent a blank check. Olia Zacour, a Mexican magnate, went one step further. He informed Mazzei that Pele could name not only his price— but also his team.

Before broaching them to Pele, Mazzei discussed all of the offers with the other members of the inner circle: Pele's brother Zoca, his business manager Xisto, and Edevar, his partner in an export-import firm. All four men play a large role in any decision regarding Pele's future, weighing advantages against risks in loose flexible dialogues not unlike the meetings of Warners' top executives. Each man has his own area of expertise. And like the Warners people, Pele's advisors seek the most profitable exposure of a unique human commodity without disturbing the delicate balance of talent and personal charisma at the heart of their venture. Hard-edged business logic is tempered by a keen responsiveness to Pele's moods, needs, and sensibilities. If he is not happy with a deal, then no deal is a good one.

In sifting through the offers, all four men had gradually come to agree that it would be in Pele's best interest to play in a country that didn't know him well, a country whose sons had not been weaned on his legend. Xisto, the market expert, pointed out that when you finish a career, people start to forget. If Pele wanted to be a successful businessman, he must keep his name out front. Edevar, the export-import merchant agreed. He felt that commercially, it is important to have a lot of press. Pele must go someplace where he only has to play five

months a year, but can keep his name in the newspapers all
year round. Zoca knows his brother's personality. Since he was
sixteen, Pele has known only how to be a star, and he must
continue to be a star. He must find a place where there are no
others.

So while Pele eased into his civilian life, the gears at his
Santos headquarters were turning. After all, a legend could
not come to a sudden dead stop. It would not do to have him
fade like a yellowed headline. Although Pele still had no fancy
for New York, his inner circle began to see the possibilities in
the offer. They realized that New York is a media hot spot, a
global marketplace—and it has never had a soccer star. It is
perfect; they will take the idea to Pele. "We must be very careful," says Edevar, "because Pele is going through a difficult
period. We cannot push."

Thus, Mazzei arranged a meeting with Pele and Rose at
their home in Santos, and the men presented their case in favor
of New York. Pele seemed stunned, growing even more confused when they outlined the accompanying drawbacks. His
daughter would lose three years of school credit. There might
be a racial problem, since he is black and Rose is white. In
America this is unusual, and people would stare. Some would
talk, and there might be letters, calls. The biggest problem, of
course, was as big as all of Brazil. For months, Pele had been
pilloried by the government, the press, and the people. For a
man who had traveled the world endless times on a wave of
love, it had been trying. Now, just as they seemed about to
forgive him, should he break their hearts?

Pele raised his eyebrows incredulously, and put down the
guitar he had been tinkering with. "But what about the people?
If I go to America, they will never understand." Zoca pointed
out to his brother that the people could not remain possessive
forever. One day Pele's son Edinho would leave home as a man.
Would he stop him?

The four men, understanding the magnitude of Pele's decision, did not press for an answer, leaving him to talk with
Rose and with his father.

In New York, Toye's obstinance lost ground to Pele's foreboding silence. The 1975 season was nearly upon him and he still had no drawing card to flash to the fans. He had to do *something*. Having been stymied in his pursuit of the greatest, he would go after the next best—in fact, George Best. While Pele was still playing hard to get, the Cosmos plunged deep into negotiations with the mercurial English superstar. Toye had already tried to buy George Best from Manchester United for $500,000 back in 1973. He had been summarily turned down; no airport meetings, no intense bargaining, just a resounding no.

At that time, Best was the naughty, natty pop idol of British soccer, a celebrity of Beatlesque magnitude. He had been named European Athlete of the Year in 1969, had led Manchester United to a First Division Championship and had starred faultlessly for his Northern Ireland national team. But it was off the field that Gorgeous Georgie made his biggest news. He estimated conservatively that his close acquaintances included some 1,000 women. His schedule tended to support the estimate, for he often disappeared for weeks at a time. Moreover, he was not known as a team player. He refused to travel with the team and missed practice and games with flouncy nonchalance. For his insouciance, Manchester United which is sensitive about such things, ordered him to sell his $73,000 mansion and move into a boarding house. He was benched, heavily fined, dropped from the Manchester team, and finally suspended indefinitely.

Across the Atlantic, Americans took little notice, all except Toye, who saw in Best not only a great soccer player, but also perhaps a great draw. Why shouldn't Best's exploits compete with those of Broadway Joe Namath? Food for the tabloids might be music at the turnstiles. Anyway, with the Big Crocodile somnolent in Brazil, Toye was ready to try anything.

On November 7, 1974, North American Soccer League Commissioner Phil Woosnam heard from Sir Matt Busby, director of Manchester United, that Best was available and in very good shape. Best had just appeared in a testimonial game in Manchester and was far and away the best player on the field. Racing for the phone, Woosnam called Toye, suggesting he seize the opportunity. Toye was, as always, ready.

Twenty-four hours later he was in Manchester to meet with Tommy Docherty, manager of Manchester United. Going straight to Docherty's elegant house on the outskirts of Manchester, he emerged two hours later with a verbal agreement for Best. The Cosmos would pay United $25,000 a month if Best were available for as much as one game. The deal included the option to buy him outright at the end of the season. However, should Best pull his disappearing act on the Cosmos, Manchester would get nothing. Toye was pleased. His newsman's habits conjured up a flurry of headlines back home: "COSMOS GET THE BEST OF IT." Two days later, he was still in a good mood, despite the fact that Best had stood him up two days in a row for contract meetings. He left for New York, with the promise that Best would follow.

In the sports world, the sizzle is often as important as the steak, which accounts for press conferences. Toye had a big one planned for Best, and Best actually arrived for it in New York on January 17, somewhat bleary-eyed from "late negotiations." "What was her name?" a newsman asked. Best smiled slyly. He was dressed in a brown crushed velvet suit which blended nicely with his lank brown hair and full beard. He could have been an ad for one of the newer "total environment" hair salons. "I don't see why anyone would object to what I do off the field as long as it doesn't affect how I play," Best told an army of newsmen at the Essex House. "Some people think an athlete should be in bed by 10:30, alone, and stay away from liquor and women. That's ridiculous. It's unhealthy."

"I'd suspend him if he changed his life-style," said Toye bravely. "He's not a soccer player, he's a celebrity. I don't have any straight-arrow types on my team."

The next morning, Best signed a piece of paper acknowledging that "I have received contracts to play for the New York Cosmos valid only for 1975." The news landed prominently on the pages of the *New York Times* sports section. The *New York Times!* They'd really done it this time. The Cosmos' credibility soared. Even *New York Daily News* columnist Dick Young weighed in with a comment, saying that Best was just the kind of charismatic superstar soccer needed to make it as a major sport.

The Cosmos asked Best to come over in early March for training, but Best was so excited, so eager, that he told Toye he'd like to play in the NASL indoor league at the end of February. On this euphoric note, he then flew back to England. At last, the final piece of the jigsaw puzzle. Now everything would fall into place. The TV people would be calling Toye for a change, bidding for this hot media property. The magazines would want to do cover stories on Gorgeous Georgie. There would be headlines in the *New York Times* and the *Daily News*. Ticket sales would soar, and how long could it be before Yankee and Shea stadiums opened their gates to the Cosmos? Toye floated on this euphoria for about a week. By the end of that week, he had not heard from Best.

He decided to phone to see if everything was okay, because there were a few more minor points to discuss. George was not in London; he was in Malaga, resting from the exertions of his trips to New York. No, he cannot be reached. Perspiring heavily, Toye made a few calls to friends in Manchester who informed him that Best was under terrible pressure from his business partners to reject the Cosmos' offer. Apparently, they felt that without George's presence in England, his string of night clubs would go under. Toye was still trying vainly to locate his superstar when the phone rang. It was Mazzei.

"Hello, Clive, Julio. Pele wants to know one thing. Are you still interested?"

Toye was shocked by this sudden flicker of hope on the tail of the Best fiasco. He had been jerked around for the last six months, first by Pele, then by Best, and his resolve had seriously eroded. In his gloomiest moments he had begun to think that the chase for Pele might be cursed, that it was destined to remain a futile effort no matter how much money or energy was poured into it. Now someone was throwing him a rope.

Toye fought to remain cool. "Of course, Julio. Certainly. I was beginning to wonder if we'd ever hear from you again. It's been over a month, if I'm not mistaken." According to his desk calendar it had been one month and five days. "I read about this business of George Best," said Mazzei. "I'm very sorry." "So am I, but he was always our second choice, Julio. We always wanted Pele first."

"Pele says he is ready to talk to you. He will be in Brussels for the Van Himst Jubilee game. Could you meet him there?" Yes!

As luck would have it, Toye and Pele were assigned rooms at the end of the same corridor at the G. B. Motor Inn near the Brussels airport. At this point, Toye was thankful for the smallest stroke of good fortune. Waiting until he was sure that Pele had gone off to a reception at the home of the minister of foreign affairs, he walked around the corner to confer with Mazzei. They talked for about an hour.

When Pele returned, Mazzei began enthusing about the prospect of a few years in New York. The children would be bilingual, and they could go home to visit whenever they'd like on the Warner jet. Pele was beginning to sniff conspiracy. "It looks to me like Toye have even my friends under contract," Pele joked with Mazzei. "Why everybody want to send me to America? You know, Professor?"

In the evening after the game, Mazzei, Xisto and Toye repaired to Toye's room. They ordered sandwiches, milk, beer for Xisto, and a bottle of Scotch for Toye. After about an hour of pleasant talk, Toye produced an envelope from his attache case and announced that he had a firm proposal from the Cosmos. Mazzei said he would show it to Pele, but he doubted anything would come of it. Toye was not worried. This time, he had a second envelope and a backup offer.

In the morning, Mazzei appeared at Toye's room and said, "I'm sorry, Clive, but Pele thinks the offer is not very good. Is not enough money, and too much contract."

"What does he want, then?" Toye asked.

"Pele will tell you himself. In his room. You come at four?"

Pele's suite bore little resemblance to the accommodations of a king. Rather, it seemed like Macy's basement during a half-price sale, with clothes and people scattered everywhere. Pele's white suit trousers split and he gave them to the chambermaid to sew. She thanked him as though he had presented her with a gold amulet. While he tore through his suitcases for a shirt, Pele's all-star teammates from last night's benefit trickled in to say goodbye. They included Jose Altafini, who first played with Pele in 1958. From behind a wardrobe a husky Portuguese voice asked Toye about soccer in the United States. It was Eusebio, the Black Panther of Portugal. Pele flipped through old photos with Altafini, laughing. In only an hour, Pele would have to board a plane to Morocco, where he was to have dinner with the king. He still hadn't seen Toye's final offer. The envelope began to wilt from the moisture on Toye's fingers.

The chambermaid charged back in, waving a bouquet of red roses, and asked if the pants were satisfactory for the monsieur. Before Pele could answer she launched into a tearful deposition, telling him that her husband bought tickets for his game months ago and died last week. Since Pele had always been her boy's idol, would he pose with her in a photograph for the boy? Pele nodded, curling his right arm around the woman's shoulders. Toye, at a loss for anything else to do, snapped the picture. The head housekeeper appeared in the doorway, loudly berating the chambermaid for bothering Monsieur Pele. Behind her Jairzinho, the Brazilian winger who teamed with Pele in three World Cups yelled a greeting in Portuguese. Toye was a wreck.

But within fifteen minutes, the room had somehow cleared and fallen silent. Only Pele, Mazzei, Xisto, and Toye were left, and Pele turned to Toye. He was now ready to hear the second offer, which Toye passed over, sinking into a chair as Pele, Mazzei and Xisto adjourned to an adjoining room. Toye's head was pounding, all the chaos and confusion finally registering at the base of his skull like a jackhammer. They've got just half an hour to get off to the airport and he can't believe their cool. Will they keep even the king of Morocco waiting?

Pele reentered the room ten minutes later and walked over

to Toye. "Okay, Clive, we talk very much. Now I make for you my final offer." He fished in a credenza drawer for a piece of hotel stationery and wrote a few numbers on the back of it. They were big numbers, bigger than Warners had anticipated. Toye tucked the paper into one of the leather compartments in his attache case, bid goodbye all around and oozed back down the corridor to his room. Mazzei phoned for the limousine. The driver did eighty-five all the way and Pele made the plane by five minutes.

Back in New York the next afternoon, Toye realized that he finally had something substantial to work with. Finally, he felt they had gotten beyond the stage of a cat and mouse chase. Once the pursuit was reduced to a question of numbers, he felt certain Warners could come up with the right ones. It was a vindication for Toye, a stamp of legitimacy on his mad global dashes. He felt secure now because he knew that the Warners offer was unique—nobody could duplicate it, especially the marketing clauses.

When Toye arrived at Warner headquarters, its legal and financial departments had already blocked out drafts of lengthy contractual and promotional agreements. All of them had several blank spaces, into which the final magic figures would be typed. Toye was uneasy about seeing those figures in black-and-white finality. Nothing seemed final with Pele. So far, all the paper had added up to nothing. Toye gathered the contracts and carted them to his office, where he placed a call to Mazzei at the contingent's next stop—Beirut. Yes, the Moroccan king had been very gracious. Yes, Pele will have a free day during a layover between Malta and Milan Pepsi appearances. Toye would meet them in Rome. By now he knew the Pan Am timetable and the first-class menu by heart.

The following morning, Roman time, Toye, Warner executive Rafael de la Sierra, and financial expert Jim Caradine checked into the Hotel Le Grand. They noticed several linen-coated men staring at them while the concierge checked their passports. Toye had been informed in telex code that Mazzei and Pele were registered at the Hotel Jolly. Since a swarm of infamous Roman paparazzi had gotten wind of the meeting, Pele actually stayed at a third hotel under an assumed name. On the other side of the city, in the lobby of the Jolly, a gaggle of anxious journalists was in a flap. They knew something was up, and like hounds who have been given just a pass at a scent, they rushed everywhere, questioning porters, rummaging through laundry bins at the back entrance, and monopolizing every public phone within three blocks.

Safe in their hotel bunker, de la Sierra read Pele a five-paragraph summary of the latest contract as Mazzei stood stationed by the window overlooking an inner courtyard and their car. De la Sierra finished, adding that if Pele was actually giving his proposal serious consideration, there would be a small preliminary detail to dispense with. Pele's seven-figure physique must be examined by a doctor to please the insurance company. An examination had been arranged with an American doctor in Rome.

Pele said he would go immediately and Mazzei made two phone calls, one to his security liaison, the bell captain, and one to his driver who suggested they hire a cab to blend in with Roman traffic, just to be safe. The cab was hailed and brought around back, and Pele left. He slouched in the back seat, cringing as his delirious, chattering cabbie did everything but drive through the Trevi Fountain to flaunt his famous passenger. Pele bought his safety by autographing the front seatcover, and slipped into the doctor's office, out again, then back to the hotel. He was tired, he said, and would order room service, foregoing dinner with Toye at one of Rome's better-known restaurants. He would just go to bed early after a light, quiet meal alone. It was almost a relief to Toye, who needed a rest too, but as he waded through the veal piccata, Pele materialized at the table, and slipped into the chair opposite him. He wanted to talk to Clive, quietly, over dinner.

But quiet, public dinners are not a part of Pele's life. Not five minutes later, the chef arrived, beseeching Pele to sign his starched hat. He was followed by a busboy who, upon seeing Pele enter the restaurant, raced home and got his soccer ball to be autographed. Just as Toye approached the particulars of the playing contract, a band of strolling musicians arrived at the table, insisting that Pele honor them by playing guitar. Pele hesitated; Toye muttered into his salad. Pele strummed two choruses of a Brazilian samba, and everyone in the restaurant joined in a standing ovation. The chef reappeared with a dish he created for the occasion—Pasta alla Pele. Each of them sampled it. "It is good, but I am very tired," Pele said. "I must return to the hotel. Then to Brazil, and rest. I will think very much about Cosmos offer. I give you answer. Only two more weeks."

Toye looked at him, wanting to believe. Detecting his apprehension, Pele threw an arm around his shoulder. "No, not to worry, Clive. The answer will not be no."

Untangling the quadruple negatives, Clive realized the answer might be yes.

During the ensuing weeks, the Cosmos office took on the air of a maternity waiting room. Toye did a lot of fidgeting. His telephone pad was covered with doodles that some enterprising analyst might make into psychoanalytic ciphers. When Pele's call was two days overdue, he began to get irritable. The media was now very aware of the Cosmos negotiations with Pele, and their credibility, already dealt a rabbit punch by the Best fiasco, was riding on that phone line. Reporters were beginning to swap Cosmos jokes much as they did with the heroically incompetent New York Mets teams of some years back. Three days past the deadline, Toye phoned Mazzei to ask just what was happening.

For one thing, the Brazilian public was putting Pele under tremendous pressure. Even his familiars eyed Pele with suspicion and accusation. During the midst of the negotiations, Pele passed an old couple he had known for several years. They sat each day in front of a store on the Gonzaga, Santos's main avenue, and each time Pele passed by they traditionally exchanged cordial greetings. The old couple got up from their post to confront him. They had heard he was negotiating with the Americans. "Pele, oh, Pele, is this true, you leave Brazil? Leave us? Please don't go. Not ever. You cannot, you are Brasilero. Always Brasilero."

Pele himself could not understand his countrymen's obstinance. They simply wouldn't hear his side. "People in the street are mad with me," he said. "Mad all time. They say no Pele, I don't want talk to you. Many times I speak with them. Listen, if Brazil go to the war, I get one gun, go to defend Brazil. But this is sport. Is not like the war. They tell me you are national monument, not for you to go. I tell them yes, I am national monument who must pay many, many, taxes."

But Mazzei told Toye not to worry. Pele had just been very busy and had made no decision yet. Toye could tell from his voice that there was still some problem. The next morning, a story out of Brazil came clattering across the wires at 11 P.M. "Pele has rejected a $7 million offer to play for the New York Cosmos." Cosmos public relations man John O'Reilly heard the news on TV and dived for the phone to tell Toye, asking, a bit nervously, "just what the hell was going on?"

Toye was hysterical. Who bloody said this? Why hadn't he been told? Did the papers have it yet? He called Mazzei in Santos. "Julio, why didn't you call me?" he screamed into the phone. Mazzei replied that he was sorry, but Pele had just made up his mind. It was not the offer. He just didn't want to play again, to wear any colors besides those of Santos or the Brazilian Nationals.

Toye mulled over the reason for this sudden reversal and realized that it probably all came down to Pele's return home and the resumption of his domestic life. Obviously, Brazil had a grip on his heart as well as his wallet. To meet Pele now on his home territory could only be more difficult. For this reason, Toye would not go to Santos alone. He would arrive bearing heavy artillery: de la Sierra and Jay Emmett. Ertegun was in Brazil anyway on record business and would meet them in Santos. A united front, and each with a specialized reason for Pele to say yes. Emmett, if necessary, would drop the biggest lure—more money, plus marketing.

When the Warner contingent arrived, the Brazilian press shadowed their every move, still on a witch hunt for any foreign agent seeking to make off with Pele. One Brazilian paper ran a cartoon of four U.S. Marines storming ashore to capture Pele. The Marines' faces were caricatures of the Warner party. Things were hot in Santos alright, and the chase hurtled on in earnest, taking on a Keystone Cops aura. Mazzei has decided on Xisto's home on the beach in Guaruja as the best paparazzi-proof hideaway. All parties left Santos at 11:00 A.M. in three separate cars. The two cars with Pele's advisors and the Warner party headed toward Xisto's place by a serpentine route that coiled through back roads and small sleepy villages. The third car was used as a decoy to lead the reporters astray. It worked. One hour after the decoy car embarked, a hundred media-men alighted in a crowd of dust, cameras, and television cables at a place they thought was Xisto's house. But they were actually twenty-five miles south of the real target, in the driveway of Brazilian racing car driver Emerson Fittipaldi. Fittipaldi came out his back door to the agitated dustbowl of his driveway. While he tried to understand the ravings of his unexpected guests, the two carrier cars hid out of sight at Xisto's beach house. Everyone went to the beach for a pickup game of soccer while they waited for Pele to arrive. It seemed like a holiday, even to Toye. While the others played soccer, de la Sierra told Mazzei that if Pele came to New York, Warners would like the Professor to come with him.

Pele arrived at 3 P.M. in good spirits, having shaken the one tenacious car of journalists still on his trail. He mixed a pitcher of a Brazilian drink called Caipirinho, and the two factions sat down to business. Pele began the negotiations by presenting Emmett with a written list of his demands. Emmett, Toye, and de la Sierra left the room to discuss the proposals. It took just fifteen minutes and when they returned Emmett tossed out the bait.

He had saved it all this time, and he was convinced that when Pele fully undersood the basic concept, the Warner offer would balloon to its full implications and leave no room for refusal. He told Pele that after careful analysis, he and Warners felt that Pele had never had marketing and licensing contracts worthy of his name. "Pele, I understand you have about five decent deals. Personally, I just can't believe that. Just five? Warners can get you twenty terrific deals."

Pele would endorse shoes, radios. He would have his own distinctive trademark, and a whole clothing line with his name on it. Pele could sell pajamas, lunch boxes, Honda motorcycles, and Brut cologne. His face would be everywhere. Emmett warmed to his subject and by the time he finished, he had conjured up a commercial wonderland. It was a bullish, high-profit package that Emmett outlined, but Pele was not sufficiently impressed.

Still, Emmett felt confident. He believed he had Pele on the hook, and began to reel in his line; it only snagged on the three-year length of the contract. "Three years is a very, very long time," mused Pele. "I am Brazilian and I want to stay Brazilian. I need to think, much more to think."

But despite Pele's apprehension, the web was drawing tighter by the moment. Outside on the small veranda, Mazzei had swung over to the Warners camp. "It will help a great deal," he told Toye, "if you can somehow get the official blessing of our government. If the government and the people approve, Pele will come to play for your team." Pele, for his part, did not view the meeting with such black-and-white finality. "After Clive and Jay come to Santos, I talk some night, with my parents, with Rose. Next day I tell Jay yes, I go, but now we start to talk. To be . . . serious talk."

Toye and the Spanish-speaking de la Sierra tried to deal with the Brazilian press. Spanish was not exactly Portuguese and Pele knew that no matter how sweet de la Sierra's words, they would not dissolve the cloud of suspicion. "He had many, many problem, Rafael. He must go make many TV shows talk and . . . discussion. People see this man and say, 'this guy want to take Pele' Rafael has to say, 'wait a minute, no, no, I don't wish to keep Pele. Not for all time.' One day he talk on TV and he gets very excited—how you say it—ner-vous. He say, I only want to stay with Pele one year and a half. He want to know why everyone think he is such bad man. Rafael feel bad. I tell him I am sorry."

Back in the U.S., Toye called each franchise owner in the NASL from New York personally and asked them to have their respective congressmen convey to the Brazilian embassy what a great cultural tie this would be between Brazil and the United States. He shuttled to Washington to meet with State Department officials. Finally, he petitioned Henry Kissinger's office, which agreed that Kissinger would send a message of encouragement to the Brazilian ambassador, Jose Augusto de Araujo Castro. This should do it—and if not, Toye had more ammunition.

On May 19 as the '75 NASL season was getting underway, he flew to Santos carrying a letter of welcome from New York's Mayor Beame and letters from 175 American children urging Pele to come to New York. One of them was from Toye's nine-year-old son Robert. It read: "Dear Pele, Please come to play for the Cosmos. If you need a place to stay, you can sleep in my bed."

Once again, Toye allowed himself the luxury of optimism. Finally, Pele seemed amenable to the idea of playing in New York, teaching soccer to American boys. The money question was down to technicalities and Pele knew his family would be well taken care of. That left just one more hurdle—the Brazilian press. They were still outraged that he would sell out for Yanqui dollars, and the logic of marketing exposure was lost on a public that had only a visceral understanding of the situation. For them it was still an affair of the heart, and with too much passion fanned by the Brazilian press, Pele just might back away once more.

Toye held a massive press conference in Santos, where he explained in painstaking detail that what Pele was doing in trying to spread the gospel of soccer would reflect very well on his country, very well indeed. Brazil would be known for something more than coffee.

Next, Toye arranged for Pele to attend a Cosmos game against Vancouver at Randall's Island on May 28. Pele arrived there by helicopter two hours before the game. From the air he could scarcely believe what he saw. The Cosmos' stadium looked like an ugly scar interrupting the green park around it. When his helicopter touched down a hundred yards behind the goal at the south end of the stadium, he was mobbed by a horde of kids wearing some of the 100 Pele T-shirts the Cosmos had ordered for the occasion. As he stepped off the helicopter, Pele was met by Steve Ross. He told "Mr. Steve" that he had heard a great deal about him. Ross said likewise, and the two made their way through the crowd to the Warner box.

The announcement that the Cosmos had an honored guest triggered a standing ovation and a blizzard of confetti from 7,331 fans, many of whom had come solely to get a glimpse of Pele, hoping their warmth could somehow influence his decision. Toye's spirits soared with each shout. "Peleeeeeee, Peleeeee." He had heard it in at least ten other countries, and he couldn't believe he was hearing it then, there in the impoverished oval of Randall's Island.

When the game ended 1–0 in favor of Vancouver, Pele was unfailingly frank. He told Ross that the Cosmos appeared to have some good players but they were missing organized teamwork. Ross asked if he could bring the team together. Pele smiled and replied, "If you think I play here and next month Cosmos win championship, forget it, Mr. Steve. Soccer is team sport." So, he had decided to come to New York? Again, a smile. "No, but I am sixty to seventy percent sure I will come."

The next day, Pele had a lunch date with Mr. Steve at Warners, but he sent Mazzei ahead to make sure his special requests had been honored in the contract. Pele wanted more money free of marketing contingencies, plus the option to buy back the licensing rights to his name after three years. Xisto had been adamant about that—a man needs his name.

When Pele arrived at 3:00, Mazzei assured him that all his demands had been met, and together with Xisto, proceeded to Ross's office. Ross immediately took the initiative. He announced that he would explain to Xisto how Pele could better manage his money. They would work with him on it after he signed the contract. Then he explained Warner's plans for accomodating Pele's family. (If Emmett is brilliant at marketing, Ross is Warner's resident genius in tailoring an environment to the needs of his stars.) He explained that above all, Warners wanted Pele to feel comfortable here. Warner Communications is a family, and Pele and Rose and the children were a part of it. Arrangements would be made for the children to attend the United Nations school. An apartment would be found on the East Side in the fifties, near the UN. They were constructing an office for Pele in their skyscraper so that he could run his businesses from New York.

Pele turned to Mazzei and said something in Portuguese, then he addressed Ross. "Yes," he says. "Everything okay. I will come. My answer is yes."

Toye went numb. The answer he'd been chasing for three years just dropped in his lap and it was almost fatal. As Ross, Emmett, and de la Sierra stood applauding, Toye remained slackjawed. Finally, he got up, walked around the coffee table and embraced Pele. There were tears in the eyes of both men.

That night, Pele returned to Santos and Toye went back to Scarsdale a free man. The yoke had been lifted.

By now, Toye had become jaded to the roller-coaster aspects of the chase and negotiations. His emotions had been tossed and beaten, leaving him with a sense of deja vu which was less painful than habitual. It was now just a question of time, a question of when, not if. Thus, when Mazzei called back to inform Toye that there were still problems with the contract, he was not surprised. At bottom, the problem was simple—a chasm of disparity in translation. When translating a fifty-page contract into Portuguese, some why's and wherefores are bound to get lost.

Two days later, de la Sierra arrived in Santos with Jim Caradine and company lawyer Norman Samnick. They taxied to Pele's office and began the long wind-up, starting at 10 A.M. Friday and working nonstop until 5 P.M. Saturday, while a bilingual Brazilian stenographer typed several drafts of a contract. Pele retired to another room adjoining his office to chat with friends. A tangle of TV crews slept outside in the reception area, keeping vigil to record the historic moment of agreement.

The nearly got to film a homicide.

At 5 A.M., a dozing Pele heard loud, strident voices from the conference room as the negotiations moved into a final convulsion. It was Samnick and Sergio DeBrito, Pele's lawyer, and things were getting nasty. Both men gleamed crimson and the veins stood out in Samnick's neck. Mazzei tried to calm them, at some risk to himself. Samnick screamed that he had never dealt with such thick people. What in hell do they want, Fort Knox? The moon? DeBrito screamed that they must have more money up front, otherwise Warners and Samnick could forget everything. Pele would not go.

It was clearly a matter of professional competition, of two high level attorneys trying to finesse one another. But fatigue and the language barrier dissolved professional cool into a near street fight. DeBrito lunged across the table at Samnick and Mazzei stepped in between just in time. DeBrito began shredding papers in a gesture of challenge. By now, Toye and Emmett were long at their respective homes after a hectic day of monitoring negotiations from the Warner building. De la Sierra rang Toye as the situation degenerated. But by 6:00 A.M. Emmett, who had spoken to Toye four times between 11:00 and 1:00 that evening, had taken the phone off the hook at his home in Westport, Connecticut. Now it was critical and Toye needed Emmett's advisement, badly. He demanded that the operator connect him with the Westport police station. It was an acute situation, he explained, someone might be maimed or killed. In the background, Samnick and DeBrito still cursed each other.

When the Westport operator refused to summon the police to settle this battle in Brazil, Toye slammed the phone down in frustration. He woke Ross, who was in Dallas on business, and told him Pele wanted more of the money up front, and Samnick and DeBrito were willing to duel over it. Ross said he'd get back to them in an hour, and called Emmett, who had since placed his phone back on the hook. Meanwhile, Emmett had spoken to Breil, who had come up with an idea. Far-fetched, but it might work. Warners offered to buy Pele's library of historic game film. Ross liked this idea and relayed it to Toye who relayed it to Samnick, who had it translated to DeBrito who relayed it to Pele who said simply, "Okay." Samnick and DeBrito shook hands.

Pele, who had not raised his voice once through this whole struggle invited everybody out to lunch. All that remained now was the official signing, and it would take place forty-eight hours later in Bermuda. There, after Pele had put the last of a few hundred signatures on the contract, Toye looked at him and deadpanned, "Okay, now where is that fifteen dollar league registration fee?" This had become a standing joke between them through the negotiations, Toye always insisting, after speaking of millions of dollars, that Pele had to give way on the fifteen, Pele playfully balking and insisting that this was the club's responsibility.

Toye laughed, "Okay, Pele, all we need is that fifteen dollars and it's official." But Pele was one step ahead of the game. He took out two American bills, a ten and a five. Then, he auto-graphed them with a flourish and handed them over to Toye, knowing all along that Clive would not part with the cur-rency, and would thus have to pay the league after all.

"Now," Pele said, "we have a deal."

Toye chuckled and shook his head as he folded the bills and put them in his shirt pocket.

5

"21"

*A*lthough it is cool and shady on the esplanade of Rocke-feller Plaza, the windows of the Warner Communications building, rising high above nearby St. Patrick's Cathedral, are smeared in orange. On the corner of Fifth Ave. and Fifty-first St. a local institution is going to work. Sorting his pamphlets and slogan buttons the "Husband Liberation" exponent slips the sandwich sign over his head and prepares to spend this June 10, 1975, lobbying for oppressed husbands everywhere. Early executive arrivals are stepping out of cabs, scaring up flocks of slate pigeons. The sun is beginning its gentle spring climb and it promises a rare and lovely day.

At 10:50 A.M. John O'Reilly and Jay Emmett are standing in front of the "21" Club, waiting for Pele. O'Reilly whistles and looks up at the windows on the second floor, where a high re-lief frieze of faces, arms, legs, cuff links, and bloody marys sug-gest that some kind of intense revel is in progress. The genteel little building in the shadow of the Warner's monolith seems about to explode and pour a river of people and hooch into Fifty-second St. Already the crackle of excitement emanating from "21" has infected the street. There are faces in all the windows of the building surrounding the old brownstone and in the street a crowd of the curious, the half-informed, and the misinformed have gathered, New York syle, to see whatever there is to see.

"It's ten of," Emmett says to O'Reilly, "where is he?"

"Well, we're scheduled to start at eleven, and from what I know about him, he's never early . . ."

"Maybe he's still on Brazilian time; what would that make it now, I guess an hour earlier . . . well, Rafael is there, I'm sure he knows what's going on."

Eleven A.M.—It is called the "Hunt Room," a fitting enough name for the place where Pele is to finally sign his Cosmos contract. Although he isn't here yet, everybody else is. The sober pine and oak paneled room is supposed to hold 130 cocktail sippers, but today it is brimming with twice as many media types, junior executives, hangers-on, gate-crashers, friends, and friends of friends. Film crews have lighted the place like a desert at high noon. TV cables and light lines are strung over the antlers of eland and antelope, tucked behind stuffed salmon on the walls and snaked around a rare collection of Bavarian beer steins. Even the walls are sweating.

O'Reilly has waded upstairs again to deliver the latest news. "Yes, Pele is on the way over right now," he says (hopes). "Yes, the press conference is scheduled for eleven, we're just waiting for him. No, there is no problem," he assures.

Not that it seems to matter to the bulk of the crowd; sterling trays of canapes and hors d'oeuvres are brought in and quickly disposed of. There's a little lake of tomato juice on the bar with ice cubes skating over it. Downstairs, Ethel Kennedy, just checking her coat, hears a low, shuffling rumble on the ceiling, looks up and wonders just what is going on.

O'Reilly is getting panicky. He wipes his forehead with his handkerchief. His Afro-perm is starting to droop in various directions from the humidity. Fortunately, he had arranged three heavy oak tables covered with white cloth as a kind of barrier protecting the podium and raised platform where the principals of the press conference will be seated. So far, there is little impatience among the nonprofessionals. True, some of

the ladies are unraveling: magenta, aqua, obsidian, powder-blue
eye shadow and mascara beginning to streak. But it's the pros
O'Reilly is worried about.

All the hardened film crews have taken up positions and
vowed not to move, baking in the lights and growing increas-
ingly short-tempered. These guys have short fuses as it is and
John can see a brawl on the way. At least there aren't any
chandeliers to swing from, but one of those Addax horns on
the wall could impale about eight people.

At about this time, it occurs to O'Reilly to wonder why the
"21" Club was chosen. Later Toye provided the answer: "It's
quite a posh place, and when I came to New York, soccer was
strictly Fourteenth St. I'll just save this as my own private
joke." But for once in his life he had underestimated Pele; even
Toye could not envision this scene.

Eleven-ten—Pele is dressed in a print shirt and cream pants,
sitting around the hotel suite with his gang. Lawyer DeBrito
is on the phone with lawyer Samnick, patiently explaining the
situation which is driving him to the brink of despair.

It seems that DeBrito has found a little snag in the contract;
a small one to be sure, nothing to do with money. In fact,
months later none of the principals will actually remember
what the problem was. Somebody suggests that it be cleared up
after the signing ceremony. Mazzei translates, Pele answers,
"No, once I sign, there is no turning back and it is bad to have
a problem. We must do it now, so there is no problem after."
He knows, he has been through this kind of thing before.
DeBrito hangs up, explaining that Samnick is on the way over
and that barring a totally unexpected impasse between the
lawyers everything will be okay. And it is. They iron out the
problem and agree to resolve it in print later in the afternoon.
At 11:50, the caravan begins to move; Rose in her pastel
damson dress and string of pearls, Pele wearing his black bro-
caded suit, adjusting the collar on his high white shirt.

Twelve-fifteen—Toye bursts with relief as he sees the crowd
in the street swarm around the arriving limousine. Photographers are perched everywhere, on railings, steps, the wing arms

of nearby brownstones. One enterprising fellow who has climbed upon a fire hydrant loses his footing, his camera bag swinging into the crowd. Up in the Warner building, people begin to leap and point, craning their necks for a good look. Pedro Garay, the Warner's security man assigned to Pele as bodyguard, leads a phalanx into the club. Toye barely has time to grab Pele's hand before they are herded towards a back staircase where an unexpected and totally unofficial greeting committee blocks the way. It seems a crew of Latin American waiters have staked out the stairs. When they see Pele they begin screaming, "THE KING! THE KING!" After a few autographs, Pele is coaxed along by Garay into a banquet office adjoining the Hunt Room. Rose and the rest of the Pele party slip into the Hunt Room, unnoticed except by the Brazilian contingent.

Cosmos midfielder Gil Mardarescu is there, looking uncomfortable in a white linen suit, with loafers and a necktie. He is beaming. "I love Pele more than my family," Gil says, "He is everything to me, my idol. He come into locker room before game last time and hug and kiss everybody. He is kind. Good, good man." Gil looks down. "This fancy clothes is respect for Pele. I never wear, I don't like. It is only for marriage, and Pele . . ."

In the banquet office Pele sits behind a desk, carefully autographing a menu for a chef. "Many people, yes Clive?" he asks without looking up, because he knows.

"Too many," Toye laughs, "we'll make it as quick as possible." O'Reilly looks in, "Okay, Clive."

When Clive steps out, the noise level increases and the chaos spread before him fills him with joy and terror in equal parts. He begins to speak, his first few words stifled and beaten silent by the commotion:

"Ever happened . . . want you to celebrate . . . great moment in soccer . . . moment in North American soccer." Rushes of incidental noise, Toye raises his voice, "The great one, the king, Pele!"

A black suit slips through the door; the face is absolutely tranquil, fixed in a shy smile, looking at everyone in the most convincing, personal way yet not really seeing anything but the silver suns flashed before him by a shifting mass of photographers. Hi everybody, glad you could make it; his hands are raised in the "V" salute. And now the action really begins; the back of the room is trying to get to the front. There is the sound of glass shattering and a small squeal of dismay as a girl who had been perched delicately on a briefcase is unbalanced and tumbles to the floor.

Tempers flare. A Brazilian TV cameraman who feels that Pele is uniquely his own tries to jockey a Philadelphia still photographer out of his way and gets a knuckle sandwich for his efforts.

Spotting this, Garay looks at O'Reilly. O'Reilly hasn't met Garay yet, so he doesn't know what to make of this meaningful glance. "I figured he was some secret agent; I mean he looks like he just stepped out of Hawaii Five-O or a kung-fu movie and I think, who the hell is that?" but before O'Reilly finds out, Garay is off to break up the fight, running along the tables in a low crouch until he hits a gap that is all cloth and no table and falls through, out of action for the moment.

A few feet away, a fellow is groaning "ooh, noooo" as he hears the brittle crunch of his eyeglasses cracking beneath somebody's feet. Toye is all but screaming now: "Gentlemen of the press, GENTLEMEN of the press, GENTLEMEN of the press, please behave yourselves."

O'Reilly, semiparalyzed, can't take his eyes off the surreal sight of eight photographers with their chins resting on the oak barrier like so many Kilroys.

All kinds of things are happening simultaneously. Dick Young, the nation's most powerful sports columnist, has installed himself on a window ledge, above the human spaghetti bowl. "How much, how much is he getting?" he keeps screaming. But Pele can't even hear him, much less understand. He is standing calmly by the podium, looking for all the world like a Third World delegate to the United Nations. But he is still smiling even if nobody else is, while in the back corner of the room, Rosie is nervously dragging on a cigarette, arms folded, conservative and inconspicuous. It is calming down a bit for the signing ceremony. As Pele takes the thick portfolio he asks Toye: "Clive, you have pen?"

"Do I have a pen," Toye incredulously, "You bet I've got a pen." A little fumbling in the pockets and he fishes out a ballpoint, a solid silver Sheaffer chosen specially for this occasion. He clicks it once and hands it over.

Back in the coatroom Cosmo Tony Picciano walks over to his teammate Angelo Anastasio, who is sipping a coke, his face inanimate. "Angelo, I heard what happened . . . I'm sorry," Picciano offers with a handshake. "Yeah," Anastasio shrugs, "it happens, what can you do?" Yesterday Anastasio was released, the first casualty as Pele set the massive gears of change into motion.

"Would you like the music louder, Mr. Pay-lay?" asks the chauffeur, swinging the sleek Cadillac into the Lincoln Tunnel later that afternoon, heading for Philadelphia. Pele looks quizzically at Mazzei, who answers for him, "No, thank you, just fine, everything is fine." The fatigue of the day is carved into Pele's profile against the immaculate white leather jacket; the face looks gray. The party consists of Rose, Pele, Mazzei, Breil, and a writer. The car shoots onto the turnpike, through the grimy industrial labyrinth of northern New Jersey, images which even the velvet seats and the polished brass buttons on the chauffeur's cap cannot dispatch.

A question is put to Pele: why is he here riding through an industrial swamp, on his way to a strange city to watch two second-rate soccer teams, one of them his new employer.

"Life itself is a challenge," Pele says, "once in a while, is necessary to have little obstacle to jump over. I retire, yes, because there is no more fantasy in game for me. Every year I come back and every year is the same. Faces change, young ones come and go lucky and unlucky. I stay same. What to do? I am thirty-four year old, is still young for a man, even for player. It is nice to have time with family, I like very much, but is impossible to do nothing; then a man become bored, lose interest in life, is maybe too old too fast. Who want to be old fast?

"If I go to Italy, Spain, Mexico, what I get? Many money. Is nice, but not so important, because is not so new. New York Cosmos . . . unique . . . for me, a different situation, maybe the only one situation which makes for me the challenge that I am not so sure about. America is only place where I am still Edson, and not so much Pele."

And what about failure, the possibility that after the first adrenalin rush of excitement and media voyeurism the crystal palace collapses and Pele becomes just another tax write-off, a gamble that failed?

"Why to think about? Whatever happen, happen. The mission to introduce soccer here may be great and difficult, even for me. But we do not know yet how big the job. Maybe not so big as we think. But no matter what happen, the seed will be in the ground, and it maybe grow into very big tree. It is only a question of the treatment for the little seed. Maybe it does not happen in my time, but this much is sure; football [soccer] is very, very important for many, many people everywhere in world. It is not like new toy, or invention. It is real; it help many people understand each other, it bring people together, even same people who fight war. Soccer is much bigger than Pele. I can only show them game, they will decide."

Slowly, he has been shrinking back into the leather, moving closer to his wife's shoulder. He lays his head on it now, and in moments falls asleep. Mazzei picks up the thread.

"Pele is phenomenon. If he goes to Spain, the people believe he is Spanish; if he go to Sweden, people feel he is Swedish. Everywhere he go, people believe Pele is one of them. He belongs to all the world, only one athlete comes close to him in fame: Muhammad Ali. But Ali is black American athlete, is very different, cannot be mistaken. Pele? Well, he is just Pele. Even those of us who are always around him cannot understand why this is the way. Why children come to him and people have no strange feelings about coming to him with open heart. Is strange, no?

"Hong Kong. We go to see border, what is called 'buffer zone' between British and Red Chinese. You know, men on both side of zone with machine gun. When the Red guard see Pele, two of them come walking across the zone to shake his hand and ask for autograph.

"Berlin. We are in West Berlin, between American and Russian zone. We just go by wall to look. Two guards in watch-tower, Russian men, wave to us, call us to them, recognizing Pele. We show them picture card of Pele, with Pele's name on it, and they motion us to throw to them. I put cards in book I am carrying and throw up to window. They throw book back down, smile and wave, happy like children. Is strange, no?

"Also Macao. We want to go shopping in street, like every-body else. How is it possible? We plan a strategy, go find for Pele a big black wig, beard, glasses. We go to downtown. He is so happy because he sit in shoeshine chair and people pass by, do not recognize him. He was feeling free, happy. We laugh much that day, oh, how we laugh . . .

"I think it is not so hard to come to top of sport as it is to stay there. This is difficult thing, after you make lot of money, become famous. Pele stay on top of sport for twenty years, nobody hate him, nobody think after some years, well, it is only Pele, who was long time ago very, very good player. Why he stay on top? Who know? I believe it is qualities of human dignity; the amazing thing is that Pele is same poor boy who came to play for Santos in 1956.

"Pele does not become a spokesman for race, or religion, or politics. He stay Pele. But there is other side to it too, the sport side. He is so great a player that when he play for a team, is question of how well team adapt to Pele, not other way. Pele has great intuition; he reads the game perfectly, he can predict what will happen. It is not coaching any more, when you work with Pele; now is just question of coach understanding, read-ing, adapting to Pele, making team so it get best from what Pele can do.

"Listen, I have theory. Great athlete I believe is very com-plex thing. I believe the great athlete is built like, how you say,

a pyramid, in three part. The top of the pyramid is specializa-
tion, the particular things an athlete does well, his exceptional
skills. The middle of the pyramid is his athletic ability, his
potential, dedication to training, fitness, disposition. . . . Then
there is the bottom of the pyramid, the base.

"This wide base I believe is human quality; love for people,
humanity, pride. This is the area on which the pyramid must
stand and I think when an athlete suddenly become famous,
then change as person is because the base cannot hold the rest
of the pyramid. The great genius in any field is at the bottom
simple man; greatness is in simplicity, not complication.

"Look at the ball. Ball is simple, yet it fascinate man, ball
sports are most popular. The ball is most perfect shape in the
world; when you hold it in your hand, you can feel the infinite-
ness, the perfection in your hand. The real situation in a ball
game is that the ball play with you, you must understand the
ball. Compare ball to ooniverse, the planets are not square,
they are round. The leetle cells, they are not square, they are
round . . ."

Pele is holding hands with his wife, high up in the box be-
longing to Leonard Tose, owner of the Eagles football team.
There are 20,124 fans arrayed below him—twice the average—
even though he showed nothing more than a ceremonial opening kick that traveled just five yards. Still, it may have been the
most important kick in the history of the NASL. Below him,
on the artificial turf, his new teammates are in deep trouble.
For the first forty minutes, the Cosmos have dominated, Johnny
Kerr leading the attack by roaming free and dangerous at midfield, dishing off pinpoint, penetrating passes to Mark Liveric,
Jorge Siega, and Fink. However, goalkeeper Bob Rigby's spectacular saves for the Atoms have kept the scoreless tie intact.

In the second half, the Atoms make a slight adjustment de-
fensively, moving winger Chris Bahr in on Kerr to mark him
tight and it pays off. The rugged English style keeps Uruguayan
midfielder Alfredo Lamas bottled up and the Cosmos' offense
evaporates. Philadelphia's center fullback Derek Trevis has had

to touch the ball but once in the first thirty minutes of the second half.

"Too individual," Pele offers, his eyes fixed on the broken Cosmos pattern down below. "They seem, how to say, disorganized. It looks like game here is much more running, not so much technique as in Brazil, but that does not mean there is no room for technique."

Here comes a potent crossing ball, defender Werner Roth leaping to spear it with his forehead, Luis de la Fuenta clearing. "The defense looks good to me, but the forwards seem slow; maybe team needs more organization, more to be . . . together."

Still, Cosmos goalkeeper Sam Nusum matches Rigby save for save and survives a second-half barrage to send the game into overtime. An inevitable individual mistake provides a sharp, unexpected ending. After neutralizing yet another reeling Atoms attack near the goal mouth, de la Fuente shoves a clearing ball over to Roth, who is turned away already, sure that Luis would not risk the dangerous crossfield ball so deep in the Cosmos' zone. John McLaughlin of the Atoms swoops in, feathers a perfect pass to Bahr across the true Astroturf, and Chris slashes the eighteen-yarder home, with Nusum rooted helpless, beaten. It is the Cosmos' sixth defeat by one goal in this nine-game-old season, a sure weathercock pointing straight at the Cosmos' stormy, volatile individuality.

But there are further circumstances in the loss, and they involve Pele. For one thing, Bradley has already lived one of the most hectic days of his life, beginning with a traffic ticket on Second Avenue more than twelve hours ago. For another, the team was scheduled to leave New York at 2:00 P.M., arrive in Philadelphia by bus at four and following the pregame meal, rest until 7:00 P.M. "As it turns out," Bradley says, "we're an hour late getting started, so we cancel the meal order and hope we can find a good place on the way. The bus driver says he knows one, and when we get there, they say they can accomodate us with no problem. Twenty-four steaks.

"An hour and fifteen minutes later, all I've got is a cup of coffee. A half-hour after that, we get served and we're late again. We finally pull up at the hotel at six, the absolute worst time because there is really no time for rest, and everybody kind of sits around getting edgy, and I'm wondering what in the world else can go wrong."

All of this, beginning with the press conference, had a disruptive effect on the team. The usual pregame jitters were now outlined in restlessness and aggravation, particularly for five Uruguayans who the Cosmos had imported for the '75 season. After the game, Trevis had said, "If he [Pele] had played, their South American lads would have played better. They hold him in awe, too." It was good logic, bad psychology.

Pele's arrival had immediately devalued the Uruguayans, who had been imported to carry a team but found themselves gradually but surely slipping in Bradley's estimation. The thoroughly English Bradley had trouble adjusting to the skillful, nearly lethargic style of the Latin Americans. The Uruguayans had further problems. They were drifters in a strange land, victim to the kinds of problems that have always attended the importation of foreign players in any nation. They were not sophisticates, so they came fully equipped with paranoia about mistreatment and manipulation. In this scheme of things, it takes nothing more than a cold steak, a lumpy bus seat, a check one day late in the mailing, to trigger whispered suspicions. The fragile Uruguayan psyche, teetering between macho pride and Darwinian survival reflex, became only more friable.

For the English-speaking players, it was a matter of one routine fractured and replaced by another, a new spider web. From this day on, nothing would be the same and if it was not evident in the mechanics of the game against the Atoms it was there in the spirit of the loss.

Specifically, Bradley's relationship with Lamas was already beginning to sour; the fabric had been torn at the deepest "human" level. Back in the second game of the season, the skillful Lamas, expected to be of such value to the Cosmos' suspect midfield, had done what Bradley himself had always considered anathema: he removed himself from a close, critical game. It was against Tampa, following the Cosmos' heartbreaking 3–2 loss to Miami. With fifteen minutes to go, New York was under severe pressure, but clinging to a scoreless tie. Bradley himself was playing because of the injury to Juan Masnick, a fine Uruguayan defender.

"Because I'm the leader type," Bradley remembered, "I was constantly shouting, especially at Lamas, who was standing in a zone most of the game. I tried to convey the importance of working harder, particularly to quell the pressure, you know, regroup and let's get moving. He was always saying yes, yes, yes, but not doing it because it wasn't his style of play. I foresaw the problems to come because of what I was saying and the answers I was getting.

"Well, we conceded a goal. Now, where it takes a concerted effort to get going and get the equalizer in those last twelve or thirteen minutes, Lamas complains about one of his toes or toenails hurting him and walks off the field. I never saw him limping, I never saw him wince when he kicked the ball. The sweat was pouring into my eyes, burning; it may as well have been tears, I was so angry. I really believe I would have noticed if he was playing in pain. So he goes and takes himself out. That was the opposite of my style of play. For me, if we are 1–0 down with fifteen minutes to go, I'm going to die to get that equalizing goal."

Trevis had something else to say following the game. "I personally hold Pele in awe. If he had played, I would have played defense and watched him just go by. I'm not fussy. I shook his hand. I haven't washed it yet and I just may not."

Atoms' owner Tom McCloskey stands at the back of the drafty, cinder-block room during Pele's postgame press conference. He hears Pele repeat roughly the same things he said ten hours ago at "21." He spoke of his "mission," a feeling that soccer in this country needs promotion to become a major sport.

"When I realized I was the only one who could do this job, I decided to accept the Warner's invitation to come here. If Brazil needed to train a boxing team, the only man for the job would be Muhammad Ali. If they needed a swimming coach, the man would be Mark Spitz. For soccer, it looks like me."

The press at this relaxed, chatty interview are charmed, as is McCloskey. He says, "A great game, overtime, Pele, a great night. I'm going home to read through the program to find out more about this guy. His press conference . . . I've never seen anything like it. It was magic."

Massive clouds of human emotions began scudding over the Cosmos' horizon in those first few Pele days, and the club's operational level gave a precise and tangible indication of a presence whose magnitude the Cosmos simply could not gauge beforehand. The Cosmos' cozy little corner on Park Ave. suddenly became headquarters for Pele-mania, a riotous outpouring of emotion and adulation, a free-wheeling get-it-while-you-can desire to Be There.

It all began for the Cosmos seven-man office staff when the *Daily News* broke the imminent consummation of the deal less than a week before the actual signing at "21." Suddenly, the Cosmos' phones were singing, and that was what it was all about in this shadowed corner of the sports market. The callers —newsmen, fans, season-ticket holders—asked, "Is it true, is he really coming?" The Cosmos played it cool. "Nothing definite, can't say when, yes sir, the story is true, no sir, please don't call back, the public will know. Thank you sir, good-bye now sir, I have another call, good-bye sir." Like that. Things were heating up alright, giving the Cosmos staff the feeling a gambler gets when the ball drops off the rim of the roulette wheel, bouncing toward the magic number.

"The most bizarre thing for me was watching our people literally smashing into each other at the office, starting the morning after the press conference," O'Reilly remembered. "It was like sitting strapped to a chair in a theater with a Marx Brothers movie going on, double speed, over and over."

The day after Pele became a Cosmo the phones exploded all over the office. O'Reilly found himself selling tickets along with everybody else, until some temporary help was called in. Fully eighty people called for season tickets for the next two years—no matter where the Cosmos were to play. On June 11, a transient brigade began showing up at the Cosmos' offices. "It was like we were giving away gold," O'Reilly recalled.

By June 13, two days before Pele's first game as a Cosmo, the lines of ticket buyers snaked out of the Cosmos' office, weaving down the emergency stairs and out onto the sidewalk. There were also the job-hunters, the snake-oil salesmen and starry-eyed, unemployed dreamers.

And the bizarre: The door swings open and a big black guy with a briefcase strides through the confusion to O'Reilly's secretary, who holds up a finger asking him to wait until she's off the phone. "Yes sir?"

"I'd like to see Mr. O'Reilly," the man says.

"Do you have an appointment with Mr. O'Reilly?"

"Well, I have to see him."

"Why?"

"A job."

"Oh, oh," Penny thinks, "another gold digger." She dials John's number, a few words are spoken.

"I'm sorry sir," she tells the visitor, "we aren't hiring at the moment."

"Oh, yeah?" He is already barging through O'Reilly's door. John looks up, startled.

"What do you want?"

"I'd like to be the Cosmos' publicity director . . ."

"Well," O'Reilly doesn't exactly know how to put this, "we already have one of those. Me."

"Okay, let me see your boss."

O'Reilly thinks this guy can't be for real. "I'm sorry, Mr. Toye is busy; he isn't seeing anybody. Besides, you need an appointment."

The man stands up slowly. Then he heels around and makes a lunge for Toye's door, which is barely open, begins screaming at Clive, scaring him halfway back to Liverpool. Then he is gone; it is over just like that, another episode. O'Reilly and

Toye look at each other, shake their heads in disbelief, and indulge in a long, hearty laugh.

Then there is the media; the reactors who follow an event as surely as a flash flood follows a thunderstorm. O'Really believes June 11 was the day the Cosmos turned the corner and became an organization of "denial," in the sense that from that day on, the team was the focus of such lavish scrutiny, rumor, and public interest that O'Reilly overnight found himself saying no to people who hadn't a spare moment for the Cosmos a mere forty-eight hours earlier.

Requests for exclusive interviews poured in from all the major national newspapers and magazines like *Sports Illustrated*, *Ebony, Esquire, People, Reader's Digest, Playboy, Oui, Jet, Black Sports, True, Newsweek, Time*; foreign publications like *Epoca, Manchete, Der Spiegel, Paris Match*, and others. The mountain was coming to Mohammad.

"All of a sudden, everybody felt that they were the top soccer sympathizers in the nation," O'Reilly discovered. "Everybody wanted the first interview with Pele because they had done so much for soccer." When John turned a request down, he was often faced by an outraged editor who threatened not to cover the Cosmos, period. Often the rejoinder was, "Fine, you never did in the first place." Every ring of the phone became a triumph in itself.

However, it could not go on like this. All circuits were overloaded, the whole machine threatened to burst. On the afternoon of June 12, the Cosmos locked the doors to their offices. The next day, the phones registered their own electronic protest as the lines simply went dead, all circuits nodded out. There was eerie silence in the office for a moment; heads poked out of every cubbyhole. There was a collective smile and sigh, but thirty minutes later, it was business as usual.

6

Debut

*P*ele's first practice with the Cosmos was indoors, at the Hofstra University gym on June 12, a rainy Thursday. He arrived thirty-eight minutes late because his chauffeur had gotten lost in the concrete nervous system of Long Island. Bradley cheerfully waived the customary twenty-five–dollar fine. Pele's first words to his new teammates were: "I've always been a team man and I still am. Please don't expect me to win games alone. We must work together."

Lamas is his first victim. Pele anticipates his best moves and strips the podal magician of the ball twice as the Uruguayan challenges him. It is a small showdown, the silent establishment of a new hierarchy. Pele also demonstrates that he is not gun-shy, stopping a bullet ball with the chest as his goalie, reserve Kurt Kuykendall scrambles to get back into position . . .

Later, Pele takes a pass midcourt, slips and dribbles by three defenders and here we are, face to face with Nusum as Pele cocks the awesome leg and prepares to unload catastrophe—but he shuffles the ball off meekly to Fink, a grin breaking over his face. "I think if he shot that ball, he would have taken my head off," Nusum says later.

Debut

The following day, the Cosmos practice at Randall's Island, their home field. It is a heavy, humid day, rain puddles in the track around the field, reflecting the faces of some thirty-five newsmen from a dozen nations. When Pele walks into the huddle, Fink begins to applaud. "Please, no, I am one of you, we must be a team, together," Pele answers in a voice stern enough to indicate that this is not just another piece of gee-whiz-guys humility. As the scrimmage gets underway, Pele asserts command. "Okay, okay," he shouts, "easy, now, look, look, look the ball." He begins to orchestrate the action; there is nothing shy in his demand for the ball, no self-consciousness in his presence among a group of people who have suddenly developed two left feet and a stutter because he is among them.

Time and place shift; Pele slips thoroughly into that other zone, the deep well of his fame, past the interface of money, geography, and race. He has assimilated, gone back into the infantry. Already he knows his teammates' names.

Johnny Kerr, from the left side, sends a shoulder-high ball crossfield to Pele, lurking before the goal mouth. The thick body sags as Pele sits back for a moment, then, with his left leg floating up, his right leg flexes and catapults him into the air, his back floating parallel to the ground. A grunt begins down in his throat, he scissor-kicks his legs sharply, meets the ball with his right instep and drives it over his laid-flat body, into the goal. The photographers are fumbling to raise their cameras, newsmen gossiping on the sidelines look up just as Pele is landing, breaking the backward fall with extended arms downward, a spontaneous cheer erupting from his teammates. The rare moment has whistled by, it is all over.

"What happened?" asks Kuykendall, the victimized goalie.

There are two fellows down on their knees, painting green over the brown patches on the field. A CBS-TV technician, watching and testing one of the thirty cameras that will be employed here today turns to his buddy and shrugs: "Maybe it'll all work, who knows?" We are in Downing Stadium, a WPA relic on Randall's Island, rising like a sludge heap out of the East River. A few stragglers on the exit ramp of the Triborough Bridge are watching those two insects in the vast empty bowl splashing paint on the grass. It is 10:30 A.M., June 15. Today, Pele will play his first game for the Cosmos, before 21,278 spectators. There will also be a live television audience, widening like a funnel from the dingy stadium, encompassing among other places Toledo, Ohio; Toledo, La.; Toledo, Uruguay; Toledo, Chile; and Toledo, Brazil; in all, twenty-two nations are hooked up for the spectacle. The live supporting cast will include Robert Redford, New York Mayor Abraham Beame, Henry Kissinger's brother, Nelson Rockefeller's cousin, 300 domestic and foreign newsmen, including a ravaged-looking fellow called Tyrone Slothrop, on assignment for an international journal called *Rocket-Trails*, written in Esperanto. Then there will be the live thousands and electronic millions who are nobody in particular; some of them are already huddled beneath the monolithic slabs of stadium wall, waiting for the ticket booths to open three hours from now. No wonder they are painting the dirt green.

Bradley and his team climb out of the bus in front of the Essex House and walk right smack into the big-time. There are photographers everywhere, children, vamping women, anonymous folks drift in from the streets to help create the scene. Smile! Sure, an autograph here, there . . . Pele, oh, he's upstairs, but that's alright, we're all part of the same show.

Bradley goes off to find the banquet manager. In his pocket he is carrying a letter from Dallas goalkeeper Ken Cooper, an old buddy, veteran of the American soccer loop de loop. Cooper knows that Pele exchanges shirts with a lucky opponent after every game, and has written to Gordon to suggest that he be the lucky opponent. But Bradley doesn't have time for that now, because he finally locates the manager and discovers that the Essex has not made preparations for the team meal.

"What?" Here we go again. Bradley is too mad to feel the deja vu creeping up on him. "I made the arrangements myself three days ago . . ." Confusion, assurances, the manager hustles off to fix things up. Meanwhile, Bradley is thinking, "There is nothing laid out, nothing ready, nothing is organized. Jesus Christ, here's Pele coming for his first team meal and we don't even have a bloody room to eat it in . . ."

It is 11:30 by the time things are straightened out and Pele sits down with the team. It is the standard pregame meal: vegetable soup, steak, baked potato, fresh fruit, toast, butter, honey, coffee, and tea. The bonus is four extra ounces of meat, a full half-pound of beef on each plate. "Well, this Pele deal is paying off okay," Picciano says to himself. Tony Donlic, a reserve player, sort of takes his steak and lets it slide down his throat whole. Bradley forces back a double-take and smiling, signs the $680 check. The mood is so buoyant, confident, relaxed, so perfectly cool that Gordon knows just what to do with his pregame speech: nothing.

"Okay, boys," he begins, "don't do anything different from normal. This is not the be all and end all of soccer. We may see more passes go astray than usual because we may not be cottoning to Pele's style and vice-versa, but that's all right. Just combine and help each other, be patient. It will come, believe me."

There follows a little strategy talk, announcement of the starting lineup: Nusum, Barry Mahy, Mike Dillon, who was purchased from England's Tottenham Hotspurs after Masnick's injury, Picciano, Johnny Kerr, Lamas, Julio Correa, Mordechai Shpigler, Mark Liveric, Pele. Now Bradley turns the floor over to the man responsible for all this, and Pele says, "Let's go to play basic soccer, not fancy, complicated soccer but basic soccer, best soccer."

At 3:30, the mercury has pushed up to eighty-five degrees and the stadium's fallow sweep is alive with clamoring, riotous colors. Both teams are introduced, then Pele comes cleat-clicking out of the tunnel into a spectacular ovation orchestrated by fireworks, banners proclaiming "o MAIS GRANDE" ("the greatest") and "THANK YOU, BRAZIL," faithful here and there waving the green and gold Brazilian flag. Pele and Dallas's all-American striker Kyle Rote, Jr., exchange the flags of Brazil and the United States in a dignified ceremony. Game-time.

Right off, New York takes the initiative, penetrating and attacking, pushing for the early goal. Pele, catapulted into the world he totally owns, seizes the flow of the game. His face is pitted in determination, absorbing the patterns around him, a hungry little black kid from the barren jungle-edge eating it up. He is shouting instructions, waving his front-line around, drifting back to a kind of combination midfielder-striker.

Early on, he takes possession of a ball near the center-stripe, dips his shoulder left and goes right around Albert "The Hatchet" Jackson. Then a cross-step over the ball, a side-poke, and he razor cuts into the clear. Suddenly the ball floats serenely towards the Dallas net while Tornado goalkeeper Cooper scrambles to regain position. The ball sails a foot high of the crossbar, saving the goalie an explanation. Trying to anticipate the spontaneous he had come out too far and ended up looking very near foolish.

As the first minutes tick, a little problem develops. Pele is so into the game that a lot of his teammates cannot at first find the rhythm or confidence to join him. Pele is directing traffic like a cop; somehow it is all hanging together, but barely. But after the first few eager, headlong rushes when the ball somehow winked at the Cosmos' ambitions, the team settles gently back into itself.

Up in the press box, Jerry Kirschenbaum of *Sports Illustrated* jots a little note: "Pele is not so much promoting U.S. soccer as exposing it." In a special section of the stadium reserved for Warner executives, Ross, edgy and excited, turns to Ertegun: "What the hell are they doing out there? They're all standing around watching HIM." Sure enough, and Pele knows his own magic isn't going to accomplish anything alone. As he courses up and down the field, he hopes only that the Cosmos hold till the half, or at least long enough to get comfortable in the game.

But they don't. Ten minutes into play, Dallas's Chadwick

and McKenzie play give and go, punching a hole in the right side of the Cosmos' defense. Chadwick shuffles the ball off and his teammate drives a tough chance past Nusum, 1–0. The goal awakens the Cosmos, who suddenly come back, find the pacing they imposed on the game in the first few minutes. It is working now, but while too many of Pele's deft passes lie unexploited, enough of them are getting through to swing the pendulum. But Cooper plays marvelously, repulsing every attack.

Twenty minutes into play, Pele delivers a subtle backheader to Shpigler, whose wicked volley is staved off by an acrobatic Cooper save. Liveric bulldogs free for a smash that shakes the post. Just when it looks like the Cosmos are homesteading in the Dallas end, disaster strikes. Chadwick, prowling the shallow midfield comes up with a loose ball from a scramble and turns it into a breakaway goal. The half ends 2–0, Dallas.

Yet for all their troubles, the Cosmos do not believe they can be denied this day. In the locker room at half-time, they are confident and calm, writing off the first half to bad breaks and jitters, and it isn't simple rationalization. They have controlled the action, taken the game and stuck it into Dallas's face. "We have had the territorial advantage," Bradley tells them calmly. "We took the game to them and the crowd was with us. Don't let's change the pattern of the game. I just want the defense tightened up and concentrating totally. We will be all right."

The team forms a small huddle in the middle of the room, hand on hand. Pele: "We control ourselves now. Everything will be no problem." Then it is back to the pitch in the waning afternoon, cooler now.

Eleven minutes later, the door finally swings open for all the banging. Pele creates a free zone in front of the Dallas goal, receives the ball from Correa and bears down on Cooper. When the goalie comes out to narrow the angle, Pele chips a soft lead pass to Shpigler, who strains, stretches and reaches the ball, nudging it with the tip of his boot toward the right corner of the goal from twelve feet out. Cooper has already wheeled around. Now it is a race and the ball trickles over the goal line to nestle into the net just ahead of Cooper's frantic dive. Shpigler leaps upon Pele's chest, bear-hugged in the erupting stadium.

The stage has been painstakingly set, the elements have all fallen into place, all but one. It is as if some vast conspiracy has manipulated the game and brought it to this exact point: twenty minutes left; the Cosmos trail by a goal. Shpigler is lined up, ready to deliver a corner kick. Here it comes, floating over the penalty area. Slowly, methodically, a figure in white with green trim appears, rising above the blue jerseys all around him, reaching, climbing the air. He hangs up there now, the head drawn back, the eyes riveted on the oncoming ball, waiting. Then the detonation as Pele's forehead attacks the ball with a violence that twists his whole body and the game is tied. It is a goal; American soccer has scored a big one.

Pele is putting the final touches on his transmutation, dabbling a spot of after-shave lotion below each jaw-hinge. The rest of the Cosmos are reliving the past two hours, shuffling in and out of the locker room, chatting with newsmen, sucking on quartered oranges.

"The team played in my point of view very nice today," Pele says, "the score of the game was a surprise for me. You like my goal? I think it was little bit lucky. The defender, I believe he slip just before, so cannot get body in position to block my shot. But it was good game, no? People enjoy game very, very much . . ."

There follows a press conference, held on the steps of the stadium, a thousand stragglers hanging around to hear him, amplified through a portable bullhorn. He apologizes for his shaky English. Kyle Rote, Jr., the Dallas striker who has been groomed as the game's first native superstar and son of an American football idol, is called upon to comment:

"One thing that impresses me about Pele is the way he's handled his fame. He's a superstar, a hero, not only in this country but in a hundred and forty-two countries. That makes him the rarest individual on the earth. It was a great honor to be on the same field with him. And I know that sounds trite."

Young Picciano played the whole game, surprising nobody more than himself. He is still awed. "I'm still embarrassed to go up to Pele and ask for an autograph. I'd like to thank him because today is my birthday and, I mean, this is a present nobody could dream up, playing with him. Jesus, he still awes me. I'm not prepared to treat him like just another player because, you know, he isn't."

Finally, the interviews are over; the klieg lights have been unplugged, and the last reporter has left to file his copy. Bradley is alone with himself, and a headful of tangled thoughts as he jams a few items into his bag in the locker room. He didn't play, but he is exhausted. He wasn't built for jawing at journalists. This kind of soccer was not what he had been weaned on.

He remembers his first soccer game, back home . . .

He was twelve years old and he pumped his bicycle thirty-five miles to see a match between Newcastle Park and St. James City. He had no coat, no money, and had not even told his mother where he was going for fear that she would prohibit him. He arrived an hour and a half before the kickoff, but the ground was already jammed, 65,000 people standing on the gently sloping terraces fanning away from the field. The colors pinwheeled before his eyes as little Gordon scampered over the barbed-wire fencing and stole into the ground.

A bluish haze covered the field, and Bradley saw the Bobbies chasing a wag who put a huge leek, emblem of Newcastle, smack in the middle of the turf. Meanwhile, another celebrant took the leek, put it down in front of the goal and kicked it—the thud of bursting fibers—goal! The leek exploded, the Bobbies got him too.

Gordon worked his way in behind the guards, and up into the back row of the side terrace, where he saw absolutely nothing but the hulking shoulders and frosty cloud-breath of the adult forest stacked before him. Fortunately, there is an English habit of taking little children from the back of the stadium and literally passing and rolling them down to the front, over heads and shoulders, to the ash track, where the Bobbies let them sit on the edge of the field.

Little Gordon was accommodated; he went tumbling and groping down a gradual slope of shoulders, whiskey breath, booster scarves, and heavy wool smelling of dark lager and tobacco. Fearfully he laughed that high-pitched squeal of child-fright. But he rolled, bouncing and bumping down to that precious field he had thus far only dared dream about.

Bradley's ensuing years were spent kicking, running, tackling, thudding thousands of times to the ash-blackened, makeshift pitches on the outskirts of Easington, the small, sooty mining town that was his home. The dreams paled, but the determination became embedded, like the fine, steelly grit that ground itself into shins and elbows at each day's practice.

Years passed and suddenly it was a ravishing spring day early in 1952, and seventeen-year-old Gordon Bradley and his now-game leg were crossing a field just beyond the shadows of the Easington cottages, just outside of Sunderland, on the northeast coast of England. He was carrying a banana sandwich, although jelly was the favorite with his fellow miners. The air was fresh with flowers and milkweed, just enough breeze to occasionally stir the languid anemones. It was a perfect day for making the angular fellow with a touch of ostrich in his walk forget that it was just over one year ago that a doctor pronounced his hopes of continuing a career in professional football useless and suggested that a depressed Bradley find some "regular" work. Here he was, carrying a shattered kneecap with fine silver thread holding it together across the meadow, waiting out its slow healing and the chance to prove his physician wrong.

But he felt remotely uneasy this morning, self-consciously overaware of everything around him for no reason he could locate. This much was sure, it had nothing to do with the fact that he hated the dirty dangerous work in Easington Colliery, a shaft 1200 feet down and 5 miles under the North Sea. After all, it was "regular" work; almost everybody around

Sunderland was a collier. These workmen remained among the most exploited English laborers, farming rock and ore out of the rat droppings and eternal darkness of "the pit." It was a vital job for a nation's industry, enough so to exempt the colliers from military service. "It was a great experience," Bradley would reflect two decades later, "one that I hated thoroughly."

The best Bradley could remember looking far back to that spring morning in the coal country was that he had a sense of "precognition." There was a distraction mixed in the air around him; it was queer-still, for no apparent reason. Bradley saw a man coming in the opposite direction. The man nodded sternly and said: "You'd want to hurry up; there's problems at the mine. There's been an explosion." Eighty-one people died on that day in Easington Colliery, among them a handful of Bradley's friends and the father of the girl he would later marry. Bradley stayed at the mine all day, helping remove the broken bodies of the dead, recognizing an ashen face every now and then before it vanished forever into a sack.

Bradley thought about quitting the mine then but did not. He stayed long enough to see a friend get his leg caught in a conveyor and torn in half as he was carried screaming through the two-foot-three-inch-high shaft. He saw a man decapitated by an elevator. He sat down to lunch in an underground hollow with a friend once, and before his banana sandwich was unwrapped, a "carving arse" (a cone-shaped stone held in place by a thin rim of coal) slipped out of the ceiling and crushed his companion. "They always told us," he remembered, "not to take our helmets off, and never to sit beneath a carving arse."

But every day after work, Bradley would slip into the company shower and wash the mine off his body. Then he would don his training suit and work his knee by running until dark. A year later, he felt ready to play again and signed a contract with Carlisle United, a Third Division club, where he labored for six years and cultivated the cherished qualities of yeomanship: hard work, expert tackling, gritty, crunching play in which he behaved like a bloodhound angrily shaking the last fleck of life from a pheasant's brilliant feathers. Few opposing forwards escaped Bradley's defense without purple-black mementoes on shin and thigh.

But at twenty-seven, Bradley felt he wasn't getting anywhere, and he had enough wit to demand more than a fresh draught of dark lager from the future. By now he had a coaching certificate and when an offer from the newly formed Eastern Canadian Pro League arrived, he saw his chance.

"I was past my prime," Bradley realized. "I was not living in the greatest place in the world, although I think the people are the greatest in northern England. Well, I wasn't going anywhere with a Third Division club; I enjoyed the game, I was happily married, had the car, the house, everything I wanted . . . everything but satisfaction. I felt I was doing a lot of existing and no living, and when the club in Toronto offered me a two-year contract, I thought how interesting . . . I decided that I would go and spend two years, then come back. I saw it as two years experience at someone else's expense and the chance to see another part of the world."

Well, the little house is still there, newly occupied when Bradley sold it following his decision to cast his lot with the NASL. Much has transpired in the meantime. Five years after Bradley arrived in Toronto, the ECPL died a peaceful death. Bradley commuted by plane to play in New York's German-American League, which is everything sandlot ball should and should not be. The Ukranian club thought enough of this punishing Englishman to offer him $10,000, an off-season job, an apartment, and a lifetime supply of hydrocortisone as player-coach. He accepted and eventually kicked and clawed his way into the budding NASL's New York Generals.

The subsequent collapse was traumatic. Bradley had just turned down a fine job offer to return to England as an assistant coach at Brighton on the assurance that the Generals would operate in 1969 against the expectations of most sane men. Bradley might have realized that in the NASL house of cards, such a confident assurance on the heels of a disaster year was a sure kiss of death. So he found himself out in the street, and ended up playing for Baltimore for $75 per game, less taxes. "It is quite ludicrious," Bradley replied on being offered the job, "I'll take it." For months, his take-home pay was $68.23 per week and all the bruises his legs could carry. The next break was the coaching job of Hota, back in the good old godawful German-American League. Bradley took it, added a few more nonnegotiable trophies to his display case and stumbled upon Toye in 1970.

Now, at age forty-two, he was a New Yorker. He wore crisp, cool Oxford-cloth shirts to his air-conditioned office and he was coach to Pele, greatest player the game has ever seen. Bradley tucked away the last of his things, zippered his bag and left for home.

Pele's eyes are closed all the way to Boston, where he will play his third game as a Cosmo, but he isn't sleeping. He has just learned that faking it is a good way to dam the persistent human stream that usually flows towards him from every section of the airplane.

Some want to chat, others want an autograph, still others are drawn to fame like metal shavings to a magnet, without even knowing it. The timid ones plan a casual stroll to the john, or the magazine rack, peering at him over the seat backs all the way. "It is said," says Shpigler, sitting across the aisle, "that a man must close his eyes to relax."

In the airport, waiting for his bags to come bumping down the chute, Pele hears a roar go up from a nearby clutch of college students. He looks over his shoulder and raises his hand in the standard "V," by reflex. The students are still slapping and whooping. Pele begins to wave. They don't even look up. The cheers are for Fred Lynn, who has just belted a home run against Baltimore for the Boston Red Sox.

The ads in the Boston newspapers all week have been proclaiming: "THE KING OF SOCCER IN BOSTON: PELE VS. THE BOSTON MINUTEMEN." The Cosmos did not even make the small print.

"They could at least have told the rest of us we weren't playing," says Roth, flipping through a magazine rack, "I could have made other plans."

Across town, all kinds of bitterness is brewing in the office of Fred Klashman, public relations director for the Minutemen. Two weeks ago, he had walked in the office of club owner John Sterge and suggested they move the game from a little bandbox called Nickerson Field (capacity, 12,500) to Schaefer Stadium, the spacious home of the football New England Patriots. "Yeah, that's a fine idea, Fred." Sterge had replied. "But you know very well that it would cost us $22,000 just to open the gates to the place."

"He said that to me," Klashman remembered, "and I remember thinking to myself, "Sure, and it costs a whole lot less to provide a handful more than the customary fourteen security police for the game, but you aren't even going to do that, are you?"

Klashman would leave the Minutemen's employ on less than friendly terms soon after the Cosmos debacle. He claims to have predicted disaster as early as a week before it occurred. Letters and phone calls from Toye and O'Reilly outlining security precautions had largely gone ignored. In the past, Bostonians had exhibited only moderate exuberance, both at the box office and in the stands; a couple of beer-sodden rowdies here and there, but never any problems. To the Boston management, Toye and O'Reilly seemed overcautious.

Nevertheless, Klashman had been told to inform the press that the Minutemen were engaged in heavy negotiations with Boston College, Harvard, and the Patriots in an effort to stage the event in the right place. But Klashman was uncomfortable with the plan. "From a public relations standpoint, here was an opportunity to put the game on the map, in my opinion, to make the Boston franchise mean something besides a giveaway coupon to some local greasy spoon with each ticket. Anyhow, when I gave the media the story about the stadium, they knew as well as I did that basically we were faking it."

So far, it had merely been a bush-league refusal to rise to an occasion. Later, when things were irreversible, it would also be seen as stupid and dangerous.

At the press conference, Mané, a former Santos' teammate of Pele's who Toye discovered and signed while chasing Pele, and David Primo, an Israeli added to the Cosmos roster just before the game against Dallas, have their curly heads bent over the latest *Penthouse* centerfold, shrieking and laughing, picking the few English words they knew out of the accompanying text. They are not very big words.

Nusum (the only black player on the team besides Pele), is graciously giving an interview to a local journalist: "Yes," says Nusum, deadpanning for all he's worth, "it was tough leaving Brazil, real tough; just go and ask that black guy from Bermuda what it's like," he says, pointing to Pele.

The press conference is called; Pele sits down with Mazzei, who fields a question beginning "Señor Pele," and ending after about six uninterrupted minutes of pure Spanish. Mazzei is off and running with the answer, when John Powers of the *Boston Globe* stands up and asks, "Can you please repeat that in English for the benefit of the two Americans in the room?"

There is really only one big question at this press conference, and that is, "What does Pele think of Eusebio?" (the Minutemen striker). It is rather like asking Hertz what it thinks of Avis.

For years, Eusebio had been number two in the world to Pele—Black Pearl and Black Panther. While American sport fans debated the merits of Mantle and Mays, of Simpson and Brown, the rest of the world fought over Pele and Eusebio, and there was more than incidental irony in the comparison.

Both of them came from backwater villages in areas of destitute poverty. Eusebio grew up in Mozambique and found his first genuine soccer shoe on top of a rubbish heap. For nearly a decade these two battled in stadiums from Zaire to Singapore and gave the world a great rivalry. Neither had professed anything but the most profound respect for the other publicly; but privately the road had forked for the men in the 1966 World Cup.

That was when Pele became the focus of one of sports history's legendary cheap shots, and the team that had to assume the collective guilt for this was Eusebio's Portuguese side. Pele was twenty-five then, theoretically at the peak of his career and playing wonderfully until the vicious double foul put him out of the game, and Brazil out of the running for the cup.

Eusebio had no part in the foul, but at the time he was the new rising star of the game, Europe's answer to Pele. In its ultimately unsuccessful drive to capitalize on Eusebio's talents and bring the World Cup to Portugal, some on the Portuguese side had abandoned all pretense of sporting integrity.

"It is bad to see this in football," Pele has always felt, "it is negative, destructive and make the game to be something ugly. To hurt another man, with purpose, this is the worst thing a footballer can do, because it take away his living, it kill his talent, all his gift." As always, Pele had maintained his own grace, submerged any hostile feeling in the vaults of his own staggering success and kept aggrandizing his kingdom. There was no room in that dominion for enemies.

The maître d' hôtel approaches Pele at the pregame meal, gives him two menus, one to order from and the other to autograph for the boys in the kitchen. After a few moments he asks:

"What is your desire, Señor Pele?"

"I like very much lobster, broiled in butter . . ."

"Oh, we make it special, just for you the way you like it," the headwaiter answers, turning to take the rest of the group's order.

He walks back through the swinging doors, into the kitchen, rolls his eyes to the ceiling and says:

"Okay, eighteen lobster specials."

When Klashman arrives at Nickerson Field at 3:00 P.M., he notices a man pacing off the distance from the field to seats. The man does not look happy, even at 300 yards. "Excuse me,

I'm Fred Klashman of the Minutemen, you must be . . ."

"Pedro Garay," the fellow picks up, "yes, sir, we met at the press conference. I'm with Cosmos' security. I want to have a look at potential danger from a security standpoint . . ."

"What do you think," asks Klashman, knowing the answer. "It's very bad sir," Garay is frank, "I am going to advise my superiors to call it off . . ."

"But you can't do that, we'll have a riot for sure, we've sold the joint out . . ."

Garay does as he says, but the Cosmos decide that calling it off would be bad for soccer as well as themselves. People have been holding tickets for three weeks; a lot of these people are fervent Latin Americans who don't like to take no for an answer, especially where their idols are concerned.

An hour and a half before game-time, people are stacked like cordwood outside the still-locked gates and it's just a matter of time before the fuses burn down and the fireworks begin. The phone rings. Klashman jumps and picks it up. "Fred," says the lone security man at the front gate, "We're in trouble down here, there's a fire in one of the concession booths under the stands."

"Jesus, we've just opened the gates and we've got an arson already," said Klashman, bouncing downstairs to check it out. It is a small fire, but it is just the beginning. People are pouring into the place now, the lucky ones with the tickets, while the SRO customers are milling about outside. A few of the seatless are scaling the back of the scoreboard, and naturally their example is followed. This will be not only the day of Pele but also perhaps the day of the locust. What can Klashman do but laugh?

At last the game begins, Cosmos vs. Minutemen, Pele vs. Eusebio, soon to become crowd vs. accepted standards of human behavior. At first, the pattern is the same. Pele roams the artificial turf in the glare of sulphur lights, arms raised in constant instructions, prowling the midfield, traffic-copping as he had done for the most of his initiation as a Cosmo.

The teams are about even, and fence a while; everybody seems to be waiting for the duel between Pele and Eusebio. When it comes, the Brazilian moves first. He takes a free kick at the eleven-minute mark, sends it screaming toward the upper right corner of the net only to have it punched away by Boston's brilliant goalkeeper, former Harvard student Shep Messing. The crowd of 20,000 jammed into the stadium erupt; the 5,000 ringing the field standing six-deep experience a convulsion.

The announcer asks the good people to return to their seats and is ignored. Security is in fact nonexistent now; instead of the sixty police and forty ushers the Cosmos suggested, Sterge has decided on fourteen cops and eight ushers recruited from Boston U., and none of them wants to mess with this crowd; too many flag sticks, beer cans, and soccer hysterics to take lightly.

Another roar bursts forth from the crowd, this one tremendous and scratchy-throated as Eusebio strikes, curling a direct kick into the upper left for Boston. An avalanche of fans spills immediately onto the field to embrace their hero, but Eusebio never stops long enough to give them a chance, running in and out of the developing mob. It takes ten minutes to clear the field, and the game resumes. Immediately, Pele goes on the attack. The Cosmos' offense is thrusting effectively, situations are opening up, spaces are clearing, the ball is running in full complicity.

Pele takes a pass in the Boston end near midfield, ducks and bobs by two defenders and slips the ball to Liveric, who unloads a hard one that Messing barely deflects to the left and right to the feet of Pele, who pushes the ball into the goal. It appears to be the tying score. As he begins the traditional goal-salute, high-leaping, yellow and green uniform thrust into the air, a mob is already forming around him, the first splashings of a monstrous wave about to break over the field.

Here they come now. All 5,000 of those who have been standing along the sidelines, waiting for the exact moment. They are roaring, ranting, waving Brazilian flags into their own Pele chant. As yet, there is nothing particularly frightening in this demonstration. Then the referee signals that the goal has been disallowed because of a pushing penalty. That's when it becomes grotesque.

The fans come pouring down from every corner of the stadium, an army of soldier ants swarming over their wronged general. Garay, standing by the Cosmos' bench, can see it coming and he breaks into a sprint, the leather-encased, lead-centered "slapper" bouncing against his hip. Already he is groping for its flapping handle. He breaks through the teeming mass, kicking, flailing, punching. Pele is moving backward as the sweep of the crowd closes on him, clutching, shouting, grabbing, eyes glazed with exultation and various stimulants. Pele's shorts are shredded, his jersey torn to tatters, his right shoe ripped off; will it find its way to a Southside trash bin, for some new Eusebio? All Pele knows is trouble right here.

"Pele, Pele," says Garay. "It's Pedro. Get down on the ground, get down."

Pedro drapes his stocky frame over Pele and clobbers a fan who is still trying to touch Pele. Reinforcements are on the way, cutting a swath through the thick cluster around their man. Marty Hamrogue, a Cosmo assistant trainer and six Cosmos' folks move in for the rescue. The crowd is dispersing, Pele is lifted onto a stretcher and carried out. Toye orders the rest of the Cosmos off the field. They huddle in the locker room, Pele lying on the stretcher, looking okay in the corner, but rubbing and holding his right ankle.

"I don't think we should go back out there," Toye says to de la Sierra, who answers, "Clive, if we don't it's going to get ugly."

"It's already ugly," Clive answers, "but I suppose you're right. We don't want a full-blown riot, but we are continuing and playing the game under protest."

Three minutes into the resumption, Eusebio runs towards the Cosmos' goal and suddenly veers off to the right and heads full speed into the safety of his own dressing room. Can't blame him, since he happens to be the second course on this menu. The Cosmos lose, 2–1 in overtime, with Pele still in the locker room. When the team shuffles back in, the door is barred and protected by a handful of security men. O'Reilly is instructed to tell the press that Pele has a bruised right knee and twisted ankle.

After the last of the inquisitive reporters and the team has departed, Pele props himself up on one elbow in the trainer's room. He looks at Breil, who is worried and shaking his head.

He winks.

7

How the West
Was Lost

*P*ele sits hunched on a leatherette sofa, elbows on knees, hands intertwined. "I am," he says, with emphasis. "I have-been," he looks up, questioning his pronunciation. "I was, I have been, I am . . ." He flashes a fragile smile at Mazzei. In a few moments, Pele will have to stroll down a short hallway, weave through a tangle of wires, camera struts and baleful spotlights and walk into America's bedrooms, as a guest on the Johnny Carson show. He is practicing his English, a millionaire pupil in a self-designed red sports jacket, Pele-special, with pleated sleeve inserts, pockets, and shoulder vents.

"Professor, you come with me," Pele suggests, but the television liaison man denies the request. It will be just Pele and Joey Fink, who is having problems of his own. Joey's sturdy footballer's knees have just quit cold on him; he wonders whether he can stand up. He looks at Pele, hoping to see the field commander, the take-charge, holler guy. Pele reaches over and pats his knee, chuckling: "Is okay, Joey, you speak, me kick the ball."

There is another conversation going on outside in the hallway, this one between Garay, Breil, and a public relations man for the Los Angeles Aztecs, whom the Cosmos will play later tonight.

"We've got twenty-one specials for security," says the public relations man, "everything should be smooth and easy."

"I'm sorry sir, unless we have fifty security personnel, no game," Garay insists, "I have seen the stadium, the wall around the field is very low, easy to jump."

"But our owner looks at dollars and cents. What good is having Pele for a game if all the profit is spent on extra security? I know what you mean, but hey, I only work for this team. My owner is a bottom-line man."

"That's foolish," Breil interjects.

"We will not have another Boston," Garay emphasizes, remembering that Pele was fortunate to suffer only bruises and recovered in time to play subsequent games against Rochester and Washington. And what games they were.

In Rochester, the Cosmos trounced the Lancers 3–0, with Pele scoring on a lovely header off Correa's thirty-five–yard drive into the crossbar. The ball deflected and Pele, sweeping gracefully in from the left, knocked it easily past the goalkeeper. The crowd chanted Pele's name, police towed away close to 100 illegally parked cars and after the game, Lancer striker Tommy Ord, soon to become a Cosmo, offered in his cockney accent: "The man still looks great to me." The legend rolled on and over Washington two days later. A record crowd of 35,621 turned out to see the Cosmos flex their new-found muscle in a 9–2 win. Pele had two goals and two assists, including a lovely shot that curved into the upper corner from twenty-five yards out, finding the single point which the goalkeeper could not possibly reach. Then the floodgates opened. Mané scored his first regular season goal in the second half and promptly sprinted to the sideline, where he knelt down and bowed repeatedly to the crowd. "The team grows day by day," Pele smiled after that one. Ike Kuhns, who covered the Cosmos for the *Newark Star-Ledger*, finished his story by suggesting that "The Cosmos appear on the verge of breaking the NASL race wide open."

Now the Cosmos were in Los Angeles, a buoyant, roistering band of soccer missionaries smashing attendance records in every stadium, smiling for the photographers, scoring goals with impudent ease, carried along on an electric high of celebrity, solidarity, and victory, Dr. Pele's medicine show. To a large extent, the exuberance was justified. Since Pele's arrival, the Cosmos record had improved to 6–6; they had not lost a game and the protest over the Boston game had been recognized; it would be replayed. Six won, six lost; good symmetry there, a new start. Surely, it would take a chronic deadbeat to suggest that the Cosmos would fade.

Yet this western trip will be the early acid test for New York. To stay atop the division, they must beat the Aztecs, an explosive team, and best Seattle, a front-runner in the West with a rabid following and thorny pride. Realistically, Bradley will settle for a split in these games. The confidence is there; the schedule has been hectic, but the team has responded well, rising to the demands of Pele's arrival.

"Okay, Mr. Pay-lay, ready?" the TV man asks.

Fink and Pele follow the guide out and onto the bright set, a shell of fluorescence in the cavernous garage of a studio. The band strikes up a snappy tune, the cameras aim and Fink is lucky that he can't see the wall of faces in the audience because of the stage lights.

Bert Convy, the guest host, is off and running with questions. Pele, trotting out that charming, shy smile stops his host in mid-sentence, touching his arm.

"Excuse me, I, ah, no speak English so very well. Please to go slowly?"

It breaks the ice; Convy slows down and Pele does some estimable tongue work, explaining why he came to play soccer in America, where his nickname originated, the usual stuff. Fink ventures that Pele's arrival has created "a new feeling of life in the league," then goes catatonic again.

"I know," Convy says, "that in South America and the Latin American nations people get so involved in the games that there are stabbings, stampedes, regular riots. Do you think that will ever happen here?"

Pele, lost somewhere high up in this question, goes thoughtful. Lifting his head, he smiles:

"Yes, I think so . . ."

"It was awful," is all Mahy can say. "We stunk the joint out," Roth offers. "For ten minutes I think we were still playing in Washington, I was sure we would have a good game," Shpigler rues. The Cosmos are huddled in the lobby of Los Angeles International Airport, anxious to leave town after a 5–1 wipeout. It had begun so well, Pele thrilling the packed house with a deft pass against the flow to Fink, who then punched the ball to Shpigler who slammed home the goal. In just ten minutes, the Cosmos were one-up, but then collapsed. Before the last festive roman candles sputtered dead, the Aztecs had mounted a counterthrust that swept over the Cosmos and would not stop. Uri Bannhoffer equalized in the twentieth minute, and then all hell broke loose. Each time New York counterattacked, the Aztecs held and surged back like a trebled echo. Nusum was surprisingly off form; the Aztecs' third goal was another Bannhoffer calling card, this one skipping crazily into the net through Nusum's legs.

Pele sat with Mazzei in one corner of this barbarous airport lobby. The harsh lights formed bright puddles on the blue plastic seats. He rummaged through his briefcase, peering through silver-framed sunglasses. "When I play in Santos, we lose sometimes like this too," he said. "It happen to every team in world. But I see things, some things now for three game. Our defense, we come too close to middle of field, give much room to other team wingers. Before, Sam always make save, so not so bad. Yesterday, Sam no make save, is different. We make little, wrong things. Los Angeles make right things." He shrugs. "It go like that some time."

The rest of the Cosmos were sprawled about the alcove in various states of semiconsciousness. The team generally travels on the morning after a night game, when everybody is pretty much pulverized, chewed up by the game or wasted by its late night aftermath. Travel day is when sunglasses begin to blossom on drawn faces, when a whisper rumbles into the ear like a rockslide, and the mouth is lined with cotton. It is the time when a fellow looks across the aisle at a teammate and hates his guts, just like that. Usually, it passes with a few hours sleep.

How the West Was Lost

So here they are, in a place with all the charm of Strategic Air Command headquarters and presto, Mané is up and strutting across the floor in a samba, screeching out some falsetto rendition of "Vira, Vira," a hot little Brazilian number, one hand on his stomach and the other in the air. Pained eyes open all around in sheer astonishment. All kinds of morning travelers are stopping and ogling at this burr-headed screamer sashaying across the vinyl tiles, shrieking out some song they don't recognize in a language they don't understand, on the Fourth of July no less . . . Most of them figure, "well, it is southern California," and leave it at that, but the Cosmos know better. It is Mané's magical mystery tour, and it is steaming along not in the least perturbed by all this depression. Before long, the lobby is alive with hooting and laughing; the wraiths are all vanquished, the flight is called.

The players have a nap at the Edgewater Inn in Seattle that afternoon; all of them but Pele, who is whisked off to a press conference. It never ends; he is used to it. He submerges his fatigue, carries his genius into the room as casually as a factory worker toting a gray lunch-pail.

"Thank you for come here on such big and important day," he tells the assembled corps. "I am [pause] very pleased to be here on day of your country's birth." They talk about the Los Angeles game, the problems of adjusting to a new team and a new country. Inevitably, the questions turn to his name, and he gives the explanation:

"I have maybe five years, and I play in street when one of my teammate start to call me Pele. I no like it, I go to fight with him. I think it is some joke, or to make fun of me. So I begin to fight against this name. Of course, the more I fight, the more they give it to me . . ."

A journalist in the back of the room rises and announces with considerable gravity:

"There is a mythological vulcan in Martinique also named Pele."

"Oh, yes?" Pele defers with a grin, wondering what on earth

"mythological vulcan" might mean. The Professor, however, is a collector of such esoterica and files it away. At the very least, it is a new one.

The tan, thirty-pound test fishing line extended straight down from the second story balcony of Pele's room at the Edgewater and knifed into the brine at an oblique angle. Pele was inside, lying down on his bed with his eyes open. Mazzei noticed as the tip of the rod dipped gently. Grabbing it, he set the hook, and began to shout: "Pele, Paaaay-laaaay."

Pele bounced off the bed, and dashed onto the balcony, leaping around wide-eyed and exuberant, as Mazzei began hauling a large, ugly dogfish up out of Puget Sound. Now Pele went down on his knees, letting the line come through his hands he poked through the aluminum slats of the balcony railing. "Po, que grande, professor, oh, que legal . . ." He knelt in a pile of bait, giving the professor all possible vocal support, half-whistling as Mazzei hauled a thrashing, three-foot-long kissing cousin to the shark over the railing, its flip-flopping tail just missing Pele's head.

By now, the two big-game fishermen have roused a few of their colleagues, who drift in looking for the action. Mané, the first one there, jumped right in, screwing the leg off a coffee table and beating the poor dogfish senseless as Pele and Mazzei baited up again, putting two rods to use.

There was a school of dogfish out there, waiting. Pele hooked one, four feet long, and got it up about forty feet before the monster shook the hook and smacked back into the water. "Professor, you see, you see," Pele demands, but Mazzei is tied into a leviathan of his own.

About this time, Roth came stumbling into the room, still rubbing the sleep from his eyes. Mané grabbed his hand and led Werner into the bathroom, poking his face into the tub, where this dogfish was laid out in full stretch to shock Roth into a waking state.

Lou Luca, chief of Cosmos' security and a man whose prodigious appetite and ample belly have become a perch for the team's collective sense of humor poked his head in. "We throw

Lou Luca in," Mané suggested, "and shark will be full for one month." Pele lost another big one, trying to lift it over the railing, making a futile grab at the fish as it went plummeting back, reprieved.

The Professor, half-mocking his own gnosticism suggested: "Now we must all sit down and eat of the fish, because we must be like family, all together. This make us closer."

"I no go to swimming here," Pele offered, "maybe shark bite me off."

Pele retracted his toes in his shoes; the soles of his feet were burning; something was radically wrong here. It's called Astroturf, and Pele is playing on it on a hot day for the first time in his life. It hurts more than his feet.

There were 18,000 people jammed into this lovely Seattle stadium on the old World's Fair ground, for a nationally televised game between the Sounders and the Cosmos. At 1:30 in the afternoon, it was already eighty-nine degrees and the field bubbled like a vast skillet. Pele suddenly realized why the Sounders were all wearing tennis shoes. This is a new world all right.

Seattle's rabid, home-grown fans, all-American red-white-and-blue types have come to bury Pele, not to praise him. Among the customary charitable banners are scattered a few good-natured taunts: "THE BLACK PEARL IS OUR OYSTER"; "WE WOULD BE HERE, EVEN IF PELE WASN'T." After all, this is a soccer hot-bed, a place where the Sounders sell out whether the visiting roster includes Pele or not.

A surprised delegation of Cosmos' officials have already been told that Luca and Garay are not to go out onto the field with Pele because the obvious security measure would not look good on television, and is not even necessary. Seattle representatives have also told the Cosmos that Pele will not be introduced last, as he usually is, "because we don't do that even for our players." Here was the missionary with nobody to convert. All of which would have been just fine with Pele, because what *really* bothers him is this little matter of the rug he is playing on.

Astroturf is an inordinately fast surface for soccer, particularly the Brazilian version which is built upon time-consuming, bewitching creativity, and space-weaving. Grass is splendid for those purposes; it holds the ball, caresses and eases it along on so many cilia. The ball purrs through it, bites and clings, obedient to every peculiarity of the clever foot. On Astroturf, the ball skips and runs, slides and races away, emphasizing the aspects of the game most cherished by English-style soccer—the lightning fast pass, the strained race in which will and aggression count for as much as intelligence and inventiveness.

Or, as Pele perceived it, "The ball, it no listen on this type field. It run away all time very fast, no pay attention to technique."

But it does pay attention to the Sounders, a rugged collection of mostly English footballers anchored by a pernicious defense, a cast of knock 'em up heavies in Dave Gillet, Alan Stephans, Mike England, Adrian Webster. That the Cosmos played Seattle even for the first twenty-four minutes was surprising in itself, what with Pele's feet burning and his body clothed in two defenders. England, a tall, gangly master of the air game played between Pele and the goal while Stephans, smaller and quicker, played in front. Pele struggled with the tenacity of a netted dogfish, writhing free every now and then to create a dangerous situation, only to have a lovely pass go fallow, the ball squirting just beyond the target on the carpet.

Still, it was the Cosmos who threatened first. Shpigler curved a corner kick in to Fink in the twenty-fourth minutes, with Joey rising above the defense to strike the crossbar with a near-miss header. Less than a minute later, John Rowlands took a perfect upfield pass from England and dribbled to within twenty yards of the Cosmos' goal, and slipped the ball to Paul Crossley who lured Nusum out of the goal mouth. Crossley shuffled the ball off to Tom Baldwin, whose thundering ten-footer hit the bar and caromed in. The Sounders then turned coy, adopting a gruesomely unimaginative defensive strategy. They had all they needed; besides they were in business to win, not just look good.

Later, the Sounders added a goal on a questionable foul in

the penalty area. There was precious little consolation for the Cosmos with the possible exception of Picciano, who picked a moment when the officials were elsewhere occupied to pop Crossley a solid jab in the nose. "Who me, what?" Picciano protested when the whole team saw that one later on the delayed telecast of the game back at the hotel.

Despite all his difficulties, Pele slipped easily into his persona after the game.

"The crowd here very nice," he said, "people understand the game, react very well to the good play. It is best audience in the league so far. All game, my feet burn, but also Seattle have very good defense. For me, worst thing is I have no time to practice with New York Cosmos. We make the mistake and pay in game. Is no good."

The next morning, the headline in the *Seattle Times* read: "GOSTO DO ESTILO DO JOGO AQUI—PELE."

The subhead translates: "He Likes Style of Play Here; Lauds Fans, Team."

The team meal on that same evening was subdued and reflective, set into the last gleaming rays of the sun upon the sound. The afternoon light flooded the dining room, polishing platters of crab claws, shrimp, fresh fruit, oysters and garden-grown vegetables. Nusum spoke quietly: "We're probably playing too much in this stretch. Four games in seven days is too much. I guess we'll just have to dig down for the reserves and keep pushing, even if we are getting a little leg weary. You know, this is the first time we haven't scored a goal since Philadelphia, the day Pele signed."

Sam was looking ahead to the Cosmos' home game against Boston on Wednesday, four days hence. He wasn't even thinking about the exhibition game against Vancouver, on Monday. It will not count in the league standings, which have seen Boston climb into first place after the Cosmos' two losses. Now, the pressure is beginning to mount, rising like early evening fog around this team that is tired and perplexed. Because of the schedule, Bradley has been juggling the lineup, trying both to preserve his best players and discover a new, effective combination. All the attention has become abrasive, the travel grinding. Pele has taken command, but his knowledge has not been easily assimilated. Liveric, struggling with his own temperament during a bad patch of play in Seattle turned angrily upon a critical teammate during the game and gesturing towards Pele, shouted, "Tell him to score goal, he is man making four million."

Fink: "We don't get a chance to practice much, and that hurts us a lot. I don't think we should use the schedule as an excuse. I think we were well rested for the Seattle game . . ."

There are further dimensions. Since Pele's arrival, some of the Uruguayans have been making appearances in the starting lineup. Bradley, trying to come up with a workable compromise between the English and Brazilian style has looked to the Uruguayans as a bridge between the two, or at least placed them on the opposite disc of the scales, weighing them with Pele against Mahy, Kerr, Fink, and the rest of the English-oriented Cosmos.

Fink: "The reevaluation is still going on. But I think we have more of a style of our own now than ever before. You know, I never thought about the problems when Pele came here. I was just plain overawed. But I still don't think the problems are insurmountable. We're not going to win all our games with or without Pele. I don't blame Gordon for juggling the lineup. It may bother a few egos, but if we win two or three in a row, the lineup will be set with the guys who played in those games. It's the fairest way. Tell you one thing, I never thought I'd be happy to see Randall's Island again . . ."

Shpigler has another perspective: "Every team has the ambition to beat Pele. I think we may have gotten overconfident after the Washington game. But you know, every game is a new story. A good pro must forget the last game quickly, especially when it is a loss. In a normal league you have a week's time to enjoy victory. Here you have one night sleep, airplane, and you must make another story."

The coffee is getting cold, milk coagulating in a thin rim on the inside of the cup. Shpigler pushes his chair back, gets up and vanishes for a nap. Across the half-empty room, reserve goalkeeper Kuykendall is hunched over, intensely questioning the attentive man in the red leather jacket and white turtleneck.

"Do you decide beforehand where you're going to put the penalty kick?"

"I am serious," Pele answers, "pay you attention now." Kurt leans over, hungry. "I show you trick next time in practice, for penalty kick. When the man is right before the ball make you to lean your body on one side, so he think space is more little on one side. Many time, from psychology, man will kick to other side, because he feel more space there. Then you dive to other side to trick him. I will kick to show for you in practice."

Pele spots Bodo jotting notes on this conversation; he starts.

"No, no write in newspaper," he panics, in genuine alarm, protecting this small deception, mark of his craft and guile.

"You put in newspaper, every goalkeeper in league know this tomorrow, is no good then . . ."

In Vancouver, there was a cocktail party at the sprawling home of Herb Capozzi, owner of the Whitecaps. Toni Sailer, copper from the sun and wearing a ski sweater, stood by the pool, as if he had just arrived from the 1960 Olympics, where he was a triple gold medal winner. Beautiful people and selected Whitecaps floated about the property, drifting in and out of the scent of pines and fresh cherries, the robust elegance of the Northwest. Pele makes small talk graciously, and at first he is treated just like another guest, despite a certain deference directed towards him. But before long he is again asked to pose for pictures and sign autographs. Eventually, he draws away and becomes involved in an animated discussion with the Whitecap players, a long chat with fellow travelers. In this company, security chief Lou Luca stands out as a home-grown New Yorker, and the ex-NYPD detective of the heartiest kind, equal parts steel and rubber. He is becoming the hit of the party. Nodding towards him, Capozzi turns to Bradley and says, "Next time, you might just as well bring twelve guys instead of him for all the difference it makes at the dinner table." He smiles, and his own ample chest sends ripples through his neo-Roman toga.

Luca's epicurean exploits were indeed impressive. That night the detective consumed four steaks, a healthy slab of baked salmon, and several bottles of wine. A handful of Cosmos were draped around the hotel lobby later in the evening. It was 11:30, curfew time, but nobody felt much like moving. "Don't go to sleep now," Mané warned Luca, "you will be so congested, no can stand up in morning." Laughter, whereupon Mazzei walked over to where the portly security man sprawled on a sofa and slapped his pockets, ostensibly looking for remnants of Capozzi's fine table. Mané, hopping around in near delirium, picked his way through Luca's threats to rearrange his anatomical parts. Eventually, Luca was infected by all this madness and cracking a wide grin, proclaimed: "Viva America."

Mazzei looks over at him: "After four steak, two salmon, three bottle wine, of course all free, is easy to say viva America."

"Oh, all time I think we are in Canada," Pele says.

Now he picks up Kerr's guitar and begins idly strumming a Brazilian folk ditty. Mané picks up on it and begins to sing along with Pele. Mazzei starts to drum on the arm of the sofa, as Garay snaps his finger now and then . . . Two songs later, everybody is part of the band, singing, clapping, tapping on empty Pepsi bottles with spoons, using various utensils as makeshift instruments. Somebody is making all kinds of metallic racket with a staple-gun borrowed from the concierge, and it all works. At 12:15, considerably beyond curfew, Bradley is still mesmerized by this spontaneous outburst. People are sitting on the floor, drumming on support pillars, samba rocking over the burgundy carpet. At the center of it is Pele, as involved in the fluctuations of his chocolate bass as he would be in a crossing ball floating through the haze of 180,000 expectant faces in Maracana stadium. Guests and passers-by are infected, the more adventuresome participating, unself-consciously. Twenty minutes later, the lobby is empty, the floor strewn with coffee cups, spoons, cigarette butts, staples, pop bottles, and the stilled notes of vanished music.

Game-time. This time, 26,495 have turned out to watch this exhibition and they are not disappointed. The play is crisp, wide open, and loose, despite a scoreless first half. Vancouver also has artificial turf, but the ball does not move over it as quickly; it is an evening game, cool and comfortable. The Cosmos take the initiative and control the first few minutes of the second half. Pele and Shpigler, intellects meshed, are dominating the midfield, the area which has been so crucial to the Cosmos' fortunes. When Pele and Shpigler have the room to operate, the Cosmos blossom; the level of everyone's game is raised, the subtle passes and instinctive moves click. Still, the clock ticks on, 260, 261, 262, 263, 264—cumulative minutes since the Cosmos have scored a goal. The drought finally broke as Pele shepherded the ball across the center line, cut left and lofted a delicious ball to Correa, steaming down the right wing. This sudden reversal of field caught the White-caps breaking the wrong way, chasing Pele. All Julio had to do was lay the ball off to Shpigler barreling through the heart of the field towards the goal mouth and there you have it, at long last, a goal.

And now the Cosmos want more. Boosted by the break-through, New York hurtles on; got it all together now, kicking the air out of the ball, Liveric splintering the post, the defense gang-tackling, Pele dunking off radar passes like a blackjack dealer turning up aces and picture cards on every throw. Watch out; Pele has the ball at midfield and the defense collapses towards him. Oops, here's one man putting a nifty sliding tackle on a place Pele only used to be. A shoulder fake, stutter-step, and quick shuffle gets him past another, while the third man melts and rematerializes behind Pele. It looks that easy. With a move that seems merely a cavalier gesture, Pele heels the ball back to Shpigler, who is there in his wake to clean up and blast his second score home. Good enough, the final score reads 2–1.

But by now, nobody is deluded into thinking that this exhibition is a quantum leap of any kind. If anything, it is a demonstration that given an inch, Pele will take a light year. It also shows the critical stature of that inch in the swing of a game and the fortunes of a team; for this is that same inch which the Cosmos have been unable to exploit against either the Aztecs or Sounders. "Is very nice," Pele said, pulling the tape off his styrofoam shinpad, "But is exhibition."

The plane stopped in Winnipeg, enroute to LaGuardia. Most of the Cosmos were bored enough to scramble off and visit the tiny gift shop but Pele remained on board, either sleeping or faking it, you never know which. Bradley leaned over his cup of tea, and blowing rings into it, analyzed:

"I've got to say the players are a bit tired. Seems as if we've been away a long, long time. I hope, and I believe, that we will be ready for Boston tomorrow. They will all have to do some thinking on it for themselves, I don't have to tell them how important that game is.

"We played very entertaining soccer last night, didn't we? It seems to me we're jelling in flashes, and that is very understandable. After all, we've had just one regular practice since the acquisition of Pele. One thing I'm noticing is that every team is laying for us now. They all want to beat the Cosmos with Pele. I could have foreseen that myself from my own experience. In 1968, when I played against him, we had twenty-four league games. But the game I most wanted to win was the exhibition against Santos.

"And you know, to him it's just another game. He's done this kind of thing all his life. I can't imagine him wanting to win a game as badly as, say, I might want to win one. This is not to say he doesn't care, because he has all the pride in the world. On the contrary, I worry that he will not become too discouraged with the progress of the team.

"We could have taken a maximum of eighteen points out of this trip for the league standings. I would personally have been satisfied with nine, but it went bad on us. The boys were tired coming out here, we then spent a hard week, and have nothing to show for it except an exhibition win and the usual record crowds.

"The line-up? Well, it's still open. Yesterday, I was impressed by Lamas, who now looks to be playing himself back into the team. But with him you just cannot tell from day to day. I have yet to figure out what makes him tick. I don't want them to be, but things are still up in the air.

"One thing, I think the boys enjoy all the attention Pele has brought them. At the moment, the Cosmos are the most well-known team in the world. When we played in Rochester, Siega's wife found out from a friend in Brazil that we won before Jorge even got home from the game. Amazing, isn't it?

"What we have to do is help Pele maintain his level, and see that he does not deteriorate if we are playing mediocre soccer. A lot of the moves he initiates, that we must carry through, are breaking down still. He will hold the ball long enough for you to do your thing, and he expects the same in reverse. It is a hard thing for impatient players, or those who are used to a faster style. But it's very bad if we don't do it, if we don't conform to the man's vision of the game.

"After all, he's better than the world's best . . ."

8

Collapse

*T*he visitors' locker room beneath Toronto's Varsity Stadium is cold, somber, and damp as a crypt. The walls are grey concrete; there is a massage table in one corner, two long wooden benches heavily scarred by cleats, a few dented lockers and little else. It is a lifeless, desolate place and on July 19, 1975, it houses a desolate team—the New York Cosmos.

"Professor, I have much pain here," Pele says, wincing. "Is no good . . . E muito mau . . . bad." He is holding his left thigh, raising it slightly as trainer Bob Ritcey arranges a pillow of ice packs. Next to Pele sits Mané, the effusive flower child, rendered mute. His head is down and his Medusan coils are tangled among his slender, dirt-caked fingers. On the floor around his feet are scattered jockstraps, dirty towels, and balls of damp, discarded tape. Ritcey comes over to see if there is anything he might do for him. Mané says no.

The rest of the Cosmos are burnt out. A fog of repressed frustrations hangs in the air. The brittle quiet is shattered by Donlic, who leaps up off the bench and begins punching the steel rafter until his knuckles ache. He is screaming. "I don't believe it. I don't believe it. No, no, no, no, noooo."

Collapse

For the Cosmos, it is all over. Just fifteen minutes before, they had lost to Toronto, 3–0, leaving them hopelessly mired in third place in the Northern Division. They were seven points behind Boston, a distant thirteen behind Toronto. There were five games left on the schedule, but the Cosmos were finished for the 1975 season. It would take an incredible turnaround of the minds and bodies of New York to qualify for the playoffs, coupled with the sudden collapse of the division leaders. And most of the Cosmos had stopped believing in incredible turnarounds long ago. Joe Fink spoke for the team in a half-whisper. "It's just impossible to see how we can come back now. I hate to say it but it looks like this is the end."

Nobody thought they would hear such talk in this, the Year of Pele. But gradually, the whole house of cards—Pele, the flashy new Uruguayan contingent—everything—had come tumbling down.

The first symptoms had begun to appear three weeks before the Toronto game. The much heralded West Coast trip was "disappointing" said Bradley. Others called it a disaster: three games, two losses in front of large, partisan crowds, and a national television audience in Seattle. By the time the team left Seattle for home, it was very close to complete dissolution. Like beaten crusaders, the Cosmos straggled back to New York, drained and broken.

For all its junkyard charm, the stadium on Randall's Island had never looked so inviting. The Cosmos had just played two games on whistle-slick artificial surfaces and had come away with one meaningless win and dozens of blisters. "My feet. This ground feel like the fire," said Pele. "Is total different game on such a carpet." There was no Astroturf back home on Randall's Island. Not much grass, either, but the Cosmos were thankful for those precious few blades, and even the dusty New York soot that rose in great brown clouds every time a player hit the ground. "The dirt at Randall's Island never looked better," said Bradley, hopeful. But when the Cosmos met Boston on July 10, they never looked worse. At least for the first twenty minutes.

They played sterile, defensive soccer and the offense performed like a jalopy; no speed, lots of break-downs. Pele spent the first half practicing his English. "Pass the ball," "Easy, easy," "Over here," and "No, no, no." He elocuted until he was hoarse. Boston scored early on and led 1–0 at half-time.

The 18,126 fans who had braved intermittent rains and dust storms were less than pleased with the score. They had come out to see Pele and the Cosmos show some magic, and all they had gotten was a listless game of ball tag. They were wet, frustrated, and ready to cheer anything that looked encouraging. Finally, they settled for booing the Cosmos off the field, down into the locker room.

Bradley shouldered the jeers on the way down the stairs, and once inside, he flung them at his team. Bradley did not like to scream at people. He usually held his anger back until it dissolved within him, unspent. But this time, the situation took him beyond anger. As a player, Bradley would hurl his entire being at defenders when his team was down 10–0 with thirty seconds to go. As a coach, he could not understand these men —especially the laconic Uruguayans. Here they were before a home crowd with a playoff spot on the line and they lay down like dogs under the Boston steamroller.

"Doesn't anyone in here have any pride?" he demanded. "When the hell are you going to start playing like professionals? You *are* professionals, aren't you?" The veins stood like knotted cable in his neck. Sweat poured into his eyes, forcing him to blink rapidly under the glaring bare bulb. Mané peered out from behind Picciano, murmuring, "meu Deus." The harangue continued. "You're *not* going to *win* this game by laying back and waiting for them to come at you. You've got to go out there and ATTACK. You . . . understand . . . me. ATTACK." The Uruguayans did not understand. Mazzei translated, quickly. Lamas stretched, and worked at knocking a clump of mud out of his cleats.

When the Cosmos took the field for the second half, Bradley's histrionics seemed effective. Correa took a well-placed pass from Lamas and rammed a fifteen-foot drive past Boston goalie Shep Messing, who only had time to move the muscles in his face. The tiny Correa sprinted up the sidelines like a possessed chipmunk, with a frozen grimace of disbelieving elation.

Ten minutes later, another surprise. Right fullback De La Fuente, a man unaccustomed to high-speed travel, came barreling up the right flank dribbling past two stunned Boston defenders. He unloaded a booming shot towards the far post, which caromed off the thigh of Boston's Carlos Manaca and landed right back at De La Fuente's smoking foot. De La Fuente screwed up his face and pounded the ball a second time, driving it past Messing's dive and into the net.

De La Fuente pranced giddily around the field, picking up Pele as his first dancing partner. The two of them locked in an embrace, mindless of the three or four other players who were trying to cut in. The crowd, alive and screaming, rose to its feet.

Minutes later Pele took the ball about twenty yards out from the Boston goal, his back to the net. He cradled the ball with his instep, thinking, looking, bobbling it from right to left as he stepped deftly by four encroaching Boston defenders. At the right moment, he slipped the ball into an open space, where Kerr was just arriving to send it home, making it 3–1. "What can I say?" said Kerr. "The moment I ran through I knew he'd put the ball on my foot." Memories of the West Coast trip began to pale like an unpleasant dream as the Cosmos left the field. "I think we've finally turned the corner," said Bradley, optimistic again.

He was wrong. The Cosmos' comeback was clubbed into frustration in the very next game. Against Portland, everything went wrong from the opening whistle. The offense did not run; it strolled, adopting the pace of Brazilian soccer—without any of the results. The forwards didn't attack—they made polite conversation, and rarely with each other. Pele darted occasionally into the open, shouting for the ball, pleading for it. The only time it came his way was when it was unloaded by a teammate about to be tackled. The defense was somnambulant. Portland forwards hurtled down on Nusum like waves crashing over the penalty area. Four times in five minutes, Nusum was compelled to make diving saves of point-blank shots from ten yards out. At half-time, the Cosmos were fortunate to be down just 1–0.

In the locker room, Bradley had nearly run out of words, and even the will to speak them. His face was a granite mask, chiseled in resignation and disgust. Werner Roth spat out a mouthful of Gatorade and slumped onto a bench. "We're getting our asses kicked all over the field," he muttered. No one else spoke. The Uruguayans huddled together on one bench.

The five Uruguayans knew they were up against a team which played Bradley's kind of game—a team that tromped over their graceful South American style as if it was a bed of delicate flowers. Portland was anchored by a core of stolid, hard-kicking British imports who liked their lager warm and their soccer blood-boiling. They had rolled over twelve of their last fourteen opponents. In the face of their assaults, the Uruguayans looked bad; the Cosmos as a team looked dazed. Pele was completely bewildered. Spinning in a frustrated dance as the whistle blew ending the half, he caught the ball in his hands and slammed it angrily to the turf.

The Cosmos came out for the second half to a crescendo of boos and hoots, the same discordant music they had heard a week before against Boston. Again the boos seemed to be a catalyst for some inspired play. Fifteen minutes into the second half, De La Fuente slammed a shot that chipped paint off the crossbar and ricocheted to the left, where a diving Pele met the ball in mid-bound to score on a lovely header. The boos turned to a rousing chant: "Pay-lay, Pay-lay."

But they would not cheer again that night. Nine minutes after Pele's equalizer, the Cosmos threw the game away with a bone-headed tactical error. Portland was awarded a seemingly harmless direct kick from twenty-five yards out. The standard defense against direct kicks is to form a human wall to block the shot. The team scrambled to assemble its blockade. "Here, here," Johnny Kerr was pointing in one direction. "Aqui, Aqui,"

Picciano motioned in another. When the line jostled into place the three shortest players—Pele, Mahy, and Kerr—ended up as the heart of the wall. For goaltender Nusum, it was a disheartening sight. "Everybody seemed so confused," he said. "It was total chaos." Portland's Brian Godfrey gratefully hooked the ball over their heads and into the goal.

"Eleven players played poorly tonight," bristled Bradley afterward. Alex Yannis of the *New York Times* noted that since there are only eleven players on the field at one time, Bradley's indictment must include Pele, no? "No," Bradley countered. "I don't mean he played poorly. I mean he didn't play up to his usual level."

The Brazilian thought he had ten good reasons why. "Tonight, nobody play with me," Pele complained, and for the first time, there was a hard edge to his voice. He was not accustomed to humiliation and loss. Perhaps he had made a serious mistake, coming here to America. Soon they might begin to laugh at him, to boo him, too. He knew they expected miracles, but how much could a man do? "I just play a little," he said. "Is very difficult, for me. Alone. The passes no come to me. No to anyone."

"It must be very frustrating for him," observed Godfrey, "He's passing a bit quicker than his teammates are thinking."

By July 19, the losses to Los Angeles, Seattle, and Portland and the driving rain that greeted their arrival at the Toronto airport might have warned the Cosmos that their next, crucial game would be a washout. The rain fell all day, but there would be no stay of execution—half an hour before the game the sun finally broke through, glazing the slick stadium. Speculation about the Cosmos' difficulties was truncated by a ban-lon sheathed blonde who prowled the stands, smiling and waving to players, fans, and the journalists perched in the press box above the stadium. "That's the Queen of Croatia," explained Brian Rowan, the Toronto fullback who would come join the Cosmos in a few weeks. "She has many, many friends on this team."

There was little bonhomie on the field by game-time—just

rancor and disaster. Twenty-four seconds into the game, Cosmos Captain Barry Mahy caught his studs in the soggy turf trying to turn upfield with the ball, and crumpled to the ground. He gripped his ankle until his knuckles whitened, to match his face. The referee didn't seem to notice, and play continued until Pele drilled the ball out of bounds to stop the game. Bradley and his trainers rushed out. Mahy was a solid, tenacious workhorse for the team. It had been said that he would take the field with a broken leg. Now it looked as if he might be leaving it with one.

"It hurts so bad," Mahy moaned, "I can't get up." He was carried off the field and as the ambulance shrieked away to the hospital, a lanky black man on the Cosmos' bench began to strip off his warm-up suit. He was De, a Brazilian who had been flown to this continent just four hours earlier to help shore up the Cosmos' crumbling defense. De owned the shortest name in the North American Soccer League, and two of the slowest feet. The latter distinction came as an unfortunate and untimely surprise to the Cosmos when they sent him in to replace Mahy.

After the Portland debacle, Toye had gone to Pele and asked if he knew any defenders in Brazil who could help and Pele had given him a dozen names. On such short notice, only De was available. Toye took him, sight unseen. "Three years ago he play with me in Santos," said Pele. "He was good defender." Toye saw a ray of hope, while Bradley hoped it was not just another South American who would blend in like a plowhorse at Churchill Downs.

Nobody was quite sure who De had played for between the time Pele last saw him and his arrival in Toronto, and no one knew how old he was. "He is about thirty," ventured Mazzei. It was perhaps a better estimate of his shoe size. As to his speed, De's style of play was deceptive. He was even slower than he looked, at least partially because he was still severely jet-lagged, and totally unacclimated.

Upon entering the game De neatly broke up a Toronto foray near midfield, pushing the ball up the left wing to Liveric. Toye was beaming. But for the rest of the game, he looked like a man in slow motion. On the bench, Picciano, whose services had been passed over for De's, shook his head in disgust. "This guy can't hold my jock," he said.

The Metros were not impressed either. Time and again, they ran plays at the big Brazilian and it wasn't long before they hit paydirt. Toronto forward Mrijan Bradvic crashed a twenty-yard drive that Nusum, diving, managed to deflect but couldn't hold. The ball squirted loose in front of the goal and Ivan Lukacivic pushed in the easy rebound. Soon after, Marino Peroni unleashed a steaming twenty-yard shot that deflected off Roth's thigh and rolled slowly into the goal a split second before Nusum thudded to the grass after it.

Moments later, Pele controlled the ball at midfield, gliding, wriggling free from one defender, locking eyes with the next when . . . crunch, his legs flew out from under him like duckpins. Bradley, Mazzei, and Ritcey rose simultaneously and started for the field when Pele pulled himself to his feet and waved them away. "Is okay, is okay," he told Bradley. But it wasn't. For the remainder of the game, Pele slowed from 33 to 16 r.p.m. But Pele at half-speed was still more of a threat than any full-bodied Cosmos player and Bradley knew that. If there was any doubt, Pele dispelled it only six minutes after he went down. First, he laid the ball off to Correa for a shot that deflected off Toronto fullback Mirlim Faslic. Liveric swooped in for the rebound and slashed it against the far post; the ball ricocheted out and Pele met it on the first bounce. His half volley sizzled by the post, two feet wide. But it was the Cosmos' last gasp. A penalty kick with eight minutes left drove the final nail into the coffin.

Toye sat in a blue and fuschia carpeted nook in the space-age lobby of the Toronto Sheraton, staring up at a chrome and glass chandelier suspended by a single strand of cable over his head. It may as well have been a guillotine. At 11:30 P.M., two and a half hours after the shattering game, things continued falling apart. The season was a disaster; Mahy, a wipeout. Pele was injured with a pulled thigh muscle. He would not be able to play for a week, and the 10,000 who had paid to see him in the next game at St. Louis would be clamoring for someone's head on a pike if he didn't show. Toye had just been on the phone for nearly an hour with St. Louis General Manager Jack Galmiche.

"Clive, it'll be an enormous disappointment for the fans here. Are you sure he can't play?"

Toye mumbled something into the receiver.

"What's that?"

"I said, Jack, even if he *could* play, what's the sense in it? Fifteen minutes of Pele just is NOT giving the public their money's worth. . . ."

Galmiche was not interested in remorse, just this Wednesday's game. "There's no way we can get him out there?"

"You can put him in a flowery suit and watch him strut around, sure you can." A pause. "But that would be fraud. I simply couldn't do it."

A few city blocks away, Joey Fink scored the remains of a strawberry crepe into neat, criss-cross patterns. "I can't take much more of this," he said, his voice barely audible above the Saturday night buzz in the outdoor café. Young Toronto was parading by in halters, jeans, tube tops, and clogs, but he didn't look up.

"Everybody's starting to get paranoid. There are new rumors every day. At least half the team will be gone after this season. It's affected us on the field. Pele doesn't like the way Sam [Nusum] distributes the ball and has told Bradley we need a new goalie. They're all set to let De La Fuente go. They think he's not putting out. I doubt Kerr and Mahy will be back after their run-ins with Bradley.

"And you can make book that the Uruguayans won't be around. They're all nice guys but they don't have it in here." He tapped his heart lightly, "I don't know what my status is. I think they'd want to keep me, but I won't come back for peanuts again. I'm through selling myself cheap."

Picciano, still smoldering over the slight of watching an un-

Collapse

tested De take his job, and bungle it to boot, didn't know who or what to blame. "The personality of this team is disgusting," he said, stabbing at his food. "It stinks."

At 3:00 A.M. the bright lights of the Sheraton's shopping arcade played in grotesque patterns on the windows of the darkened stores along the corridor. Fink and Picciano clack, clack, clacked their way across the tile like noisy survivors. They stopped, the ghostly silence broken by a clump and a scrape, a clump and a scrape. It was Mahy, grappling with a set of rubber tipped metal crutches. He had just returned from the hospital, and his eyes had a glazed Darvon cast.

"Only hurts when I laugh, heh, heh," he winced with all the body language of Emmett Kelly. "Some night." Mahy grew thoughtful. "I call from the hospital. One-zero at the half. Ten minutes later it's two-zero and I figure, well that's it. Finally, I hear three-zero. Three to ZERO." Mahy shifted his weight on the crutches. His denims had been slit to the knee to accomodate the cast. He shook his head, sighing. "You never like to leave a game, but it doesn't hurt half as bad if you're winning. You lose and you think what you yourself might have done to save it. Everybody likes to think they're the most important man out there."

He winked at Fink and Picciano. "But I guess we all know who that is now, eh mates?" The three of them made their way to the elevator bank, stopping every few feet for Mahy to catch up.

At 7:00 A.M. that morning, the lobby of the Toronto Sheraton was empty. Almost empty. A security guard eyed its only two occupants curiously. Two black men, one very tall, one not so tall, sat huddled next to a pile of luggage. It was De and Pele, waiting for the bus for the 7:45 flight to New York. No one had told them that it was 7:45 P.M.

Over the next three weeks, the Cosmos dragged themselves to a 10–12 overall record. In the newspapers and in the corridors at Warner Communications the only thing left was the grim task of picking the season apart, dissecting the losses, the arguments, the firings, and the hirings into a cat's cradle of tangled why's. Pele was connected to all of them. It was he himself who had said, "For the Cosmos, I maybe make more problems than I solve."

And now, he could look coolly at the collapsed dream and analyze it as if he were just another perceptive spectator. "Is no good to have such a big change in the team during the season. When I arrive, everything change and the situation is not so fair to New York Cosmos. Even a good player must now prepare for big change, and try to overcome problem on field, not in practice or training. This very bad.

"At Santos, I play for many, many year, and the team develop this way. We know the physical capabilities of each other, we know the little habits and tricks, little psychologies each man have and how to use it best for team. This is very important, because the game is based on things like anticipation, intuition of the imagination of other player, many things which are as much feeling and experience as technique.

"But this is what I expect, a difficult time to adjust the game, particularly with the mix on the team of English and South American player. It is big job to make this combination to work; maybe too big a job for anybody unless the players can bend with no problem and sacrifice their own habit of play.

"Gordon also have many problems—with the language, the communication, all the job he must do when I arrive. It all make for him very, very difficult time. Sometime it look like he want too much to be friend to the players, and not enough of the coach who tell everybody, 'now you must do this, and no explanation.' Gordon is very good man, he have big heart and he know what is the problems of most footballers. But he take on too much, or is given too much to do outside the field. As coach, he must make the meal plan, check on the bus, see if plane on time and everybody understand what he say about everything. All these little problem add up to big problem."

For Bradley, the problems had begun long before Pele ever arrived. To the Cosmos' coach, it all boiled down to the problem of management, or how to wear six hats, walk softly, and win without the aid of a big stick while your general manager is chasing halfway around the globe for an answer to the prayers of a whole sport.

From March to June, the critical preseason months, Bradley was left to handle player accommodations, training arrangements, and transportation logistics. Then there was the scouting. "We made a few mistakes in evaluating players this year," admitted Toye. "With all my time devoted to Pele, Gordon was forced to fly to Europe or South America for a day and sign a player on the basis of one good game."

Now at the end of the season, only half of those players remained on the roster. Half of the team, and Bradley. Constancy had always been his foremost virtue. Through the worst of the season's tumult, he had remained miraculously even-tempered and patient, as is his nature.

With the advent of Pele, Bradley had become overburdened. The extra duties had diluted his ability to concentrate on his coaching. And what was there to coach? His team would shuffle positions and players in a jerky, coast-to-coast version of musical chairs that made constancy impossible.

Some of the regulars had become distractingly ill-tempered through the last three months, including a few of distinctly English background whom Bradley had counted among his closest friends. They were all from the same school—kick hard, run, shoot, and run some more. When Bradley began diddling around with the languid South Americans' game, they lost their patience, and Bradley lost a good deal of their respect. The rift culminated in the release of Kerr, and the alienation of Mahy, two players who had begun the season as entrenched veterans. They felt let down by Bradley. Gordon felt they had been inflexible, wall-eyed to the diplomacy and patience the checkered complexion of the team demanded.

Everybody on the team had his own opinions:

"Gordon's problem is that he is too nice a guy," said Fink. "He stuck with some players all year who didn't give a damn about winning."

Werner Roth, a tough, aggressive player who took over as

captain after Mahy's injury, had heard loud rumblings from players discontent with Bradley's style. "But I think it's too easy an excuse to blame the whole thing on Gordon," Roth said. "He made mistakes. He never came in the dressing room and got down on us when the situation demanded it. He thought he could motivate some of the players by appealing to their sense of pride instead of kicking them in the ass. The trouble is, there was no pride. For half the team, the season was an education in Yankee bucks. Like Professor Mazzei once said, it looked like some players thought they were on vacation, and would have an easy time of it."

At the crux of the problem was the Uruguayan experiment, which had slowly pulled Bradley in various directions, as if he were a piece of taffy. There were really two Cosmo teams, one consisting of the Latins, and the other of players with an English approach to the game. The Uruguayans, each a marvelous player in his own right and under his own conditions, were imported gems who turned out to be glass under the heels of the North American Soccer League.

The emphasis in the NASL had always been to recruit talent in England, scouring the lower league divisions for players whose career prospects seemed decided, destined to not climb above the level of sturdy craftsmanship. The backbone of the NASL consisted of Englishmen, from coaches like Bradley on up to executives like Woosnam and Toye. As a result, the English style of play dominated, and still does. This game is predicated on long passes and speed, on advancing through the air instead of on the ground, on hurtling attacks, strategies developed after and hauntingly reminiscent of the Second World War. The British temperament on the field of play, had developed into an impetuous one. At its best, this type of soccer is a volcanic, spectacular game, punctuated by incisive passing and explosive action. At its worst, it is a futile series of headlong rushes from one end of the field to the other, bordering on nonsense.

The primary virtues of English NASL imports like Mahy and Kerr were hard work, an unusual capacity for inflicting—and

Collapse

absorbing—punishment, and an aura of jaded recklessness. The vagabond British players possessed a poignant spirit of futility, as outlaws might, kicking, screaming, straining with ferocious effort. Before he joined the Cosmos, Bob Rigby was goalkeeper for the Philadelphia Atoms, who won the NASL title in 1973. He spoke for the going NASL philosophy of the time as well as anyone when he said, "You can take all the finesse players in the world and put them on the same team for all I care. I'll take a dozen beer-guzzling Englishmen from the third division and kick the piss out of them."

So it seemed heretical when, in early 1975, the Cosmos revealed their plans to use five high caliber Uruguayan players along with the usual contingent of mad dogs and Englishmen in an attempt to merge the methodical, artful South American style with the rugged English version of the game. Ultimately, it was like trying to mix oil and water.

"I found that basically, the Latin American players are more emotional than the Europeans or Americans," said Bradley. "They are all very good at skills, nothing to learn there, and they perform their skills just like a belly dancer would perform on the stage. Just beautiful. They love to have the ball, they love to play with it. You can see it in their faces.

"On the other hand, what I was noticing was that they would not be prepared to do the amount of physical running that the European players are used to. I was told in advance about this, and I was warned to make adjustments for it. I feel that although they were beautiful at manipulating the ball, there's another side to the game. That is hard work. They weren't keen on that type of thing, like running back to cover a teammate who's been caught out of position.

"Perhaps they were even willing, but they had never been taught how to do that, how to play a running, hard, work-rate game. I'm not being critical of their style, it's just something that is opposite of the European game. I expected more from them in the way of work, and I didn't get it, not because they were lazy, but because they were different. Not worse, but different.

"I also realized that I couldn't change their style if I wanted to. I could make them play our game, but it wouldn't be fluent, we wouldn't get away with it."

The position of the five was inevitable; they had been thrown into a foreign culture, an alien style of play, and into an organization that was just groping toward solid professionalism. Small wonder, then, that they held back, snickered, regretted the situation they had put themselves into for the sake of a few gringo bucks, and felt superior, smug, in a small-minded way.

As late as August, the Uruguayans displayed an amazing ability to learn nothing during their American sojourn. Not long before the end of the season, Bradley and the Uruguayans shared an automobile on the way home from practice one day. One of them wanted to stop for a moment at a supermarket, so they pulled over. Bradley watched in amazement as the player strolled up to the automatic "Exit" door, and began leaping furiously on the rubber carpet, puzzled by the door's refusal to open, until a woman on the other side left the market with her goods and the player with a swollen nose.

Like Bradley said, the Uruguayans were not worse, but different. Differences, of course, went beyond just the Uruguayans. With seven nationalities represented, communications hadn't gone well from the start. At the beginning of the season, Bradley had handed out mimeographed sheets containing the usual skeletal action terminology of the game in Spanish and English: *Atras*—forward; *alto*—high; *mio*—mine; *cuidado*—caution. Apparently, no one bothered to learn the translations. The sheets had long since been thrown away, glanced at hastily and then filed with yesterday's newspapers, candy wrappers, coffee grounds, and empty cans of baked beans. It was a telltale sign. Once he arrived, Pele would shout himself hoarse trying to scale a barrier that, if anything, had grown taller in the passing three months.

If Bradley had experienced problems shepherding his crazy-quilt team in the early part of the season, they multiplied ten-fold when, at last, the messiah arrived. There were complaints that Pele was buried at midfield, never given the ball, and unable to score.

"We have a gem in Pele," Bradley told reporters after the Toronto game. "But we don't have the players around him to properly complement him. Too often, the passes Pele gets are what we call hospital balls, ones that he has to go for, a defender has to go for, and somebody winds up in the hospital." More often, Pele would wind up stranded, blanketed by opposing defensemen, bereft of the ball. "I am trying to set up patterns of play for the team," Pele said. "When we set up these patterns, I can go forward more, to make score."

For his teammates, Pele's presence was less a matter of some fine tuning than a complete overhaul, with several veteran players getting junked in the bargain. The casualty list was authored the same day Pele affixed his name to a Cosmos' contract. The first dismissals were simple house-cleaning, but slowly grew into a litany mirroring the various failures of the club. Upgrading the personnel around Pele triggered the second wave of releases, while the third reflected the schisms that had torn the club's heart out. It began with the release of inexperienced hopefuls like Anastasio, Carlos, Scott, and Marderescu and ended with the departure of Kerr, once the right hand of Bradley himself.

"The day Pele arrived, it shattered everything we had built so far for the season," said Werner Roth. "There are so many pieces lying around I wouldn't even know where to start looking for them."

9

"I Have Many, Many Friends"

*T*he massive 747 climbs into the sun, the Golden Gate
Bridge below, heading for the Arctic rim and London.
The Cosmos are scattered throughout the plane, locking themselves into various stages of sleep. They are embarking on an
international tour, to showcase Pele and this band of soccer
vagabonds who have suddenly become a team worth seeing.
By the end of the tour, Pele, the son of a poor journeyman
soccer player, will have shaken hands and chatted with one
king, one president, and two prime ministers, logged over 50,000
miles, appeared on the front page of over sixty newspapers and
magazines in five languages, signed well over 500 autographs,
escaped down several service elevators and three flights of fire
stairs. He will have played before 263,500 live spectators and
millions on television. All in six weeks work.

There is another dimension to this tour. It is the biggest
gamble in the history of American soccer. The Cosmos, a
team that could not even make the NASL playoffs, are hurtling
towards a round of top-flight international competition and into
the eye of a skeptical world. Yet even while the Cosmos' first
season (really a half-season) with Pele was crumbling beneath
their feet the gears were turning in the Warner Communications building.

Clive Toye knew that he needed players, and needed them badly, if the Cosmos were going to make any kind of impression on international soccer. First shoring up the weakest line, the midfield, Toye acquired Brazilian Nelsi Morais from Santos and Ray Mifflin, a subtle, creative player who had excelled in Peru's 1970 World Cup team in Mexico. He also added two defenders, Thannasis Rellis and Mike Faslic, from Greece and Yugoslavia respectively. On the front line he added John Coyne, an Englishman with a singular ability to collect "garbage" balls. All of these, it was hoped, but particularly the competence of Morais and Mifflin, would spring Pele to play a more dominating, dangerous role as striker.

Despite improved personnel, the changed cast left a distinct sense of deja vu. The Cosmos now had players representing nine nationalities and six languages, a pitching, rolling ship from everywhere steaming toward a hazy destination. The tremors of Pele's arrival had grown into a quake which had yet to subside, as evidenced by the number of people it had tossed and shaken out of complacency, out of the team, or simply transported into Pele's own life.

Heathrow Airport is gloomy at 8:00 A.M., as the Cosmos deplane in oppressive, gray humidity and jam into the small shuttle bus for a ride to the terminal and an hour-and-a-half wait for the connecting flight to Copenhagen.

Pele and Mazzei sit in the most obscure corner of the lobby by reflex, even though there is no crowd, just a ragged assortment of night-flyers in transit, most of them foreigners.

One by one, they recognize Pele. First a Spanish businessman, then an Italian steward, come to shake his hand and request an autograph. He is also approached by an Iranian, and an Indian couple. A Brazilian appears from somewhere and they embrace, murmuring "Felicidades." There are two Swedish journalists waiting to interview Pele, even though the Cosmos' destination is Sweden.

One of the journalists produces a photo taken in 1958, the year Pele catapulted into instant, international celebrity. It is a picture of the Brazilian team running a victory lap with the national flag. One corner of the flag is held gingerly by a wide-eyed, round-shouldered, and very young Pele.

"Do you remember all them?" he is asked.

Pele stares silently at the picture for a few moments, then answers. "Yes, of course, most of them are still in football."

He recites their names: this one is president of the football association at home, this one is a coach in Rio. Another runs a soccer school in São Paulo. This fellow has blown his money and plays every day on the beach, slightly pathetic, still marvelously deceptive. Vava, an old friend is coaching in Seville, another is coaching in Istanbul. Yet another is a general manager, while this one owns a sports shop. This one died five months ago. Pele muses for a moment, then points with a smile to the slump-shouldered youth. "This is only man still playing."

It is an irony. Pele, who has been Brazil's highest individual taxpayer, who literally freed himself from financial worry before reaching his majority and straddled the world at the tender age of sixteen is the only man on that team who still sits rear of the coach on the bus. He is the only one who still gets kicked and elbowed by an ambitious antitalent, who has to have the light out by 11:00 P.M. on the night before a game. But also this: He is the only one who has survived without a surgeon probing his knee joints, without tiring of the endless stream of hotel rooms, airplane food, the often rambling, bored, inane conversations endemic to the barracks life of soccer.

"I have been very lucky," he muses. "All this time, to be able to go higher, to make new things in my career. Sometime I am tired, yes, but not of the people, my friends." Our flight to Copenhagen is called, but as we stand up, an elderly airport porter whose rumpled uniform is worn and shining from too many pressings walks uncertainly up to Pele. Taking off his official cap, he asks for an autograph. Pele grips the hat by its sweaty inner band and writes on the liner, "Do Amigo, Edson = Pele."

After arriving in Copenhagen, the team boards a bus which will take them to the harbor and across to Malmo, Sweden, where the Cosmos will play their first game. Pele stays behind;

there is the usual press conference in the airport for Swedish and Danish TV. "No problem," he says.

After this interview, one of the journalists tells Pele that he speaks English very well. He replies, with a smile, "No, not very well, but you are my friend." There is another press conference on the ferry, where he is told he speaks English very well six more times, and answers the same questions. The rest of the Cosmos are strung out along the deck, staring at the impending Swedish coast, turning their faces up to the sun, jostling each other and absorbing the scene with a jaded sense of having been here before.

"It's like the twilight zone for us, you know what I mean?" says Picciano. "You know, like the same movie over and over, here and there, everywhere we go. I tell you, I don't know how he can take it, you know what I mean? Man, I think I would go nuts." Pele is up in the bow now, heading a ball for photographers, a smile on his face, at play with the salt spray and sunlight.

Eventually, the team bus pulls up in front of the Aarkaden Hotel in Malmo, and after a meal everyone drifts off to his room for some sixteen hours of heavy sleep. The first day of the tour is ended, and it has set the tone for the next month. It is one day, more typical than extraordinary, in the life of Pele.

Standing before the door to his room, he says "Good night, see you at the airport tomorrow morning. Early." He is still smiling.

Pele is standing in a "folk park," immaculate in a crisp white suit with a bright red shirt underneath. He is waiting for Olaf Palme, Sweden's prime minister, on this sun-dappled, autumnal afternoon. Palme, a big man, winces as he steps into this dazzling light. His hair is gray blond, his face lined, and his eye sockets underscored in charcoal. Beside him, Pele appears a child, with the gaily painted strut of a roller coaster rising behind him. They exchange handshakes, embrace for the cameras.

"I told my sons that I would meet with President Ford and

Premier Brezhnev, but they were uninterested," Palme smiles. "Yesterday, I told them I might meet Pele and for the first time they looked at me with something like admiration."

Pele laughs, he gives Palme two autographed picture cards for his sons. "You play football too?" he asks.

"Yes, as a matter of fact, I was an adequate goalkeeper at one time."

"Good," answers Pele. "We need a goalkeeper for our game tomorrow."

It continues like that, as the two public figures move into a grassy area where they kick the ball back and forth for a few moments, drawing a crowd. An old woman, her teeth sunken into a poor mouth, straggles up behind the prime minister, shaking her fist at his back in an exaggerated, figurative threat. Then she spots Pele and as their eyes meet for a moment, she drops her arm and exposes her disarranged teeth in a wide grin.

Ten minutes later, the car is pulling away from the folk park and the driver, peering into his mirror, asks: "Have you signed many autographs?"

"Yes," replies Pele, "I have many friends."

"One more?"

"No problem. I give you one of my cards, with picture and my name. Okay?"

The Volvo rolls along the canal, the afternoon sun flooding in and out as we hum through the trees. "It is nice, what the prime minister say about his sons, no?" Pele asks. Without waiting for a reply, he yawns mightily and turning his head to the side, falls asleep.

The bus is heading towards the stadium where the Cosmos will play their first game. As we pull into the parking lot, a steady stream of youngsters falls in along the bus, shouting, "Pele, Pele." They are waving autograph books, leaping to hammer on the windows. Pele, the embracing smile on his face, stands in the aisle giving the peace sign with both hands.

Evening is falling as the bus presses up close to the player's entrance to the building, a crush of mostly young people surrounding the bus like a living, noisy moat. The rest of the Cosmos get off first; it has become habit that Pele is the last on and the last off to facilitate a quick, easy getaway.

Now he is up to the window, cautioning the crowd to "watch the wheels, watch the wheels." He is signing autographs slipped in and out of the window until Garay gives the signal. With faithful Pedro in the lead and a Swedish official on either side, Pele and the human triangle around him wade off the bus just twenty feet from the stadium door.

In the lead, Garay is trying to push his way through the crowd, an undulating, splayed wave closing around the knot of four adult faces. Pele, utterly calm, is trying to sign autographs, rock-steady while the two Swedish men alongside sway like bushes in the wind.

Inch by inch they are making their way through the crowd to the dressing room door, Garay creating openings in the shifting mass of clutching hands. Suddenly, Pele pops through the door like a tight cork. As a security guard struggles to close the door Pele walks over calmly, reaches out into the faces and locates the child whose pen and crumpled piece of paper he still holds.

He gives back the child's equipment, the door slams, and we are left alone in the dark hall of echoes leading to the locker room. "When I was little boy," Pele says, "I always go to stadium for to try to get the autograph. Sometime, the player just push aside and go by. But other player, he stop, smile, give autograph and maybe touch my head. They are the men I always want to be like."

The locker room warms gradually to its new occupants; a pitcher of hot tea steams in the corner, its aroma mixing with the smell of wintergreen and the collected ointments of trainer Mike Saunders. Bradley walks over to where Pele is absorbed in lacing up his studded shoes. He is holding an autograph book and pen. "Pele, I need six, please . . . make them good, they are for the officials of tonight's game."

Pele laughs and recalls the time in Brussels when he was suddenly confronted by a referee bearing a yellow card for no apparent reason. "He ask me for autograph, what I do? If I no say no to referee, is no good politics in game. I run fast off to side of field, quickly sign, and run back to game and give back to him."

The Cosmos, jet-lagged and unused to European offsides rules lose 5–1; Pele scores their only goal. Moments after the final gun, Garay leads a phalanx of police and officials surrounding Pele off the field. Dazed by a late game check that rattled his teeth, Shpigler staggers over to the massage table and collapses upon it. Saunders passes a cup of amyl nitrate under his nose, trying to bring him through. A doctor indifferently shines his small probe-light into Shpigler's eyes. Pele is bent over his Israeli teammate, peering at him as the hot breath bakes his face.

"Shpigler, you okay? Shpigler, you okay?" No answer. "Shpigler, you okay?" Still no answer. There will be no answer for twenty-four hours, at which time Shpigler will reappear for dinner, dressed in his quiet, elegantly cut Parisian pullover, recovered from a concussion.

It is 2:00 A.M.; the team is sleeping, but Garay stands in the dim light of the hallway in the Aarkaden, the glow from a single shaft of light filtering through the crack in the door and falling upon the tips of his well-polished black shoes. Pele is in the next room, sleeping some ten feet away. The flame of a match leaps toward the tip of Pedro's cigarette and he begins to talk: "I make him lock the door every night, because he likes to leave it open. Every night, I check to make sure the chain is on the door. It has become a little joke between us."

The conversation drifts to Pele's Brazilian concept of time, and his absolute refusal to do things at a pace he finds unnatural. "Oh, it is easy to wake Pele. He is not really slow, he is just a philosopher. You see him in a game and he is totally different, intense, swift, cutting like a knife at every opportunity. In his private life, he does not like to be pushed or rushed into anything. 'What is there to hurry for,' he says, 'everything will be okay anyway.'"

"I only see him when we must go out of town. In New York, he is with his family all the time. He likes to live a quiet, secluded, intimate life. Family life is sacred for him. I think it would be impossible for him to enjoy his life without the peace he finds with his family.

"When you see him with Rose, you are amazed at how normal they are. It looks like they are just married, on their honeymoon. He always says he inherited his peace from his father and I believe him.

"He is also a perfectionist who is not overpowered by his fame, but is humble and responsible. He never complains to me, and rest, for him, is just time to recharge the batteries.

"You know how we were all supposed to take a boat ride today? Well, he said to me, 'Pedro, if I go, I will spend the whole day giving autographs, and I will also ruin it for the other players.' See, he sees from more than one perspective.

"One thing I will never understand is where he gets his patience in dealing with people. I believe he is the perfect Catholic. He keeps a rosary besides his bed, and he is very religious but he never shows it off. He makes the sign of the cross when he goes in and out of a game, but he never takes out the cross he wears around his neck.

"The word depressed is not in his vocabulary, he never shows signs of psychological changes, moods. I watch all this very carefully, because I want to know who he is, to know him better, to help him in any way that I can. When I was knocked down in Toronto, he was concerned about me, I see it in the pictures they took.

"I know how to read pictures, I learned that in the CIA. They taught me how to read pictures, so I could recognize somebody if their physical appearance changed, in the way they held their cigarette, or how they pushed their hair back. Well, I know how to read pictures, and I saw that Pele was concerned about me.

"Something else. In the Beverly Hills Hotel I borrowed his rosary. I was praying and the phone rang. He walked by me and said, 'Don't pick it up, I will. Pray now.'

"In San Jose, on the anniversary of my father's death he did something else. I could not help it, I become very sentimental when I think of my father. Tears come to my eyes. He noticed it and understood, very humanely. Pele just touched my hand and said, 'Sometimes we need that too. Let yourself go, it helps sometimes.'

"That was all, no questions, no speeches."

Three hours later, the team leaves for Gothenburg. The bus is full, waiting only for Pele, who is once again besieged by local officials, journalists, fans, friends. Staring out the window, sunglasses shielding his eyes, Roth offers: "It's amazing how many nobodies put their arms around him."

"Brrrrriiiiinnnnnnggg, Brrrrriiiiinnnnnnggg." The team wakes with a collective start, leaps in alarm. Pele is standing in the back of the bus, grinning from ear to ear, holding aloft a big red alarm clock he has purchased as a souvenir for his son Edinho. "Come on, wake up," he demands. "No, please a few minutes more," he mimics. "Nobody sleep on this trip," he concludes as the bus pulls out and heads for Gothenburg. Moments later, he himself has fallen into a deep sleep.

Lena Hagen sits patiently, standing near the elevators alongside the restaurant in Gothenburg's Hotel Europa, an ordinary looking woman whose curves have filled out healthily. She could not be mistaken for anything but a comfortable housewife, absorbed daily in the small chores and pleasant inflections of domestic life.

"When he was free after the match, Pele and I would go out, hand in hand," she remembers, recalling the year of 1958, the year a sixteen-year-old Pele took his first trip on an airplane and lived the final, tender days of his anonymity.

"He write his name on my arms, and I didn't want to wash. He signed a pair of white shoes I owned and I wore them thin . . .

"How strange it is, he looks the same now as he did then, as if nothing has changed. He looks like a boy who likes to play football. I see how I have changed, and it makes me feel old.

You see, he still has that, how do you say, gentle look around the eyes? He seems preserved, unchanged.

"Perhaps there is a little change. Back then, I remember that he looked a little bit sad and he was often going around alone. Everybody was taking pictures of his famous teammates, Garrincha and Didi, but not Pele. He was left alone, and not many people bothered with him.

"I was fifteen years old then, and I had very long blond hair. He said he liked that very much. There was a place called Hindos, near his training camp, by the sea. I took him there, we went walking by the water. It was a very nice time.

"Of course, he left. He wrote me cards from some countries where he played, and I followed the growth of his career in all the newspapers.

"I wrote one or two letters to him, and he answered them. Yes, of course I felt more than friendship for him. I believe it was the first big love of my life, something I will never forget. How strange it is to see him now, what he has become. Who could have known?

"Oh, I remember how I cried when he left Hindos, I will never forget how I cried that day."

Lena attended the game that evening with her family, and saw the Cosmos play the best game of their season in the 3–1 win. Pele played an inspired game, scoring two goals, and with time running out the Cosmos' bench signaled that a substitute for Pele was coming on.

Pele waved to the crowd and sprinted from the field towards the tunnel leading to the locker room to avoid the crush of the crowd. It happened with some six minutes left; a sudden veer and wave and Pele with Garay alongside, were heading for safety.

Then he spotted Lena, standing with her daughter in the nucleus of a growing crowd. He stopped, all haste vanished. The face, intent on escape, now lapsed into recognition and as the sweat poured from Pele's forehead he gently bent down and embraced Lena's daughter, kissing her on the cheek. He said a few words to the child, then stood up and greeted her mother in kind. "I must go now," he apologized a moment later, jostling through and reaching the locker room just ahead of the crowd, which roiled around and finally engulfed Lena and her daughter.

The train rocked softly through the night and rain, the rails ticking, a metronome pacing the tired Cosmos into sleep enroute to Stockholm. The team arrived at the Hotel Foresta the next morning. It is a curious place in the Swedish equivalent of a suburb, far from downtown Stockholm, high on a bluff over a river, appearing isolated and magical when seen late at night from across the water.

Pele's afternoon is devoted to the Swedish press, one of whom is a tough, serious woman named Berit Nelsson. She wants to ask Pele some provocative questions, in private. He consents to the interview. Twenty minutes later she has her story.

"I asked him about politics, and he said football involves all his time and he cannot be involved in politics," she explained. "I asked him if having a white wife ever created problems for him and he said he wouldn't think of her as white, just, well, Brazilian.

"I told him about a rumor I had heard, that he was trying to have his children accepted as white, through some formal process. He looked at me as if I was a monkey; he was shaken. He asked, 'How would this process be? I have never heard of it.'

"Finally, I asked him if he had ever made a rational decision to try to do the best for everybody, as he seems to do. I asked him if he is seeking approval and admiration consciously.

"He answered: 'I have been like I am for the last twenty years. Can a man decide he wants to be something he is not and live that way for twenty years? I don't think so. He would be found out as a liar and pretender very quickly.'"

Finally, her own impressions: "I like him very much, he is the only famous man I have met who does not have an attitude. If you treat him like he treats you he is all open, a very warm human being."

Two evenings later there is a game, which the Cosmos lose

3–2 despite two more goals by Pele. After the game, it is the usual scene, a scene few players who have never been Pele's teammates could have anticipated. The surreal, untimed chorus of "Pele, Pele," haunts the locker room, the bus, the hotel. The inflections, the distances, the pitch, the emotions are all different, all the same, the constantly muffled drumming of "Pele" on everyone's ears. He stands by the window of the bus now, smiling, patiently passing out autographs. "Pele, Pele, Pele," down the block, the bus pulls away. "Pele, Pele, Pele," the crowd slips away. "Pele, Pele, Pele," two kids have climbed a drain pipe where they hang on precariously, fixed to the dirty brick building in the heart of the industrial sector. Pele waved and turned his head slowly, watching the kids until they disappeared into the night.

The Cosmos are apparently stranded now. Games scheduled for Turkey and Iran have fallen through because the promoters have not come up with the guarantee money. Toye is in Rome, trying to negotiate an alternate game and the team is strung out in Stockholm, plagued by a gnawing, debilitating boredom. Three days pass. The players have a light workout in the morning and that is the day, save for the meals which are welcomed mostly as signs that time is indeed passing.

A curious thing has happened here: Team unity and morale have vanished. Irritations flare. Stockholm is very expensive, the days seem endless, orchestrated by the abrasive monotony of too many foreign languages, too many missed connections in the middle of a good joke, too many suspicions.

There are few diversions: slot machines and a low-stakes roulette wheel, an occasional girl, the spontaneous poetry of Mané. Rellis, always seen in a lurid yellow Alice Cooper T-shirt, feels that Liveric treats him condescendingly.

"I will do nothing now," says the otherwise charming little Greek, "but when my leg is good, in three days, I will speak to him with my leg." Actually he does not really say that so much as gesture and coach it out of Shpigler, his buddy, who enjoys some kind of extraverbal, telepathic system of communication with Rellis.

Coyne is building a good old-fashioned hate for Paredes. Bob Rigby, the fiery American goalkeeper on loan from Philadelphia who would later become a Cosmo, has amazed everybody with his unqualified skill, but he is so driven to distraction that he is discovered in the gray predawn hours, hurling copper coins at the ducks in the river some 200 yards down and away.

It has become evident that above all, the footballer's personality is defined in action; games are his grip on the world, a narcotic justifying the rootless, wandering that make up so much of his life. The time between games is only a suspension in the purgatory of hotel rooms and airplane food, sleeper cars hurtling through a landscape he will never see and villages which are not his own, heading forever toward the next game, the existential fix. More than three days between games and the player begins to recede into himself, sick of looking at his teammates across the table and asking them to pass the butter.

Pele hibernated between meals and called his family in Brazil daily. One night at dinner, an eight-year-old Swedish boy, Stefan, cautiously left his parents' table and approached Pele.

Pele: "Okay, we can talk now a long time, food is coming later."

Stefan: "I'm going to play football where you play."

Pele: "In Brazil?"

Stefan: "That's where?"

Cautiously, the child took Pele's relaxed hand from the table top. He caressed it, kneading the fingers, toying with the protruding veins, unself-consciously.

Pele: "Yes, Brazil is where I start. What position you play?"

Stefan: "Number ten."

He skipped away and returned moments later.

Stefan: "We're having pancakes."

Pele: "Yes, they are good. You like pancakes?"

Stefan took Pele's hand again.

Stefan: "Yes, yellow and brown, not black."

Pele: "Yes, that is how they are."

Pele's artful approach to the game was constantly tested by the North American Soccer League's rugged, jackhammer defenders. PHOTO BY TIM CONSIDINE

Pele begins his dribble, already preparing his next move.
PHOTO BY TIM CONSIDINE

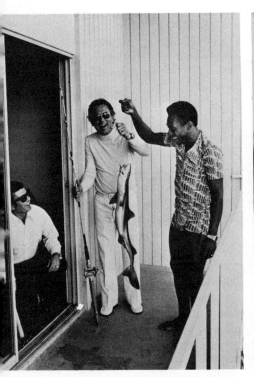

Bodyguard Pedro Garay looks on as Mazzei and Pele catch a dogfish from the terrace of their hotel room in Seattle. PHOTO BY TIM CONSIDINE

Pele patiently explains a subtle aspect of the game to journalists during a press conference on the West Coast trip. PHOTO BY TIM CONSIDINE

Mark Liveric is down.
PHOTO BY TIM CONSIDINE

Pele is down. The season is gone.
PHOTO BY TIM CONSIDINE

The tour begins; a supine Tommy Ord drills the ball goal-ward following a pass from Pele. PHOTO BY TIM CONSIDINE

Ord is congratulated by Shpigler, Liveric, and Pele following the goal. PHOTO BY TIM CONSIDINE

Pele from Shpigler: a goal against an all-star team in Oslo, Norway. PHOTO BY TIM CONSIDINE

An amazed goalkeeper can only watch a Pele goal with wonder and resignation in Gothenburg, Sweden. PHOTO BY TIM CONSIDINE

The team had a handful of pressure-free moments, when Pele would pick up a guitar and use it to help dispel the struggles of the 1975 season. But even then there was always somebody watching. PHOTO BY TIM CONSIDINE

"I Have Many, Many Friends"

Later that evening, Pele and Mané visited a nightclub, where Pele astonishingly remained unrecognized. However, somebody recognized Mané, or thought he did anyway, asking Pele confidentially: "Is that Charles Bronson you are here with?"

And finally, the next morning, news. The Cosmos are heading for Oslo that evening, and will continue from there to Rome. With the tangible promise of games the team is lifted, the ribbing begins again, the hostilities evaporate.

Oslo. "I feel like I'm living in a fishbowl," says John Coyne, slouched in a leather armchair in the lobby of the Hotel Continental. Before him is a window filled with faces, people standing in the rain, hoping to see Pele. "I can't take it anymore," Coyne laughs, and leaves for lunch.

The team meal is upstairs in an elegant dining room, its tables are resplendent in cut crystal glassware and lavender tablecloths, signature plates, and silver salt shakers. Scooped high into one of the walls is a Botticelli-like shell, containing a piano. All of this civilization rubs off on the Cosmos; nobody is throwing rolls around or sipping his soup without a spoon. The maître d' bows elegantly and asks Pele to sign a menu. Later, when the tables are cleared, Pele toys with a demitasse spoon and ponders the question:

"I have met very many famous people, is hard to say which one impress me most. Maybe the papa XII, he is the one, maybe. I have, how you say, private meeting with him one time. Also you know, the rosary I have is given to me from one of the priests in the Vatican. Is good rosary.

"But there are so many others. I like very much Bobby Kennedy, he seem to me very good man, easy to feel I know him. Very relaxed. Also many prime minister, Nixon, Ford, others. Papa Doc in Haiti, I remember very well this man. He very old when I go to make visit. He shake very much and when I give him hand, he say only, 'Pele, Pele.' Then I have tea with him, but he seem very, very old to me. Also, he have many problem in his country, bad situation . . ."

187

There is an interruption; Pele is called upon to arbitrate a dispute among his peers.

"Pele, which is better, Disneyland or Disneyworld?"

He thinks a moment, answers, "Disneyland still better, Disneyworld much bigger, but no finished yet, only bigger space." The debate goes on without him. Pele talks of the satisfaction his life has given him.

"How many people I make money for? This is something I think about, which make me feel that some good has come from my career, my life. Look the people in the stadium, selling little flag and banner, Pele flag, Santos flag, Cosmos flag. Look the restaurant, where they put picture of me in window and people come to eat, or restaurant in Italy where chef make 'spaghetti a la Pele,' with pasta, vodka, and caviar. Many other people too. They sell shoes, skirt, jeans, everything because I put my name on it, or because I wear same thing. I make money for many people. This hotel, now we have press conference, so people come here, maybe stay to eat, drink. Is nice, yes?

"People, journalists always ask, 'Pele, why?' Generation after generation come to see me play. In Sweden, people who see me twenty years ago must come again because children say, 'Please, father, let us go to see Pele.' Or eight- or nine-year-old, never see me play before, but they want to come watch. Why? My talent, that is simple thing, is gift from God. Also I am very lucky because maybe my personality fit to my talent, is close, maybe same thing.

"Funny thing, I never want to be famous, this I know. As child, I could not imagine how this happen to me. When I am child, I only want to be football player like my father. I want to BE my father, second division Brazilian footballer. One time Italian reporter say to me, 'Pele, I know you now twenty year, and you stay always the same.'

"My opinion, I think I am famous without individuality. Others, they have names in art, music, smaller, more special area. It is like the politics, fashion change, new thing come all the time. Is little bit different for me, I have no special area, no slice of something. I think people do not know me as 'Pele, the Brazilian footballer' but only as Pele. For them, I am just like other people, only I have some different talent and many, many luck."

The game against the Norwegian all-star team is played in a steady rain, with bulging clouds scudding across the pine slopes surrounding the stadium. Pele has two more goals, bringing his total to six in four games, and the Cosmos coast 4–2. "Pele is in his glory on a field like this," Bradley said afterwards, "it is wide, unlike most of the NASL fields. The space is very important to him, to his style of play. Also, I think he knows the load is on his shoulders." Bradley paused just long enough so that it seemed the following words simply fell out of his mouth, by accident. "Each of these games could be his last in places like this . . ."

"I think this was last game we have a chance to win," Pele analyzed in the elevator up to his room. Tomorrow the team leaves for Rome and a game against Roma, a legitimate international powerhouse. It will be the acid test for the Cosmos, the most challenging obstacle they have yet faced. It may even be premature, for despite the addition of quality players like Mifflin and Pitico (a Santos player who joined the club after Nelsi broke his leg in Gothenburg) the Cosmos remain by and large less a team than eleven characters in search of a style. "We will see" Pele says, "but win or lose against Roma, is important to play well, to make good game, with imagination."

Bradley, O'Reilly, and Mazzei joined us in Pele's suite. O'Reilly opened the small refrigerator-bar, peered inside, asked the company for their preference, and began passing bottles around. Pele reached in and extracted a bottle of Schweppes. "I drink Schweppes," he said casually, with mock naiveté, "that is what I pay for. I know nothing of beer or champagne. I no drink beer or champagne."

This took nobody by surprise; stories of Pele's thrift are legion. It gave everybody a good laugh and launched Mazzei into an anecdote.

"It is said that when Pele's fist is closed, it is so tight that nobody can open it," he said. "Yeah, you think is funny? I tell you little story.

"Pele have good friend, great Santos player called Zito. One day, I watch them at bar. They both order Guarana, a typical Brazilian drink, and stand there, speaking, speaking, speaking; nobody puts a hand in the pocket. Finally, somebody else come along and puts the money down and they look up in surprise together, at exact same moment and say, 'Oh, what a surprise, thank you, thank you.' "

Pele chuckles, takes a more serious turn. "I see many players come and go, and money is very difficult for them. I see sometimes poor boy, who come to Santos to make contract. First time he gets money, he go out, buy twenty-five shoe, fifty shirt, new car, everything. Then he have injury, maybe lose little speed and career is finished. He stay just a poor boy with many clothes. Look at some young Cosmos player. We first arrive in Sweden, they go out in street, shopping. They no think about the money, always shopping. They look, see something they like and say give me, no worry about price. Some player learn, some do not. Is many sad story with money."

One of the players is missing. This is pointed out by his roommate, Tommy Ord, who packed both bags in the morning fully expecting his mate to show up at any moment. Now, he can't hold out any longer. "Ah, Gordon, got something to tell you . . ." Bradley's face goes blank, tenses up. The bus is ready to pull out, heading for the airport and the flight to Rome. The Cosmos are leaving this country in ninety minutes, hopefully all of them. Gorden leaves messages at the hotel for Gulliver; nothing more can be done. The bus pulls out.

The announced boarding time is 9:15. Still no Gulliver. It is funny, sad, bad, or heroic, depending on who you happen to be listening to at the moment. At 9:12, Gulliver comes clinking through the lobby like a stray tomcat. There is a collective sigh of relief, followed by the inevitable epigrams. "Look the guy," says Liveric, "all year he have face white like ghost, now he has

"I Have Many, Many Friends"

suntan." You can see Gulliver blushing even at this distance.
Bradley is waiting for him, the first man he must face. Even he
can't help it. The granite crumbles, the corners of his lips go
racing towards his earlobes.

Gulliver had been carried away by the quality of Norwegian
hospitality at a farewell party last night and ended up with a
roommate nobody would ever confuse with Ord. He fell into a
light sleep around dawn and could not be roused into consciousness until 8:30, when he realized that here he was, in a strange
bed in a foreign city on a thumping morning, without the
foggiest idea of how to ask somebody for a match, much less
directions to the hotel. Oh yes, what was the name of that
hotel? Fortunately, he remembered and all is well one hectic
cab ride later.

Or almost all is well. Mané, whose favorite expression has
become an emotionally rendered, "I wish I never met you,"
followed by whatever he wants to say analyzes Gulliver's plight.

"I wish I never met you girl, because now, now, you cost me
many, many money." Ersatz sobbing. Right he is, $200 worth,
to be exact.

Suggests Liveric, "Why don't you write her, tell her to send
two hundred dollars?"

"Because I don't know her name," Gulliver sighs.

After everybody has exhausted the humor of this situation,
the Cosmos begin dropping off to sleep on the plane. Ord is
looking at a Norwegian newspaper; the front page has a
marvelous photograph of Pele and Tommy leaving the field
together.

"I wish I could read Norwegian," he says, looking at the
caption.

Rowan pokes his head up from the next row. "I'll tell you
what it says: 'Pele with unidentified Cosmos player.'"

The night is slipping by softly, licking at the perimeters of
the Via Veneto, never quite penetrating to disturb the bubbling
life of the sidewalk cafés, the noon-time countenance of the
boulevard's weary hedonism. Mazzei and his companion finally

get up from the table and head back for the hotel, leaving the incandescent umbrella behind. It is pitch dark now, the city is sleeping. Mazzei adjusts his voice to a suitable whisper. They are talking about what Pele may or may not mean to people 100 years from now.

"There are already two stadia named for Pele," Mazzei reflects, "one of them with a big bronze statue of him before it. The government wants to go ahead and build a vast Pele recreation complex, with a big Pele museum. We have thought about things like that already. You know, many movies, a kind of computer you can ask questions to, like, when did Pele play his first game for the Cosmos? The computer gives you immediate answer. Also maybe an autograph machine. You know, put in the nickel and you get autograph, "Edson = Pele," just like he sign. Pretty good idea, no?"

It is 4:30 P.M. the next day, a perfect time, when Rome is spread out before you, a timeless, decaying ruin of maize and honey. The bus is purring, just about ready to pull out and head for the vast olympic stadium and the pressure can be felt now, pushing against the windows, regulating the silence in the bus. Nobody quite knows what he is getting into here; all the Cosmos know is that out there somewhere will be hordes of rabid Italian fans and a fine soccer team, both fully expecting a rout, a dismemberment of this upstart American club. The only thing missing is the roll of muffled drums. Pele boards the bus, along with Daniel Sierra, a Brazilian singer appearing in Rome. We head into the golden wake of the city.

This silence will never do. Sierra begins to tap his foot and leads into a traditional Carnaval number. Pele begins to sing along gently. It is an invitation. Mané and Pitico, old Carnaval hands, join in without prodding. Then Pedro, Mifflin, Rowan, everybody. The bus approaches the stadium, still a mile away although the streets are already thick with people who turn, stare, point, marvel at the sight of a bus rolling along, powered by music.

Pele is keeping rhythm, drumming on the window, so involved in the song "Felicidade" that he breaks a sweat. The whole club is deeply into it, drumming, tapping, mouthing words. The crowd gets thicker, Pele is flashing the peace sign left and right, nobody quite knows what to make of all this until they recognize Pele's face. It is a perfect moment, a crystal high of solidarity and spirit, a perfect definition of all that is best in a footballer's life.

"Nope," says Rigby, "hasn't changed a bit." He has just returned from an inspection of the field, where the fans behind the barbed-wire fence and empty, concrete moat showered him with boos and makeshift projectiles. The last time Rigby played here, a month ago, the U.S. national team lost to the Italians, 10–1. They remember this guy all right.

The Roman journalists have an extraordinary greeting for Pele, particularly in light of the depthless chauvinism of Italian fans. It is a poem, delivered by Massimo Sirano, of *Il Messagario*, the largest daily newspaper in Rome. It translates:

> Dear Pele
> The Roman team says to you welcome
> by her fan's heart
> Now "a fete" for you
> The star who still awakens the football
> splendor.
>
> Every sportsman by your coming
> Is remembering in a dream your achievements
> Now that the imagination is nearly lost
> And very few athletes play
> Using their brain.
>
> To this Rome team we invited the Cosmos
> For a friendly tension;
> I wish you could give her
> A very nice football lesson
> So that she'll be able to win
> The Italian championship again.

Pele would like nothing more than to do just that, but he will not even see the poem until later. Right now, he is with the team in the locker room as the Cosmos huddle in feverish concentration. A bad loss here would be an embarrassment to the Cosmos, to Pele, to the NASL and American soccer dreams. The credibility of American soccer is to be decided in the next two hours, and everybody knows it.

Bradley, anticipating stage fright, cautions: "Everything will be all right if we keep the score tied at zero for the first fifteen minutes. After that, things will go fine, don't worry."

During the warmup, Mazzei chooses to remind the players that "the game start zero-zero, so you in a very good position." Pele sends a sly smile over his shoulder to Shpigler, another veteran of games this big. "Shpigler, explain to me why zero-zero is good for us, and not good for Roma?"

Five minutes left to game-time. Maybe it is a sense of occasion that leads Rigby to choose this moment to ask a friend to snap a quick picture of himself with Pele.

As they approach his locker, Pele looks up incredulously and asks, "Now, before this game?" Rigby is painfully embarrassed, but a moment later Pele breaks out laughing and bare-chested, throws his arms around the goalkeeper's shoulder. After the picture is snapped, Pele decides it would be a better picture if he was wearing his shirt. He slips the jersey on and goes looking for Rigby. Taking his time, he makes sure the pose is just so and it is time.

This is the real thing, and even a player of Pele's experience is affected by the scene as the Cosmos go clack-clacking down the tunnel and onto the field. The towering arc lights flood the stadium with an electric blue haze, turning 60,000 Roma partisans into a concave, expressionistic mural.

For the first ten minutes, the Cosmos are bullied, playing in a sort of trance, as if the game iself was a movie unrolling before their eyes. The Italians mark Pele closely, trying to force the action to the wings and into the hands of their own accomplished fullbacks. But the Cosmos survive the shaky start Bradley has anticipated. They spurn Roma's attack, with Roth and Masnick shutting down the defensive middle. After fifteen minutes, the crowd is brooding, feeling hurt and betrayed by beloved Roma's inability to pulverize the Cosmos. Now New York swings into the game and it is fine thrust and parry soccer until the twenty-second minute, when Roma's Carlo Petrini scoops a badly cleared ball and sends a fifteen yarder whistling across the goal mouth at a perfect angle, leaving Rigby helpless. The half ends, 1–0.

Four minutes into the second half, Shpigler sends a free kick whirring into the penalty area. Coyne and a defender rise simultaneously, battling and misheading the ball. It lands over near Masnick, who has moved in expecting just this. He thumps a volley that deflects off an Italian and bounces right to an opportunistic Coyne, heading across the penalty area. Bang, he lets go and the score is tied 1–1.

But the Italians press back, the fullbacks penetrating deeper and deeper, forcing the action and getting two clean goals in a span of six minutes to put the game away. From there it is anticlimactic, and despite some exquisite play by Liveric, Pitico, Mifflin, and Pele, the Cosmos cannot penetrate the defensive shield thrown up by Roma. Final: 3–1.

"For a team that has been together only a few months, the Cosmos are great," Roma coach Nils Liedholm says afterwards. "If Pele has the right kind of players behind him, and it looks like he has a few of them already, the Cosmos could be one of the best teams in the world by the end of the next two years.

"Remember, this is very different for him [Pele]. At Santos, he knew his teammates inside out, he played without his eyes, by instinct. And that is where his real genius is displayed."

Liedholm should know. He was the idol of the Swedish team that Brazil defeated in the 1958 World Cup.

Although it takes the Cosmos an hour and a half to shower, change, and make their way to the heavily guarded bus outside, thousands are still lingering along the road out, hoping to catch a glimpse of the man they call "Il Re."

They are three deep on the sidewalk, and rag-tag *ragazzi* are darting back and forth, like moths attracted to the bus headlights. The windows are kept closed for security reasons. Now they are fogged up.

Pele and a writer are talking about the game; what it might mean for American soccer, what it will mean to the thousands of Europeans who will read the result over coffee in the morning and perhaps raise their eyebrows at the respectability of these American upstarts. The European leg of the tour is over. The Cosmos have finished 2–3 through the most rugged, tiring segment.

Suddenly, Pele squeezed the writer's arm and said, "Look, look at all the people." He wiped off the window with his sleeve, and for five minutes, peered through, searching the row upon row of intent and expectant faces outside.

Gently, he waved and smiled, now and then. The dulled echo "Pele" rose continuously, reverberating through the humid Roman air. He just continued staring. What was he looking for? Would he find it written on all those faces, the secret of his fame, a reflection of his own face, or the hunger he once felt on the other side of that pane of glass?

"My friend, I have many, many friends," he said, with a voice bordering on resignation.

10

Jamaican Farewell

*I*t seemed much longer than six months ago that the Cosmos
—without Pele—had landed here at François Duvalier airport in Haiti. Back then, in April, a loosely organized, anonymous pack of footballers had touched down with all the impact
of a dry leaf spinning off a branch to train, play exhibition
games, and demonstrate their glaring inadequacies as a team.
So much had changed in six months, months that had flashed
by like heat lightning on a surprised summer night. "I don't
recognize these guys," said Joe Namphy, a Haitian who had
met the team on their earlier visit. He watched the squad
deplane, three days after their season and tour had reached a
climax in Rome. "I guess Pele's presence has had quite a profound affect . . . ," he speculated.

On their earlier visit, the Cosmos had been treated casually.
This time, they were accorded homage due royalty. The airport terraces were packed solid with smiling Haitian faces. A
reception committee greeted Pele with a huge bouquet of car-
nations, while camermen from the national television networks
hopped about photographing from every angle. A Haitian func-
tionary handed Pele a ten-dollar bill to autograph, which he
took, slipping it, laughing, first into his pocket, then signing it
and waving the peace sign with both hands.

It was no simple bus for the Cosmos this time, but a motorcade led by a car with a large loudspeaker on top of it. "Sen-sa-shonal," blared the loudspeaker, "Pele et New York Cosmos, sen-sa-shonal." The parade streamed through Port-au-Prince, enormous crowds lined the streets, overshadowing the filth and squalor looming behind them with spontaneous outpourings of cheer and good will. Sen-sa-shonal.

The four of them stood on a veranda at the Cosmos' elegant quarters, the Royal Haitian Club and Casino. There was Henrick, an immaculately attired Haitian secret service man who could easily be mistaken for a Belgian industrialist; Lionel, the trim Haitian president of the Victory Football Club; Mazzei and Steve Richards, a slightly rumpled Englishman who had taken over the Pepsi Pele program. The solemn attitudes of Henrick and Lionel suggested that something was very wrong here, a suspicion verified by the embarrassed glances and methodical shrugs of Mazzei and Richards.

This was the problem: Jean-Claude Duvalier, also known as Baby Doc, had sent Henrick and Lionel to fetch Pele to the palace for a formal introduction. Pele, however, was tired from the long journey which began three days ago in Rome and all the hoop-la in Haiti. He was having a massage and did not particularly want to meet anybody, not even Baby Doc. He was also disturbed by the fact that he had received no notice of this meeting. Henrick and Lionel just showed up to fetch him, as if he was just another minor bureaucrat.

"You must understand," said a melancholy Henrick, "we mean no offense. We are dealing with a factor beyond our control. When our president tells us to do something, we do not ask questions."

Richards mulled over this remark and slipped into the same weighty mood. "I have just been in his room and Pele is offended." Pause. "Remember, he is a king in his own right."

"Oh, this will cause big problems for me," said Lionel nervously.

Then Mazzei has an idea, as Mazzei often does. Pele has to

eat lunch, so why not issue an invitation on behalf of the president, asking Pele to lunch with him at the palace? Lionel and Henrick, unused to the notion that they could speak for Baby Doc, blanched at this casual and rather reasonable solution.

Bradley came over and joined the group. He firmly told Henrick and Lionel that everything must be done with proper notice; the order of the team was to be disturbed as little as possible. Further complication. Everybody began gently juggling the weight, shifting blame and responsibility with diplomatic rhetoric.

"Oh, Pele would like to meet the president," Richards assured the Haitian delegates. "But he must have notice. It is as if your president was summoned to meet, oh, ah, God, on five-minute notice. He would be happy to go, but is disappointed that the notice was so short. You can be sure that Pele wants to meet your president. After all, he met his father. But you should have arranged it with more respect for Pele."

Finally, the compromise was struck. After his massage and lunch, Pele and Mazzei left for their visit. Half an hour later, they were walking back up the steps of the hotel.

"It was nice visit; he ask about the football in America, about New York Cosmos. I tell him, "no problem," everything okay. He is, ah, little bit afraid," said Pele, drawing his body back in a shrinking gesture. "How you say, embarrassed."

"Was it a nice palace?"

Pele and Mazzei exchange glances.

"Yes, very nice," nodded Mazzei. "But . . . there is one thing, very strange. We see many, many gun. Machine gun, antiaircraft gun. You walk in garden, and there are barrels of gun in the flowers."

Two more days of rest and boredom passed, listless "free" days spent by the pool sipping citronade, punctuated by occasional forays to one of the local clubs or lackadaisical gambling in the casino. They were the only diversions as the Caribbean cast its sunny net over this weary team. The three days were highlighted by the performance of Steve Marshall, traveling secretary for the Cosmos. Marshall, a regular Falstaff, lured a few local molls back to the hotel and orchestrated a bash of such proportions that he was named "Captain of the Copacabana All-Stars." Then, finally, it was game day again.

The Cosmos began shuffling into Saunders's room at 4:30 P.M. for the ritual of taping. The room was a tumble of crates and trunks, drying shorts and underwear, rolls and rolls of tape wound tight or, unraveled across a bed or dresser. The smell of ointments balmed the air. The boys felt at home here and lay about on the trunks, crates, and beds in various states of undress.

Some of the players were discussing a possible pension plan, looking to a future most of them are loath to contemplate, to admit will happen.

"Yeah, in England they have everything for the players," remarked equipment manager Charlie Martinelli. "Insurance, long-term pension payment, the whole works, that's the kind of deal everybody should have."

Liveric, lying moodily on a bed in a towel suddenly exploded. "Ah, pension, nutting. Don't tell me, everywhere you play is same, all over world, and if you think no, you stupid. When you finish play, they all say same, fug off you, ged out."

Roth raised his eyebrows, peered over: "You're in a hell of a mood . . ."

"Always same," continued Liveric. "When I am quiet, everybody say what the matter? When I talk, everybody say I am in bad mood."

Liveric turned over, watching Saunders meticulously wrap Mifflin's right ankle. "Pretty soon everybody on this team will be Jewish," he forecast gloomily.

Failing to get a rise out of Saunders, he went on. "Since Jews come, this team worse."

It worked. Saunders stopped, looked up. "Don't talk about the Jews, who the hell wants to live in Yugoslavia anyway?"

"Ha. Who want to go live in Israel? Nutting to do but fight and kill Arabs, all time."

Saunders just shook his head and kept taping. Mifflin looked at him, rolled his eyes.

Picciano walked in just about this time, and Liveric took off on the trail of a new scent.

"And the Italians," he said, "since the Italians come, no more socks for nobody."

"Shut up already and don't yell so much," said Martinelli. "And I hope you have a lot of socks, because you ain't gettin' any from me anymore."

"Hey," discovered Picciano, "don't talk no more, this guy's writing everything down."

The last words in the notebook were: edginess, boredom, pregame tension, homesickness, fatigue.

The team shuffled into Pele's suite at five for the customary pregame meeting. Only Pele and Bradley were missing. Shpigler and Mazzei played cards, Rellis leaned against the wall, eyes vacant, looking for his wife or Greece, it seemed like ages . . . Rigby, alone in the corner was already doing his pregame stretching when Bradley finally walked in.

"Okay boys, before we start, the president of the Haitian Soccer Federation wants to say a few words to you."

The door opened, and in strolled perhaps the most menacing fellow any of the Cosmos had ever laid eyes on. His face was lost in malevolent, Ton-Ton-Macoutes-style wraparound sunglasses and a full beard. Around his shoulders was a filthy raincoat, and a rumpled hat was pulled down over his forehead. The gun he surely carried could not be seen. A silence gripped the room. The man began to speak: "Je voudrais parler . . . ," but he stopped short, choked might be a better word, and burst out laughing.

"Pele, you idiot," screamed Rigby, triggering an avalanche of epithets and laughter. The tension was gone.

The bus waited outside. If anything had been proved throughout the tour, it was that the ride to each stadium provided new thrills. This driver was a particularly spirited fellow. He pointed his machine toward the stadium and in moments we were pitching and rolling, police escort motorcycles fore and aft, hurtling on like a balloon blown full of air and then released. The bus swerved left and right, careening through streets boiling with people. Somewhere on top of the bus bounced François Reichenbach, the academy-award-winning documentary film-maker and his gang of very decadent looking assistants, ostensibly shooting footage for a Pele biography. But right now, they were too busy worrying about their own lives.

By now, the Cosmos were high once more and they proceeded to beat Victory, 2–1 in a thrilling wide-open game, highlighted by a classic goal which lifted the Cosmos into a 1–0 lead. It came in the fifty-fifth minute of play, when Pele took a ball from Mifflin and dribbled it to the Victory end line, halfway between the corner flag and the goal. While the defense looked for a move coming out, or at least a pass back towards Ord at the top of the penalty area, Paredes slipped in under the fullbacks, right in front of the goal at the far post. Pele shot an exquisite line drive that curved across the goal mouth, just beyond the reach of the Victory goalie. Paredes headed it into the open net from ten feet out. Ord scored the winner, a flukey ball that caroomed off Coyne's foot and landed right in front of him for a point-blank cannonball. It was a loose, relaxed game, spinning along with crisp, clean artistry. This satisfied the Cosmos; it conformed to a sense of emotional winding down as the tour approached an end. Little did the Cosmos know what lay in store for them in their next two games.

The old man carrying the painting approached the breakfast table cautiously, no one among Pele, Mazzei, Richards, and Breil noticed him until he was standing alongside with a Haitian football official who had come along as an interpreter.

Introductions were made, and the two visitors sat down. Gervais Ducasse, a distinguished painter of the Haitian primitive school was obviously nervous. A thin man with chiseled features and a full shock of snowy hair, he spoke no English and his gnarled hands shook with age.

The portrait was not a particularly good likeness; all of its charm lay in the naiveté of the work, the angular, vaguely cubistic rendering of Pele's head. Mazzei happened to have with him a book on Haitian Primitivism, left as a gift by George Nader, the owner of a local gallery. He asked Ducasse to autograph it, and the old man complied.

Then an uncomfortable pause fell across the table, followed by a whispered conference between Mazzei and the interpreter. Nobody knew if the painting was offered as a gift or for sale. To make matters worse, Pele did not see anything very attractive in the portrait. When Ducasse got the drift of Pele's judgment, his shattered pride and painful unease translated into a facial twitch.

More whispering, this time to Pele by Mazzei. "No, I no like," Pele said, shrugging, unwilling to buy the work. Breil suggested that they make an offer "for some different paintings," aggravating Ducasse even further. "Hold on to the painting, I'm sure you can sell it," Breil suggested. But it was a far more delicate matter than that. It only made things worse when Breil pulled out a glossy *Sports Illustrated* magazine cover of Pele and said, "This, can't you do something like this?" Ducasse held the slick photograph, staring at it uncomprehendingly.

"I love your pictures, they are very beautiful," Pele offered, flipping through the book. "But Mr. Pele does not like this painting," sniffed the translator.

"No, I do not have to like the painting, even if I am Mr. Pele," came the blunt answer.

A connection had been missed here. It was a failure of communication, and one of the few times Pele had not perceived a professional pride analogous to his own, did not tap the proper diplomatic vein. Instead, an onerous deadlock settled in.

Finally the old man sat straight up and thrust the painting towards Breil defiantly. "He want you to take it as a gift," the interpreter said. Breil asked Ducasse to sign it. The painter turned the portrait over, affixing a date and signature with a trembling, childlike scrawl, and shuffled off. (Later, Pele and Breil would visit Ducasse in his modest home, where Pele would be so reminded of his own impoverished childhood that the party would stay for well over an hour and eventually spend $1,000 on paintings, two of them destined to adorn a wall in Pele's New York apartment.)

But the painter had hardly disappeared across the patio when another artist staked out Pele's table. This one was a local drummer who had his makeshift band along. The only quality in this man's face was a charitable, charlatan vivacity. He relaxed his grin long enough to dedicate the next number to "Mr. Pele," and launched into a typical calypso number, something he must have hammered out for God knows how many real or imaginary dignitaries on innumerable occasions.

When he finished, he rose, took off his hat, and bowed deeply to Pele, eliciting a smile. But when he straightened up, he left the hat outstretched before him. Pele applauded gently, "thank you, my friend, thank you." The drummer, not done yet, shuffled his feet and arched his eyebrows, looking straight at Pele, making it clear by his twisted grin that he expected negotiable gratitude. For a moment Pele and the drummer locked eyes, silently. Then Mané and Pitico, who had been watching the whole thing from poolside, doubled over, screaming and whooping, and the drummer put his hat back on his head. "See how many friends I have," Pele laughed.

This time, the Cosmos did not have time to build an appetite for play. Less than twenty-four hours after defeating Victory, they took the field against Violette, tired and anxious to get it over with. Bradley had had the foresight to rest key players like Shpigler and Mifflin the evening before, so at least the midfield was fresh. But the defense was dead and Masnick in particular was not looking forward to another evening with the aggressive Argentines, Montironi and Barionvevo, who had spent the year playing in the Haitian league. An electric atmosphere greeted the Cosmos in the purple mountain shadows rimming the stadium; the crowd seemed gripped by anticipation. All 24,000 tickets to the game had long since been sold, but so many fans were standing on the perimeter that a ball kicked over the fence would bounce across the thirty feet of track between field and grandstand on heads and shoulders, never touching the ground.

From the beginning, it was evident that Violette came not merely to play, but to win by any means necessary. It was a rugged evenly matched game, distinguished by close marking and vicious tackling. Still, the Cosmos controlled most of the first half and took a 1–0 lead in the thirty-eighth minute. Liveric played a ball beautifully out of the corner, advanced along the end line and flipped it out to Mifflin in the center of the field, fifteen yards from the goal. Mifflin faked a pass left and surprised everyone by sinking his foot into the ball, sending a soft, purring floater that curved into the upper left corner of the net. It was a brilliant goal, second only to Pele's best tour effort in Gothenburg.

The Cosmos held that lead until the seventh minute of the second half, when Montironi bulled and dribbled free in the corner, drew Cosmos' reserve goalie Kuykendall out and fired the ball home behind him. Although the Cosmos reached back and extracted everything they possessed in a savage attempt to break the tie, they could produce only a handful of frantic assaults. The game ended 1–1. Drained, the Cosmos began to stagger from the field, glad it was over, heaped onto each other's shoulders, thighs rubbery and minds blank. Then came the word from the officials. There would be two fifteen-minute overtime periods. Violette would get its pound of flesh.

It was an unbelievable decision, but Bradley argued to no avail. It must be played. The Cosmos sat or lay on the turf during the five-minute intermission as thunderheads massed over the stadium. They were oblivious to the crowd, squirting Gatorade into their mouths and all over their faces, too exhausted to care much either way. Masnick wandered around in a daze, shaking his head, muttering elegant Spanish imprecations. Pele, sitting calmly in the center circle spotted a shiny object suspended on a wire stretched across the field, grandstand to grandstand. "Look, Shpigler," he said, "a UFO." Then the rain came and the team lay back, sweat and rain running off them into the parched field, their mouths open to the sky.

The first overtime was sheer torture. The ideas were there for the Cosmos, but the legs were not and the resolution came in the second minute of the second overtime. Pierre Bayonne, dribbling into the penalty area was tacked by Roth. The referee said foul, Montironi converted the easy penalty kick and it was almost over. But not quite.

The Cosmos could have folded peacefully right there, but for some inexplicable reason did not. A deep pride, something this enigmatic and confused team had rarely displayed during the tumult of the past six months, now gripped them and would not let go. They felt that the officials had taken the game away from them by awarding a questionable penalty kick. They wanted it back.

With just thirteen minutes left, they hurled themselves into the attack. They dominated and forced, kicked and clawed. Masnick's leg turned black and blue from his battle with Montironi. Pele, eyes ringed and wide with fatigue was equally driven, pushing himself to his own physical boundaries with the intensity of his leadership, the incisiveness of his progress upfield against the clock, against the odds. But through it all, he retained his implacable calm and almost stole the game back in the waning minutes.

He ran right up to the Violette goalie after a save, stared into his face and stood chest to chest, unnerving and intimidating him into committing the infraction of running more than three steps without touching the ball to the ground. Pele whirled on the referee for a judgment and got it. There was just under a minute left in the game, and half of it ticked away as Pele lined up his free kick from the penalty spot. Violette formed its protective wall, the Cosmos tried to cramp it, punches were exchanged. The referee dived into the fray and somehow Pitico ended up with a red card. The seconds ticked away. Pitico spat on the card and shoved it into his trunks, refusing to leave the field. Pele tried to line up the kick again, but the jostling continued and the final whistle sounded.

"We controlled the game," Bradley fumed later. "The kick they awarded Violette was a penalty, but we had four like that ourselves. Why were they not called our way too? The officials had no control over this game. It was a mob, a riot. It was a disgrace."

Pele's version: "We lose the game because we lose. We miss three, maybe four good goal. Is our fault only. If you make the goal, referee can say nothing."

He was also asked about his emotions, the complete detachment he demonstrated right up to the moonstruck end despite the intensity of his play. "What is there to gain?" he replied. "Anger cannot change the game, only the goal change game. The proper moment only make the difference, is all which matter."

It was well past midnight when the bus finally pulled up at the hotel. In the back of the casino, the palm fronds and hibiscus arms quivered in irridescent patches of red and blue. The pool shimmered from its own concealed lights. Fifteen pairs of cleats clicked on and Liveric, the first to appear, stood for a moment at the edge of the water, totally exhausted, in full uniform, and slowly let himself fall in. Within ten minutes, eight Cosmos were suspended in the water, flickering through the pool's lambent grasp in a surreal scrimmage against their own fatigue.

Shpigler finished the tapioca, a curious flight dessert that melted in the mouth without leaving a trace of flavor. He looked out the window, down at the changing blues of the Caribbean depths. He was very tired. He had come to the Cosmos after finishing a hectic season in the French league, joining the club just before the arrival of Pele. He had survived the trauma for a number of reasons beyond his soccer skills. These included his absolute professionalism and a flexibility rooted in his ability to analyze the game, the team, the personalities around him with the objectivity of a detached witness. Now he wanted to talk about it.

"You know, I never thought about playing with Pele. I knew that he was the greatest of players, but I didn't realize how different he would be in so many other ways. He is so far above, or apart, from us that I am always astonished. He believes he can do things in a game where other people do not even see possibility. This is imagination. As a player, physical execution can take you to the top. But the imagination to see possibilities nobody else is aware of, that is rare. He is like the great artist who creates something new, only he does it in soccer, where the emphasis is on conforming to patterns, to accomplishing things by the better execution of certain preconceived ideas.

"In my philosophy, to succeed at anything is great. Pele must be a great personality or he would have stopped somewhere in the past, like so many others. Somehow, something new, unique always turns up for him. Now it is American soccer and the Cosmos. But it is not a job for just any man, it is specially for him.

"People use the word 'luck' all the time. Pele also uses it a lot, maybe too much. He speaks of scoring the right goal in the right game and calls it luck. But he does it so much that it cannot be luck. Maybe it is a talent for luck. He must be someone who can carry all this success on his back and still walk straight.

"There are so many sides to him. He is usually in complete command, but sometimes you will see him turn to Mazzei while he is talking, with the complete look of a child and say 'Professor?' Isn't this something, how after all this time he still calls Mazzei 'Professor,' as if he was a little boy who still had so much to learn.

"Maybe because I am the nearest to Pele in age and because I know what success is I have a little better chance to understand him. With Pele, in certain situations, I can look into his eyes and guess how he is feeling correctly two out of three times.

"We can communicate, and I realize that he is a man who can say everything with one word, one look. I like that, when communication is like good passing in a game, tak-tak-tak, easy, fluid . . .

"I know people are always asking if he is putting on a face, wearing a mask. This is very hard to know, because he knows how to hide himself when he must. But if he put on a face to the public he would lose himself. I read about Liz Taylor and see how she tries to play other people. But Pele is himself, he is playing his own role.

"If you want to make the best movie of Pele's life, Richard Burton cannot play the lead. It must be Pele. Movie stars play somebody to be great, but the greatest movie I ever saw never told me what it is like to wake up in the morning for an actor. With Pele, I see just that.

"What a team this has been. I like it very much, because I like the variety, because I like people. But I feel very sorry for those who cannot express themselves, it is like living in an open jail.

"You see Mané, Rellis, they are special. They can communicate without language. Some of the others speak the same as everybody but are more difficult to understand. The only thing that gets me is some of the people who are traveling and do not have a place they want to go back to, a place to belong to. I can only imagine the suffering.

"I know I have a castle at home. If I am having a problem, I only have to think about it and I feel better. Maybe it is just a cover for a gypsy life, I don't know. And I wonder how much further I can go.

"People have always asked me what I will be doing when I finish playing. Well, knowledge of that question made me live my life a certain way. I am not worried yet, but time is going. It is a story of ten years now, and I have a wife and children at home.

"When I finished with the Army, everybody said now is your chance, Morteli, take out some money, make business for yourself. But I played soccer for the same club since I was nine years old, and it is all I ever wanted to do, play, enjoy the game, make something out of it." Shpigler grinned. "I did. I became the highest goal-scorer in Israel's history, a little Pele for the people at home.

"The satisfaction is knowing that what you are doing makes people happy. Yet when people ask what I do and I tell them, they look at me like I am an actor, a bum.

"You know, some people believe you must get up at six in the morning and make work with your hands, make shoes. I know I caused problems in Israel, because the little children there want to grow up to be like me. But I cannot help that. I just cannot make shoes; I will never make shoes."

Later, the Cosmos sat in a reception lounge in Jamaica's airport, waiting for passport clearance. It was a tired and depressed company, lost as wooden chips in the backwater of a rushing river. Mike Faslic, morose and menacing, rummaged in his briefcase, the only baggage he carried on the tour. Mané popped up from a corner and grabbed everybody's attention by inquiring, "Mr. Kissinger, what are you doing?" This triggered a hilarious, nonsensical conversation between the two of them. "You like . . . very much . . . Mr. Kissinger . . . I wish I never met you, because, because, now I never forget you. Why because?" To which Faslic answered, "Yes, Toronto very good, but no speakee for money . . ." It went on like that, until everybody realized just how ludicrous the whole situation had become. Shpigler looked over to where Reichenbach the moviemaker lay sprawled in the corner, snoring. "Here is the real movie," he said defiantly, "Where is your camera? Ah, you are sleeping . . ."

There were nearly 50,000 Jamaicans milling around the stadium just outside Kingston and those were the people who couldn't get in. Another 60,000 jammed the concrete oval, a few hundred of them perched like bright grackles on the billboards ringing the top of the bleachers. It was a pastel evening, clouds lying overhead like inverted pools of mauve rainwater.

The Jamaicans had their own Pele in Alan Cole, a gifted

player, but one who never lived up to his enormous potential on the international circuit. "Hey, mon," boasted one of Cole's countrymen, "he's our Pele, and that's no lie mon, watch him on free kicks, he gives his players a gift, mon. He going to run all over your Pele, mon."

Unlike the gentle, happy-go-lucky Haitians, the locals here came less for entertainment than war. The crowd was tinged with malevolence, a bitter, flashing edge colored by racial antagonism. This became evident from the early stages of the game, when the first racial insults drifted towards the Cosmos bench and culminated later with Toye making a quick run for the chief of police as a frenzied, taunting mob closed in.

The game went badly for the Cosmos from the start. The Jamaican club (called, ironically enough, Santos) wanted victory just as badly as Violette but it went about claiming it with even greater desperation. Bradley had to go in for Masnick early when the Uruguayan pulled a groin muscle in the fifth minute. In the twentieth minute, Cole dropped a pinpoint pass into the Cosmos' backfield and his teammate Errol Reed drilled home a clean twenty-yarder.

New York, despite some brilliant moments, was unable to finish any of its threats. Again, the Cosmos lapsed into a kind of collective inferiority complex, signaled by an unwillingness on the part of most of the players to take a decisive shot, seize the moment, convert possibility into a goal. Again, they seemed to be looking for Pele and reaching for things that lay just beyond their grasp. They spun out baroque, pleasing patterns, trying to play Pele's game but turned up counterfeit, self-consciously imitative to the point of parody.

Bradley, from his position at center fullback, saw it all. He saw Santos players wade in, hack, tackle, and shoot while the Cosmos again fell into passive confusion. Why couldn't it be easy, just once? After all, here they were on what was supposed to be the soft leg of the tour, and suddenly it looked like any hungry gang of straight-ahead Sunday players could eat their lunch. Everything that had been built in Europe was falling apart before Bradley's eyes and he couldn't stand it. The half ended 1–0. There were no subtle strategies discussed in the steaming locker room. Bradley toweled off and asked for the team's attention.

"You're not putting yourself in the game out there. I have no shouting, see no teamwork. You are playing like you are in a trance. Shoot! You're at the eighteen-yard box, tapping the ball around. Shoot! I don't care what else is going on, or who you are thinking may get free, dammit, shoot! If you shoot enough, one will go in, but you must shoot! We've got to show some urgency out there, especially around the penalty box. Accept the responsibility, shoot! We cannot let a team like this beat us, it makes a mockery of the sport. Shoot! There is no desire, no fire out there, shoot! I know one thing as sure as I'm standing here, and that is that you will not win this game unless you shoot."

Pele had taken a knee high in his right thigh, and it was decided that he would play only fifteen minutes of the second half. At the 14:34 mark, an ambitious fullback smashed into him, and they tumbled to the ground together. Pele did not get up, and two minutes later, he waved to the crowd as he hobbled off the field and into the locker room on the shoulders of Garay and Saunders. In the following few minutes it seemed as if that weight had been lifted off the Cosmos' shoulders.

With Pele gone, the rest of the forward line scrambled to take the initiative. Now nobody was afraid to shoot, and an attack, as undaunted as it was unattractive, materialized. Mifflin and Pitico distributed the ball from the midfield precisely and Coyne, Shpigler, Liveric, and Paredes began to play savage, dangerous football. The action relocated in the Santos end as the Cosmos began pounding furiously upon the goal, deterred only by some excellent goalkeeping and a failure to command that critical second or inch which amounted to the difference between a hard-luck miss and a score.

Amazed at the sudden resurgence, the crowd abandoned its smug overview and turned participant, directing its own stormy defense at the Cosmos. In the span of just fifteen minutes, the stadium had become a seething emotional cauldron.

Liveric strained to reach a Shpigler pass in the thirtieth minute of the second half, just managing to achieve it at full
stretch. He pushed it feebly towards the goal, where the keeper,
already committed and stretched prone at the end of his dive
succeeded in batting it away with his fingertips. Three minutes
later, Liveric again threatened, dribbling by one man and taking on the tackle of another. For a moment, the two were hopelessly tangled. Then Liveric collapsed, like a limp dishrag, as if
on signal from the referee's whistle for a foul. He had caught
the full impact of a churning knee in his chest and he was out
cold.

Saunders rushed onto the field, waved amyl nitrate under the
fallen Cosmo's nose. But Liveric's head only slumped from side
to side, unresponsive. His eyes were closed, the cheeks flushed
except for a porcelain white spot at the center of each of them.
He was carried unconscious to the locker room where Pele lay
on a bench, his right leg heavily bandaged, a half-smile on his
face.

The game sounded so different through the damp, musty
walls. Without the splash of light, the driving rhythm of the
ball, and the exhilarated faces draped round like a dropcloth,
it assumed the character of a restless beast. Nothing of the
game penetrated into the room where Liveric lay on a training
table; all that could be heard was the rumbling of the crowd, a
sustained growl building now and then to an apocalyptic rush,
as if the stadium was sliding off the edge of the earth.

At each new crescendo, Pele raised his eyebrows inquisitively,
as if to ask, "goal?" Nobody could be sure, least of all Liveric.
He was still far away, locked into a nameless sleep. The doctor
snapped open a vial of pain killer and shot it into the player's
limp arm. Slowly, Liveric began to come around, moving his
head from side to side, occasionally opening his glazed eyes. He
wanted to speak, but his throat was too dry. No way to tell anybody he needed a drink of anything.

Rigby held his teammate's hand, spoke to him, stroked his
head with a wet compress as the doctor probed the winger's
chest and stomach gently, with the index and middle fingers of

his right hand. Everybody wondered how the game went, was it over yet? No way to tell. The doctor tested Liveric's blood pressure, grunted satisfaction. Slowly, his patient began to recognize the surroundings. He felt Rigby pouring a cold orange liquid into his mouth.

The door burst open and the Cosmos tumbled in, ghost faces from the sea. Liveric could not focus properly and still felt as if a transparent peel had been grafted onto his body. The score had remained 1–0. Pitico walked straight into the shower and turned on the cold water.

It was Bradley who broke the silence of scraping spikes with a human voice. "Listen," he said, standing over a tray of drinks on the table, his voice tense and bitter. "That was a pathetic display out there and I'll tell you right now, if any of you want to play for the Cosmos next year you will have to go out and sweat blood out there."

The words hung in the humidity, while voices from outside and a sense of cloying human bodies pressed the room on all sides. There was tumult in the hallways, jeering, taunting, screaming, and pleading voices echoing and pushing against the door. The Cosmos sat exhausted and disconsolate, feeling nothing but the claustrophobia of this infernally hot chamber that alone protected them from a mob.

Pele sat in a corner, giving autographs to the game's officials. "They spat on me," Garay muttered, "they insulted and spat on me. How I would like to get just one of them alone, to teach them about respect . . ." The words drifted off as he worked to get the shoe off one of Liveric's plastic legs. The only ventilation in the room came from a rectangular shutter fitted with aluminum slats high above the door. Dozens of arms poked through the shutter despite its height. Faces pressed against it. "Hey Pele, hey mon, you got boots? Give me boots, mon."

But Bradley was far from finished. "I didn't see anybody out there giving a hundred percent," he charged. "Before you go out and ask Marshall for this favor or ask for spending money, or when your check is coming, go out and prove that you deserve it."

Again, the chorus came: "Hey Pele, you got boots, mon? How about a picture? Hey Pele, up here." Bradley couldn't take it anymore. He grabbed a tall cup full of Gatorade and hurled it against the shutter, driving back the limbs pushing through it. The cup exploded, orange rivulets ran down the wall.

"You're always arguing about the officials, breaking curfew, taking a vacation . . . well, let me tell you, from now on everybody fights for their job. This team we played tonight was nothing. We came here with a collection of big stars from all over the world and we lost to a local club that's all but picked up off the street.

"It kills me, it just plain kills me."

Abruptly he began to peel off his uniform with intense, possessed determination and the other Cosmos followed him, dressing down. Only Pele smiled, as he had his picture taken with a Jamaican official, then turned and said something softly to Mané. Liveric revived long enough to utter a few words, reaching for his first grip on something real. "What is the score?" he croaked. When it was time to go, two men hoisted him upon their shoulders and walked him out into his own expressionistic nightmare, populated by scores of sworling black faces posed in eerie grimaces, the name "Pele" penetrating his consciousness like a submarine dirge.

Thousands still milled around the stadium as the Cosmos phalanx fought it way out. All the roads were jammed and the bus crawled along, the heat inside reaching sauna level. As it crept along, the bus became a cipher for the crowd's passion. They beat on it with fists, sticks and bare arms; they hurled stones and bottles, leaped to punch the tightly closed windows in a schizoid show of exuberance and malice. The Cosmos weathered it in silence, and blank watchfulness, as the scheme reversed and they became the spectators. Liveric, still struggling to leave the sensory antechamber, found enough voice to ask how long it would be. "Pele no good, mon, Pele is an old man," cackled a teenager running along with the bus. But the old man didn't hear him. His eyes were closed against the world and his mind was elsewhere.

The nightmare in Jamaica did not end the tour; there were still eight days left and two games, one in Puerto Rico followed by a surprise return to Haiti, after a tornado in Santo Domingo forced cancellation of a game there. Those last eight days would slip by quickly, free of the tension but also lacking the solidarity, struggle, anticipation, and unique pressure that charactized the Cosmos' first year with Pele. There were still touching moments:

• Pele, sitting by the pool in San Juan, examining a recent chest X-ray looked up, smiled and said "Everybody know how I look on outside. Now look on me inside."

• Before one practice in Puerto Rico, Liveric and Kuykendall argued about the former's robust life-style. In what was either a monumental rationalization or a rare moment of abreaction, Liveric snapped: "If I think I can be Pele, I stay in room forty-eight hour day and sleep. What you think, you stupid . . ."

• After one practice, which was consumed mostly by a long team meeting translated into Spanish by Mazzei, Kuykendall said, "We lost half this season in translation."

• Mané poured Pepsi all over himself to convince the team that it was a powerful, unknown tanning agent. He succeeded in convincing nobody, but he did get a bad sunburn and attracted most of the flies in San Juan.

• Pele played hurt in the game against the Puerto Rican national team, scoring just once in the 12–1 romp. Two days later, he telephoned his father Dondinho from Haiti. He recalled part of that conversation:

Dondinho: "How many goals for you?"
Pele: "One."
Dondinho: "Shaddup. You are making joke?"
Pele: "No, it was penalty kick."
Dondinho: "Penalty kick? How come team make twelve goals

and you have only one, on penalty kick. What is matter with you?"

"I try to explain," laughed Pele, "it was a bad team, I was little bit injured. I relax some and let other player make goal. But he no care for nothing of that. He want only the goal."

• A second painter showed up with a study of Pele. This one portrayed Pele dressed in ermine, with a crown on his head. But he carried a can opener instead of a scepter, and climbed a stepladder towards a great bottle of Pepsi. Scattered around him were people representing every race and color, bearing banners that read either Pele or Pepsi. In the blue sky were the words: "PELE, KING OF FOOTBALL, PEPSI, KING OF DRINKS." There was also an insert in the sky, a round picture within a picture in which two astronauts were cavorting on the moon, clutching bottles of Pepsi. The inscription read: "On the moon and on the earth, Pepsi is the best." Nobody quite knew what to make of this vision. Pele shook the painter's hand and accepted it. It sits today in Mazzei's office, beneath a pile of posters, waiting for the right wall.

There were simple visual images which achieved poignancy only within the emotional framework of the moment. Consider Tommy Rellis, the little Greek, sitting on a bus in Haiti, wearing his Alice Cooper T-shirt, a blue wet-look jacket and an enormous straw hat with "Souvenir of Puerto Rico" stitched on the brim in hot pink script. He sat alone, staring at the lavender mountains, no way to tell anybody what he was thinking now.

Yet it was in Jamaica that the tour really ended because the game itself was, by virtue of its distortion, a powerful metaphor for the Cosmos' first season, the year of Pele. It encompassed all the problems they had faced and not had time to overcome. It represented every cruel ambush they suffered, magnified the deep desire of their opponents to break the bank at Monte Carlo, to beat Pele, to inject life and pride into the soccer backwaters both in the U.S.A. and abroad. Europe had been graceful, relatively easy. The teams there were solid and established, armed with a sense of their own worth, no matter what happened on that particular evening. But when the Cosmos arrived in the Caribbean, it was back into the pit where there was no concern for the problems of American soccer, the mission, the celebrated organization that lured Pele out of retirement. They were blind-sided when they least expected or deserved it. Their potential was stopped, their vulnerability exploited. They were stripped and beaten. Perhaps only one man had recognized how really difficult a task lay before the Cosmos back in sultry June, and that was Pele. Now they all knew.

In the end, the Cosmos learned that Pele was precious cargo and that they were his vessel. He would not carry them to glory alone. That was beyond his power. But he could lead and direct, if somebody could stand on the flank and absorb the punishment. Most of the Cosmos were ill-equipped to stand on the flank and they paid the price. Still, they grew and learned, despite the harsh glare of attention that trailed them everywhere. In the end this celebrity also became an obtuse reward for their tribulations. The only man who remained immune was Pele.

He stood above and beyond, not through his own choice but the choice of the world around him. It was the cause and effect of his celebrity, this uncanny ability to be recognized everywhere as somebody "special," touched by fate, genius, or by the luck of his charmed life. It would always be like this for him, because it is he. Gradually all of his teammates understood that even Pele himself never professed to know why. He offered instead a constant gratitude which only increased his charm.

The air was crisp the morning after the Jamaican game, a cleansing breeze had washed away the metallic taste of the previous night. The Cosmos waited impatiently for the bus, standing in front of the hotel. Liveric had recovered overnight; he appeared, poured into a baby blue jean suit that softened the harsh angles of his body. "Is nutting," he said, "part of game."

Toye came out of the lobby and offered to buy Pele a fast drink before departure. They walked over to the outdoor bar, and sat down, chatting beneath the ample arms of the same almond tree under which they first met. Only five years had passed, but it seemed like such a long, long time ago. "Pele, I have a feeling that this is just the beginning. I think we are going to be one of the best clubs in the world someday. Really, what is there to hold us back? Maybe we should order some champagne, or at least a good Scotch; you drink too much of that Pepsi anyway."

Pele leaned over smiling, grabbed Toye's shoulder and after a moment's pause shook his head and said, "Clive, you are still crazy, my friend. But I think maybe you are right."

Epilogue

On June 10, 1976, one year after the signing of Pele, the Cosmos were atop their division of the North American Soccer League, engaged in a shin-to-shin struggle for the divisional title with the Tampa Bay Rowdies and Washington Diplomats. Pele himself dominated the scoring tables and continued to garner both headlines and record crowds in NASL cities; the bold investment of Warner Communications came to fruition in the form of packed stadiums, increased media coverage and the blossoming of soccer interest in cities as indigenously American as San Diego and Minneapolis. All along, the NASL had nurtured a conviction that Americans would accept soccer on its own terms; all along the league had diligently cultivated possibilities that had once seemed outrageous. Now the dream was becoming tangible.

In San Diego, the newborn Jaws put 18,128 fans into their stadium for an exhibition game against the Cosmos. In a nationally televised game on June 5, 46,611 spectators jammed Tampa Stadium to witness the crucial struggle between their beloved hometown Rowdies and New York. At a party following the Rowdies' unexpected 5–1 victory, a euphoric young lady insisted, "I have some friends who know soccer very well and even they told me Pele was not as good as everybody said he was . . . certainly no better than our Marshie" [Rodney Marsh, the Rowdies flamboyant English midfielder].

While the remark was ludicrous at best, it served to point up the fact that the NASL was winning hearts out in America's provincial capitals, developing a loyal following that would

burgeon long after the last generation that had seen Pele play
would recreate his exploits in reverential tones.

On the eve of Pele's first anniversary as a Cosmo, 46,164 fans
filed into Metropolitan Stadium in Minneapolis to see the man
who had never played there before, against their fledgling Kicks.
And that's what it was all about; kicks were coming faster and
harder, in front of more people, on more television screens than
ever before.

The NASL cracked its attendance record of 1,695,651 on
July 11, with five full weeks to go on the season schedule and
projected a total attendance of 2.5 million for its 240 regular
season games. The presence of Pele had permeated the entire
league, lifting its fortunes higher even in places where rabidly
partisan fans hoisted signs like "WAY-LAY PELE," or "THE KING
IS DEAD." Six teams—Seattle, Portland, Minnesota, San Jose,
Tampa Bay, and New York were drawing over 15,000 fans per
game while Dallas, the most thoroughly American squad from
field level on up flirted with that mark. The Cosmos' own home
attendance average of just over 16,000 represented an increase
of more than 50 percent above 1975.

The instant prestige that Pele's appearance in an NASL uniform added to the league increased in a dozen ways. Following
Pele to the booming league were English internationals like
Bobby Moore, Bob McNab, Marsh, and Geoff Hurst. The
enigmatic figure of George Best reappeared on the NASL horizon, in the orange and white uniform of the Los Angeles
Aztecs.

Early in 1976, the Cosmos added a second luminary of international soccer to their roster, Italy's Giorgio Chinaglia, a hulking striker with a shot so lethal and talents so uncontested that
his performances for Lazio of Rome often galvanized half the
city on the morning after. But there was particular significance
in the decision of this Italian international to cast his lot with
the NASL. At twenty-eight, Chinaglia was in the full flower of
his career, happily married to an American girl and looking to
these shores for his future.

He found it in a Cosmos' offer the vulpine Italian press said amounted to a three-year contract valued at $850,000. This was in addition to an estimated $800,000 the Cosmos paid Lazio for the rights to Chinaglia's contract. The amount may appear exorbitant but Toye called it "a steal." The Cosmos had paid what in Italy would amount to the transfer fees for a promising fifteen-year-old, and got away with it only because Chinaglia had told Lazio that he was emigrating to America regardless of consequences.

This then was not a man with a missionary vision reaching to the furthest edge of his potential as a personality, but a raw, explosive talent, above all else a player, a blue-chip commodity on the sporting flesh market. Together Pele and Chinaglia worked marvellous combinations and formed the greatest one-two combination in NASL history.

As for Warners' bold plan to write Pele's name across the commercial marketplaces of the world in big, electric letters, the licensing branch of Warners had assembled over a dozen clients in less than one year. By mid-1976, Pele's face or name appeared on arm and hat patches, electric and air-powered soccer games, soccer shoes, balls and shin guards, lunch kits, novelty hats. He helped sell men's cologne on television commercials with Muhammad Ali and Jimmy Connors, endorsed trail bikes and motorcycles for multi-national Honda interests. This was all in addition to his prior commitments to Pepsi and a long list of Brazilian products. Pele did not so much go into a market as become one.

And what of the 1975 Cosmos, whose lives were shaken or shattered by the awesome demands of Pele's presence? The ones who survived with a real chance in '76 were Werner Roth, Mike Dillon, Brian Rowan, Ray Mifflin, Nelsi Morais, Bob Rigby . . . the rest of the crew were flung or returned to places as far from Manhattan as Athens, as painfully close as the dusty soccer fields of Brooklyn and Queens. Joey Fink was traded to Tampa. Mark Liveric was traded to San Jose, where he found happiness on a club replete with fellow Croatians who understood . . . Johnny Kerr helped the Diplomats battle New York for the division, Tony Picciano was released, and sought gainful employment wearing long pants. Sam Nusum was traded back to Vancouver, with no regrets. Shpigler could not come to terms with the Cosmos, and went home to Israel, where he met Pele early in 1976 while working on a soccer documentary. Pitico returned to Brazil to excel in the midfield for Portugesa Santista, while Tommy Ord was traded to Vancouver. All of the Uruguayans went home. Mané, who had done so much to buoy flagging spirits also returned to Brazil, and crafted an astonishing comeback with Santos.

The Cosmos began 1976 with a new coach, Ken Furphy, a veteran of English First and Second Division soccer, while Gordon Bradley was promoted to vice-president. Furphy recruited some stout-hearted men, but proved too inflexible to balance the international character of the club and negotiate the peculiarities of the American soccer environment. While the Cosmos' abundant talent kept them in first place, the ground beneath Furphy eroded and the team was quietly turned over to a new coach in the last month of the season. His name was Gordon Bradley . . .

So the Cosmos had come full circle in at least one sense, demonstrating that the job was never really finished; rather it had only started back on June 10, 1975 when a thirty-four-year-old Brazilian soccer star walked into the Hunt Room of 21, flashing his universal smile, holding his hands up in the "V" sign.

But for the Cosmos and the NASL, the castles in the air kept drifting closer and closer to field level; occasionally they could even reach up and touch one as they did with each brimming stadium, each well-known signature on a standard NASL player's contract, each child dribbling a soccer ball on a grassy patch infused with all the magic of Maracana Stadium.

The dream was sustained and grew with the 1975 Cosmos—from Pele, who undertook the job, to the least skilled of the Cosmos, who were sacrificed to it. And for skeptics or doubters, there were always the words of Pele, who said, "Why to worry? Time is not so big a problem. If the job is made the right way, the time always come."